OFFICIALS AND STAFF

INDIANAPOLIS MOTOR SPEEDWAY CORPORATION

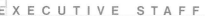

Mari H. George
Chairman

Anton H. "Tony" George
President & Chief Executive Officer

M. Josephine George
Nancy L. George

Katherine M. George-Conforti
Jack R. Snyder

EXECUTIVE STAFF

Brian Barnhart
Vice President IRL Operations
Jeffrey G. Belskus
Executive Vice President & Chief
Financial Officer
W. Curtis Brighton
Vice President & General Counsel

Laura George
Staff Advisor
Mel Harder
Vice President, Operations
Fred J. Nation
Vice President, Corporate
Communications & Public Relations

Bob Reif
Senior Vice President of Sales &
Marketing and Chief Marketing Officer
Peggy Swalls
Vice President, Administration
Kenneth T. Ungar
Chief of Staff

SPEEDWAY STAFF

Karen Ahrens
Payroll Processing Manager
Terry Angstadt
Assistant Vice President IMS
Marketing
Don Bailey
Vehicle Coordinator
Kelly Bailey
Manager of Brickyard Crossing
Resort & Inn
Ellen Bireley
Manager of Museum Services
Dr. Henry Bock
Medical Director
Martha Briggs
Manager of Accounting
Jim Campbell
Director of Safety
Randy Clark
Manager of Food & Beverage
Theresa Cooksey
Manager of Sponsorship
Fulfillment
Donald Davidson
Historian
Derek Decker
Manager of Event Marketing
Jennifer Dixon
Director of IMS Marketing
Dawn Dyer
Manager of Creative Services
Chuck Ferguson
Director of Information Systems
& Telecommunications
Julio Fernandez
Director, IMS Radio Network

Brenda Ferryman
Manager of Mail Services
Tom Fix
Director, IMS Productions
Kevin Forbes
Director of Engineering,
Construction
Dave Gass
Director of Engineering, IMS
Productions
Joseph George
Manager of Accounting
Purchasing Systems
Lynn Greggs
Director of Accounting &
Administration
MaryAnn Hawkins
Manager of Catering &
Conference Services, Brickyard
Crossing Resort & Inn
Pat Hayes
Manager of Contract
Administration
George Hobbs
Manager of Special Events &
Hospitality
Marty Hunt
Manager of Track Racing
Operations
Paul Kelly
Manager of Communications
John Kesler
Director of Marketing
Partnerships
Jon Koskey
Manager of Technology

John Lawson
Manager of Safety Administration
Lisa Lewis
Manager of Human Resources
Bruce Lynch
Director of Retail Sales &
Operations
Buddy McAtee
Assistant Vice President,
Broadcast Communications &
Business Development
Richard McComb
Director of Finance
Ron McQueeney
Director of Photography
Annette Miller
Licensing Manager
David Moroknek
Senior Director of IMS
Marketing & Consumer Products
Sherri Nierste
Assistant General Counsel
Ken Noe
Manager of Hospitality
Gloria Novotney
Director of Credentials
Adrian Payne
Manager of Internet
Development
Dan Petty
Manager of Retail Merchandising
Nicole Polsky
Manager of Licensing & Retail
Marketing
Bruce Ralston
Manager of Telecommunications

Paul Riley
Manager of Facilities
Rollie Schroeder
Manager of Brickyard Crossing
Pro Shop
Michael Sherman
Manager of Safety Operations
Scott Smith
Assistant Vice President,
Indy Racing Marketing
Frank Slover
Director of Engineering, IMS
Productions
Jeff Stuart
Golf Course Superintendent
Dennis Vervynckt
Assistant General Manager,
Brickyard Crossing Resort &
Inn
Cindy Vrshek
Manager of IMS Marketing
Tom Weisenbach
Senior National Account
Manager,
Marketing Partnerships
Greg Woodsmall
Director of Flight Operations &
Chief Pilot
Adrian Young
Manager of Software
Applications

INDY RACING LEAGUE STAFF

Bob Beasley
Director of Indy Racing Team
Services
Mark Bridges
Technical Manager
Phil Casey
Technical Director
Ruthie Culbertson
Manager of Indy Racing Events
Joanna Edwards
Manager of Indy Racing Driver
Development
Matt Godbout
Manager of Fan Development &

Research
Ron Green
Director of Media Relations
Tiffany Hemmer
Director of Racing
Administration
Marty Hill
Manager of Indy Racing
Accounts
Adam Jacobs
Manager of Indy Racing
Integrated Marketing
John Lewis
Director, Racing Operations

Kent Liffick
Director of Indy Racing
Strategic Alliances
Les Mactaggart
Technical Consultant
Matt McCartin
Director of Indy Racing
Marketing
John Pierce
Safety Consultant
Jim Reynolds
Manager of Fuel Services
Kimberly Miller
Manager of Media Relations

Johnny Rutherford
Special Projects & Consultant
Jayme Sabo
Manager of Indy Racing Event
Advertising
Chris Tracy
Manager of Medical Services
Al Unser
Driver Coach & Consultant
Chuck Whetsel
Manager of Timing & Scoring

CONTENTS

First published in 2002 by MBI Publishing Company, Galtier Plaza, Suite 200, 380 Jackson Street St. Paul, MN 55101-3885 USA

 © IMS Corporation, 2002

The information in this book is true and complete to the best of our knowledge. All recommendations are made without any guarantee on the part of the author or Publisher,
who also disclaim any liability incurred in connection with the use of this data or specific details.

We recognize that some words, model names and designations, for example, mentioned herein are the property of the trademark holder.
We use them for identification purposes only. This is not an official publication.

MBI Publishing Company books are also available at discounts in bulk quantity for industrial or sales-promotional use. For details write to Special Sales Manager at
Motorbooks International Wholesalers & Distributors, Galtier Plaza, Suite 200, 380 Jackson Street St. Paul, MN 55101-3885 USA

Edited by Paul Johnson
Layout by Stephanie Michaud
Designed by Tom Heffron

Editorial Contributors: Tim Tuttle, Jonathan Ingram, Dick Mittman, Kris Palmer, and Michael Dapper, Joe Crowley

Printed in China   ISBN 0-7603-1320-2

Thank You

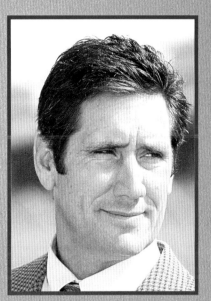

ndy Racing again proved to be the most exciting racing in the world during the 2001 season. This was dramatically emphasized at the season-ending Chevy 500 at Texas Motor Speedway where Sam Hornish Jr. edged out Scott Sharp and Robbie Buhl nearly three abreast in the closest three-car finish in Indy Racing history.

Sam had already made racing history a week earlier at the new Chicagoland Speedway when, at 22 years of age, he clinched the Northern Light Cup as the youngest series champion in a National North American racing series.

It was a tremendous year with 13 races, eight of those being decided by less than two seconds. We added six new markets—Chicago, Miami, St. Louis, Kansas City, Nashville and Richmond—and sold out three of them.

We saw the return of Team Penske to the Indy 500 in a dramatic fashion having Helio Castroneves and Gil de Ferran finish first and second, giving the team its 11th "500" title.

Buddy Lazier became our first driver to win four races in a season. Other winners included veterans Greg Ray, Scott Sharp, Al Unser Jr. and Eddie Cheever Jr.

In 2002, we have more growth, adding races at California Speedway, Nazareth Speedway and Michigan International Speedway, bringing our schedule to 15 events, all to be broadcast on ABC/ESPN. Chevrolet will be joining the series with a new Chevy Indy V-8, succeeding Oldsmobile, which is leaving with 49 victories. Firestone has signed a long-term contract as exclusive tire provider, and the Infiniti Pro Series will debut in mid-2002, offering a needed step-up to the Indy Racing League.

We invite you to "Take a Ride With Us" in 2002 and experience the excitement of Indy Racing first hand.

On behalf of the Hulman-George family, our staffs at the Indianapolis Motor Speedway and the Indy Racing League, our sponsors, crews and drivers, thank you for supporting Indy Racing.

Sincerely,

Tony George

Tony George
President and CEO
Indianapolis Motor Speedway

by Tim Tuttle

Opening day at Indianapolis always arrives with a feeling of heartpounding excitement and eager anticipation of the days ahead. This year it also carried a renaissance-like aura. For the first time since 1995, Roger Penske's team and Michael Andretti were entered, and two-time 500 champion Arie Luyendyk and former Indy Racing League Champion Tony Stewart were returning after a one-year hiatus. The defending Indy 500 team, Target/Chip Ganassi Racing, was returning as well. They were headline-making additions to the field comprised in the majority by drivers and teams from the Indy Racing Northern Light Series, which has the 500 as its crown jewel.

Greg Ray, the 1999 Indy Racing champion, had the fastest lap in a busy first session at 224.301mph in Team Menard's Dallara-

Oldsmobile. The Texan was 3.3mph faster than Eddie Cheever's Dallara-Infiniti, which turned a 220.968. Ray was mighty impressive out of the gate, but it was the appearance late in the day of Penske Racing teammates Gil de Ferran and Helio Castroneves that was historically significant.

Penske's team won 10 500s between 1972 and 1994. But in 1995, it failed to qualify with drivers Al Unser Jr. and Emerson Fittipaldi. Penske did not enter the next five 500s, deciding to concentrate the Championship Auto Racing Teams (CART)–sanctioned series instead.

De Ferran and Castroneves, after driving in a CART race earlier that day in Nazareth, Pennsylvania, flew to Indy in time to take some shakedown laps in their Dallara-Oldsmobiles. De Ferran ran 13 laps in his primary car with a best lap of 219.243. He was the eighth-fastest driver on Opening Day. De Ferran also managed to get out in his backup, running five laps topped by a 205.644. Castroneves, whose Dallara had battery and telemetry problems, was limited to 10 laps in his primary car. He ran 216.608.

Hopeful of adding another Indianapolis victory to his resume, 1998 Indy 500 winner Eddie Cheever Jr. (51) took to the track for early practice.
Walt Kuhn

"It's great (to be back)," Roger Penske said. "Everything went smoothly today. We got three cars out and around the racetrack. Both drivers are pretty happy." De Ferran and Castroneves had accomplished their primary goals, making sure their cars were ready to roll for a full day of practice on Monday. "It was a good day for us," de Ferran said. "It's good to shake down the cars." Added Castroneves, "Things didn't go the way we wanted in Nazareth (Castroneves finished 11th, de Ferran 23rd), but we got to come over here and shake down the cars. It's going to be a long week and there is a lot of work to do."

Greg Ray ran 34 laps, posting his best lap in the closing minutes of the session, which was cut short seven minutes by rain. "We wanted to see what we could run before the rain came, and in the heat," team owner John Menard said. "It's supposed to rain the next couple of days."

Ray's lap of 221.837 came less than an hour before posting the lap that was faster than his 2000 pole-winning lap of 223.658. "The wind kind of died down; we put on a new set of tires and we changed some things on the aero(dynamic) package," Ray explained. "It was a combination of all those things. One day of testing doesn't mean anything. It is just all of the information you gather over five and a half days of running (before qualifying). It isn't about getting it exactly right, but about not missing it."

Lyn St. James, the second female to drive in the 500, took three farewell laps (best of 179.626) after announcing her retirement. St. James was the 1992 Indy Rookie of the Year, but her real claim to fame was out-qualifying Nigel Mansell, the 1992 Formula 1 World Champion, at Indy in 1994. St. James started sixth that year, her career best, and Mansell seventh. St. James drove in seven 500s, with 11th in 1992 her highest finish. "It's time," St. James said. "Sometimes you have to step back and take stock of what reality is. I've had a wonderful career. For me to be a rookie at 45 was an accomplishment in itself. I was starting my career when some drivers are considering retirement. To sustain that for nine years is more significant to me than the gender issue."

DAY-AT-A-GLANCE

Date: Sunday, May 6
Drivers on Track: 33
Cars on Track: 38

TOP FIVE DRIVERS OF THE DAY

Car	Driver	Speed (mph)
2T	Greg Ray	224.301
51	Eddie Cheever Jr.	220.968
91	Buddy Lazier	220.221
52	Scott Goodyear	220.084
98	Billy Boat	219.765

Arie Luyendyk couldn't resist the lure of Indianapolis. He tried to close out his career in 1999 with an organized farewell program at the Indy 500. Hired by ABC as a commentator for the 2000 race, Luyendyk realized he would rather be driving in the race than talking about it. The 47-year-old Dutchman was welcomed back by Fred Treadway, the only owner he had driven for in the Indy Racing Northern Light Series. Immediately, Luyendyk showed that the layoff had not taken away his deft touch at the Speedway.

Luyendyk was seventh fastest at 219.481 miles per hour on Opening Day and jumped up to 221.340 for second on the charts on Day 2. Rain eliminated the final three hours of practice, but the 1990 and 1997 Indy 500 winner had already put in an honest day's work. Luyendyk did 60 laps in Treadway-Hubbard Racing's G Force-Oldsmobile. "So far, things have gone well," Luyendyk said. "I'm having fun and I'm making laps that make sense. We're making full fuel runs. I stayed in shape by racing shifter karts and I tested at Las Vegas and here, but yesterday I still hurt in some new places. Today was much better."

Greg Ray topped the practice for the second straight day, with 222.976 miles per hour in Team Menard's Dallara-Oldsmobile. Ray, who did 21 laps in the designated 2T car, also had the third-fastest lap in the 22 car at 221.130 in six laps. "We've been trying two different setups," Ray said. "I was pleasantly surprised with the 22 car. I had a feeling I wouldn't like the setup, but it was coming off the corner strong. I was very pleased with how it handled."

Eliseo Salazar had a productive day in A.J. Foyt's Dallara-Oldsmobile, completing 53 laps with the best at 220.634. He was the day's third-fastest driver. "I'm delighted," the Chilean said. "We have a brand-new car. We ran one car the first three races (in the IRNLS). We got this one out and went 218 pretty easy and then pushed it some. I was a bit apprehensive because it was a new car."

Michael Andretti turned his first laps at Indianapolis since 1995, running 217.636 in a Team Green-owned Dallara-Oldsmobile that was prepared primarily by technical partner Panther Racing. "I think the goals were just to get settled in a little bit," Andretti said. "We had something to go by with what (Panther's) Sam (Hornish Jr.) had done. I think we had some of the trouble that he had yesterday."

Others making their 2001 Indy debuts included Robby Gordon, who lapped at 220.028 in A. J. Foyt/RCR Childress Racing's Dallara-Oldsmobile; Jimmy Vasser, 219.381 in Chip Ganassi Racing's G Force-Oldsmobile; and Tony Stewart, 215.474 for Ganassi. "I'm pretty happy," said Gordon, who ran 24 laps. "I haven't driven an Indy Car in over a year, so to come out and finish in the top 10 (sixth) on the first day, that's pretty good. We haven't even tried to go fast yet."

Vasser was ninth on the timing chart at 219.381. He ran 29 laps. "We did a few laps just to get used to it," he said. "The car was set up pretty conservative. It's great to be back at the Speedway."

Stewart ran 215.474 in 24 laps. "We just knocked the cobwebs off," the NASCAR Winston Cup regular said. "We didn't set the world on fire and we didn't get too many laps in. This is a whole new team for me, and we have to get to know each other."

Rookie Cory Witherill spun entering the short chute between Turns 1 and 2 and put the nose of his Indy Regency Racing G Force-Oldsmobile into the inside wall. Witherill wasn't hurt beyond a bruised elbow in the initial incident of contact of the month.

"The right-rear tire went down," Witherill said. "I felt something when I was coming off Turn 4. It was pushing really bad and something didn't seem right. I was going to bring it in, but then when I entered Turn 1, it started bouncing around and spun."

Mario Andretti, who won the May classic in 1969, leaned in to exchange practice and setup thoughts with his son Michael, who craves an Indy 500 win of his own.
Dan Boyd

DAY-AT-A-GLANCE

Date:	Monday, May 7
Drivers on Track:	32
Cars on Track:	39

TOP FIVE DRIVERS OF THE DAY

Car	Driver	Speed (mph)
2T	Greg Ray	222.976
5	Arie Luyendyk	221.340
14	Eliseo Salazar	220.634
8	Scott Sharp	220.340
51	Eddie Cheever	220.037

by Tim Tuttle

The search for speed shifted into high gear on the third day of practice. Mark Dismore and Kelley Racing were the trailblazers, running the fastest lap of the month so far at 224.823 mph. Four more drivers were over 223, and another six were above 222.

Through the initial two days, Greg Ray had been the only driver with a lap of 223 or above. Dismore's top-of-the-chart lap was a classic

Two-time Indy 500 winner Arie Luyendyk (5) could not resist the attraction of the Speedway. He came out of retirement to run at Indy in pursuit of his third victory in the 500. Steve Snoddy

Happy Hour effort, four minutes before the track closed at 6 p.m. and achieved in excellent moderate-heat, low-humidity conditions. "We are so far ahead of where we have ever been at Indianapolis," Dismore explained. "I'm really excited."

Dismore said it was only the beginning of cars upping the ante. "What I did today will not win the pole," he said. "There are a lot of teams that are not showing all they have got, including us."

Arie Luyendyk had a busy and productive day that nearly ended badly. He ran 72 laps in Treadway-Hubbard Racing's G Force-Oldsmobile and posted his best lap of 223.986 on his 71st. On his 73rd lap, Luyendyk was confronted with smoke coming out of Turn 1. Rookie Casey Mears had crashed. "I saw the smoke and knew that wasn't a good sign," he said. "I had to decide where to go. I didn't want to go high and get into the debris, so I turned just a little bit left. When I slammed on the brakes, I spun. I put my head back and waited for the

hit that never happened. I was lucky, but also smart to keep the wheel as straight as I could. I'm just happy not to have hit anything."

Luyendyk was enthusiastic about the rest of the day. "I was really pleased with that speed," he said. "I had actually turned what I thought would have been my best lap of the day (222.475) earlier in the heat, and I thought that was really good to go that fast at that time of the day. I was flat all the way around (on his 223.986), so it's obvious to me we're making good progress with the car and that's the most important thing this early in the week."

Mears did a 180-degree spin into the wall, first making contact with the left rear of his Galles Racing G Force-Oldsmobile. Mears, complaining of lower back pain, was transported to Indianapolis Methodist Hospital for precautionary X-rays and was released four hours later. The impact was measured at 86 Gs.

"He said he had a slight understeer and then the car bit in the corner and he lost it," owner Rick Galles said. "It was a good whack. It just goes to show you how strong those IRL cars are."

Mears had also crashed 11 days earlier at the IRNLS race at Atlanta. "I'm pretty much sore all over," Mears said the following day. "It's my knees and my back that hurt, but my back mostly. It's pretty sore."

Jeff Ward, Buddy Lazier, and Eddie Cheever Jr. also topped 223. Helio Castroneves, Jimmy Vasser, Greg Ray, Eliseo Salazar and Scott Goodyear were above 222.

DAY-AT-A-GLANCE

Date: Tuesday, May 8
Drivers on Track: 35
Cars on Track: 45

TOP FIVE DRIVERS OF THE DAY

Car	Driver	Speed (mph)
28T	Mark Dismore	224.823
5	Arie Luyendyk	223.986
35	Jeff Ward	223.716
91	Buddy Lazier	223.315
51	Eddie Cheever	223.146

by Tim Tuttle

Scott Sharp and Tony Stewart escalated the need for speed into a new orbit in the fourth day of practice. Sharp posted the fastest lap yet of the month—226.137 miles per hour—and Stewart moved into the No. 2 position at 225.004.

The Kelley Racing driver downplayed the relevance of his lap in relation to what it could mean for qualifying, when cars are alone on the track. "I got a great tow from Airton Daré," Sharp said. "I caught him on the front straightaway, and he dragged me all the way around the track. It was a pretty awesome draft I got. They (fast laps) are fun more than anything. Obviously, that lap was great for numbers, but not too realistic." Sharp was happiest about having a trouble-free session. He completed 52 laps, the most of any of the four days. Sharp's Dallara-Oldsmobile had engine problems on two of the three previous practices. "We finally got a chance to run all day," Sharp said.

Stewart's G Force-Oldsmobile made a major breakthrough. His fast lap before Wednesday had been 221.810. "We had a great speed for today, since when we started this morning we were going backwards," Stewart said. "(Teammate) Jimmy (Vasser) and I stood around and scratched our heads, talked about what direction we needed to go and the team listened. We gained a lot. This is by far the fastest I have gone in these new IRL cars. You still need to get around the Speedway without lifting. Right now, I'm cracking it [lifting], mostly for my safety. Today was a monumental jump for our team. After the pow-wow, we made big changes and they (Ganassi team) really worked hard."

Jaques Lazier also made substantial progress, running 223.310 to rank fifth for the day. His previous best for the month was 221.289. "I tell you what, today we did a lot of fine-tuning and it resulted in a great speed," Lazier said. "We've been consistent from the first time we hit the track. Right now, we are just trimming the car out. We've (Lazier and TeamXtreme) been together for three weeks and to be fifth fastest for today is amazing."

Robby Gordon had his best lap at 223.032, sixth for the day. "I'm pretty happy," he said. "The speeds keep climbing and I am getting more comfortable. A. J. (Foyt) and I are communicating better about setting up the car to suit my driving style. Today the car felt the best it has so far. Scott Sharp's lap was pretty impressive."

Penske teammates Helio Castroneves and Gil de Ferran ranked eighth and ninth for the day. Castroneves ran 222.527, de Ferran 222.271. "So far, my first few days at the Speedway have gone well," Castroneves said. "It's been quite a learning experience for me. Every day, we learn more and more about the car. We're slowly improving, but we're not there yet. We did some full tank runs today as well as some qualifying runs. Everyone at Marlboro Team Penske has been working flat out to try to find more speed in the car."

It was de Ferran's most productive day of the month. "Team Penske had a good day," he said. "We made gains from yesterday, posting our fastest lap so far this week. We were also able to get a qualifying simulation done, which we weren't able to do on Tuesday."

Jaques Lazier (77) drove hard through the short chute in an attempt to find the speed needed to qualify and, if possible, make a run at the pole.
Ron McQueeney

DAY-AT-A-GLANCE

Date: Wednesday, May 9
Drivers on Track: 35
Cars on Track: 38

TOP FIVE DRIVERS OF THE DAY

Car	Driver	Speed (mph)
8	Scott Sharp	226.137
33	Tony Stewart	225.004
2T	Greg Ray	223.848
5	Arie Luyendyk	223.499
77	Jaques Lazier	223.310

by Tim Tuttle

Bogged down in the middle of the pack through his previous three days of practice, Michael Andretti made a run toward the front with a lap of 222.927 mph. It was the sixth fastest of the day and a marked improvement over his best of 221.668 going into the session.

Andretti was not exactly jumping for joy, but at least his Dallara-Oldsmobile was becoming more competitive. "We're finding it a little bit at a time," he said. "The race setup is good, but we would like to find some more speed for qualifying." To start near the front, Andretti knew he would have to be able to keep the throttle flat to the floor. "We are still pushing," he explained.

The conditions of the day were not conducive to going fast. By midafternoon, the ambient temperature reached 88 degrees. The scheduled seven hours of practice were interrupted by 15 cautions that eliminated two hours and 22 minutes of track time. Of the final 66 minutes, 43 were lost by five yellows, virtually eliminating any chance for those famous Happy Hour flying laps.

Greg Ray's 224.542 was the session's best, accomplished just past noon. He completed only 11 laps. Gil de Ferran ranked second at 223.579. "We're continuing to go through our plan for the week and are working on both qualifying and race setups," the Penske Racing driver said. "We're taking baby steps, and we were able to post our fastest lap."

Jeff Ward drove his backup G Force-Oldsmobile for the first time and was third at 223.432. "Everything went fine," he said. "The car seems really good. We put on some suspension parts from the old car after lunch and made it better."

The Speedway's safety crews were kept busy, but Jeret Schroeder's crash in Turn Two was the only high-speed major impact. He backed PDM Racing's Dallara-Oldsmobile into the outside wall. Schroeder was not seriously hurt. "I'm just a little sore," he said. "The car felt great. I got into the middle of [Turn] Two and it just snapped around on me quickly."

Jim Guthrie, in Blueprint Racing's G Force-Oldsmobile, made low-speed contact with the inside wall after spinning on the warm-up lane between Turns One and Two as he came out of the pits. "You never think an accident can happen in the warm-up lane," Guthrie said. "This is the stupidest thing I have done in 27 years of racing. I was already in Turn Three in my mind and wasn't paying attention."

Rookie Brandon Erwin also spun exiting the pits, without making contact, in McCormack Motorsports' G Force-Oldsmobile. Erwin grazed the wall in Turn Two to bring out the caution for the second time in 11 minutes. "It's been a very tough day," Erwin said. "We're trying some new stuff in our front-end package, some new springs. We had a major push in the front end. I was pushing it just a little too hard and ran out of room coming out of Turn Two. I guess a soft brush against the wall is a lot better than a hard hit here at Indianapolis."

Helio Castroneves also ran too close to the wall, scraping paint off his Dallara-Oldsmobile in Turn One. "I was just going flat out and unfortunately the car had too much understeer," Castroneves said. "It was just a little kiss. I don't think we damaged anything. To go fast, you have to use the whole track. That's what I'm trying to do."

Driver Gil de Ferran (left) conferred with "The Captain," legendary team owner Roger Penske, happy to make his return to the Brickyard for the 2001 Indy 500.
Jim Haines

DAY-AT-A-GLANCE		
Date:	Thursday, May 10	
Drivers on Track:	35	
Cars on Track:	42	

TOP FIVE DRIVERS OF THE DAY		
Car	**Driver**	**Speed (mph)**
2T	Greg Ray	224.542
66	Gil de Ferran	223.579
35T	Jeff Ward	223.432
33	Tony Stewart	223.188
5	Arie Luyendyk	223.009

by Tim Tuttle

Greg Ray was flying early in the sixth day of practice, streaking to 225.403 mph on his 10th lap. It was the Team Menard driver's fastest thus far, second overall to Scott Sharp's 226.137, and held up for the best of the day. Ray finished on top for the fourth time of the week.

For all there was to like about the session, Ray found it equally lacking in terms of progress toward winning the pole and the race. "We had a good car this morning," Ray said. "I guess it was after lunch when we ran our best lap, around 1 p.m. We thought we could go a little quicker. We threw everything but the kitchen sink at that car, but it didn't help."

Part of Ray's problem was heavy track activity and 14 cautions that wiped out half of the seven hours. He ran only 10 more laps in his primary (2T) Dallara-Oldsmobile after the 225.403 and was never able to put a four-lap qualifying simulation together. "You try to find clean laps, and there are a lot of cars out there—that makes it difficult," Ray said. "I'm sure it's exciting for the fans, but it's frustrating. We never had four clean laps."

But traffic wasn't Ray's only problem. The team had tried all week to break the 226 barrier. "We had a plan coming in and it hasn't worked out exactly right," Ray said. "There were some things we thought we could do in the car that didn't work, some technical things that were not better for the car on this track."

Sharp had the second-best lap in the session at 224.715. The Kelley Racing driver completed 19 laps. "It was a rougher day than expected for everyone," Sharp said. "It was real hard to get momentum with all the yellows and accidents. Every time something happened, more fluid and oil dry were added to the track. Combine that with winds from the east and west, it was hard to put two fast laps together. Overall, I feel pretty good about what we got done."

The session was toughest on Eliseo Salazar, Stan Wattles, and Davey Hamilton. They hit the wall hard but were not seriously injured. Salazar's Dallara-Oldsmobile went beneath the white line in Turn One and lost control of its back end going into the short chute. The Dallara made right-rear contact with the outside wall, rode along it, and impacted the wall again in Turn Two. Salazar spun to the inside, where he was able to walk away with only a bruise to the right side of his face. The Dallara's right side was heavily damaged.

Wattles did a 180-degree spin and hit the outside wall in Turn One with his Dallara-Oldsmobile's left side, which had extensive damage. Wattles did not stop until he was in Turn Two. "I was just getting the car up to speed, trying to find another 1 or 2 miles an hour," Wattles said. "I was going to stay on the throttle and just got too low

going into Turn One. I hooked it and the car came around and slapped the left side."

Hamilton spun exiting Turn Two and rammed backward in his Dallara-Oldsmobile into the inside wall. The rear of the car was destroyed.

Helio Castroneves bent the front and rear right-side suspension on his Dallara-Oldsmobile when he made a light impact with the outside wall in Turn One. "Unfortunately, I kissed the wall a little harder today," Castroneves said.

"Maybe it's my line. The reason I clipped the wall is the understeer, I guess."

Having won the pole for the 2000 Indy 500, Greg Ray (22) was confident of posting a qualifying time that would return him to the front row for the 2001 race. *Walt Kuhn*

DAY-AT-A-GLANCE

Date:	Friday, May 11
Drivers on Track:	39
Cars on Track:	46

TOP FIVE DRIVERS OF THE DAY

Car	Driver	Speed (mph)
2T	Greg Ray	225.403
8	Scott Sharp	224.715
51	Eddie Cheever	223.981
5	Arie Luyendyk	223.673
35T	Jeff Ward	223.504

The Choice Of Champions.

Firestone Congratulates Sam Hornish Jr. and Pennzoil Panther Racing.

Sam Hornish Jr.
2001 Champion
Indy Racing
Northern Light Series®

Sam Hornish Jr. made history September 2. With the points he earned in the Delphi Indy® 300 at Chicagoland Speedway, the 22-year-old driver clinched the 2001 Indy Racing Northern Light Series® championship. No other person has won a major league open wheel championship in the U.S. at such a young age.

Driving the Firestone-equipped Pennzoil Panther Dallara/Olds car, Hornish recorded 10 top-three finishes this year, including wins at Miami, Phoenix, and Fort Worth. He led a total of 765 laps, earned the pole at Gateway and finished all but 7 laps. And he still has history to write in upcoming IRL competitions.

The 51,000 employees of Firestone salute Sam and the Pennzoil Panther team for their success in 2001 Indy Racing Northern Light Series competition. We have a feeling we'll be seeing more of him—even if it's just a blur at over 200 mph.

The Choice of Champions... Firestone.
The exclusive tire for the Indy 500®
and the Indy Racing Northern Light Series®

2 0 0 1   I R L   W i n n e r s

March 18	Phoenix, AZ	**Sam Hornish Jr.**
April 8	Homestead, FL	**Sam Hornish Jr.**
April 28	Atlanta, GA	**Greg Ray**
May 27	Indy 500®	**Helio Castroneves**
June 9	Fort Worth, TX	**Scott Sharp**
June 17	Pikes Peak, CO	**Buddy Lazier**
June 30	Richmond, VA	**Buddy Lazier**
July 8	Kansas City, KS	**Eddie Cheever Jr.**
July 21	Nashville, TN	**Buddy Lazier**
August 12	Sparta, KY	**Buddy Lazier**
August 26	St. Louis, MO	**Al Unser Jr.**
September 2	Chicago, IL	**Jaques Lazier**
October 6	Fort Worth, TX	**Sam Hornish Jr.**

Firestone
52 WINS
A RACING LEGEND AT THE INDY 500.

INDY RACING
Northern Light
Series

Firestone®
America's Tire Since 1900

firestonetire.com
tiresafety.com

Firestone is a proud supplier of tires to the Indianapolis 500® and the Indy Racing Northern Light Series.® Since the league was founded in 1996, the annual points championship has been won 5 times by drivers on Firestone® Firehawk® racing radials.

Indy 500® is a registered trademark of the Indianapolis Motor Speedway.

when our
network
engineers
need inspiration,

they spend
a day at the
track.

Photo: courtesy of The Indianapolis Motor Speedway

WorldCom is home to the fastest

speeds available over the Internet

today. So is it any wonder we're a

proud sponsor of the INDY Racing

League® and INDY 500®?

generation d.

by Tim Tuttle

To the pole winner goes the spoils. Scott Sharp, 2001 pole winner (right end of check), earned numerous prizes as well as $100,000 and the best seat in the house for the Indy 500. *Roger Bedwell*

Scott Sharp kept his right foot planted to the floor even as smoke poured off the right front tire. The Dallara's rear tires were sliding to the outside, trying to take an arclike path that would snap Sharp around and send him into the outside wall. It was the edge of adhesion, the limit of the laws of physics, and not a place for the timid or tentative. This first lap of a qualifying run for the 85th Indy 500 was not the time to lift.

"It all came down to how gutsy you were in Turn 1," said Tom Kelley, Sharp's car owner.

Sharp had plenty, streaking through that first corner on his way to a 225.783 mph opening lap. The next three confirmed his courage and car control on the most important Indy car qualifying day of the

year. Sharp clicked off laps of 226.020, 226.423, and 225.923. His four-lap average of 226.037 put him on the pole, worth $100,000 from MBNA; an Oldsmobile valued at $40,000; and prestige that lasts a lifetime.

"I carried some serious speed in the corners," Sharp said. "On my first lap in Turn 1, I saw smoke off the right front. We were loose and I had to turn hard to make it. My car actually was fairly loose, I'd say, for the first couple of laps and then it was perfect after that. I pretty much kept the hammer down all four laps."

Sharp had not been able to complete a four-lap qualifying simulation in practice, prevented by caution periods. He had the fastest lap of the week, 226.137 on Wednesday, until MBNA Pole Day morning practice, when Tony Stewart tore off a 226.996 mph lap. And Sharp didn't think his top lap was that strong, crediting a draft from another car for assistance.

"We didn't spend a lot of time on low downforce (a qualifying setup) this week," Sharp said. "I got up this morning and I didn't know where we were going to sit. I felt the best we could finish would be on the pole and the worst we could finish was probably sixth or seventh. It just was going to be how we could put our four laps together."

Sharp and engineer Jeff Britton decided against running in practice, which was held in 50-degree temperatures. "We've tinkered around like that the past two years and got messed up, and I was determined not to let that happen again," Sharp said. "But you can't believe how hard it was to stand there and watch a bunch of guys (actually two: Stewart and Greg Ray) throwing 226s on the board."

It was still cool, in the mid-50s, for the 11 a.m. start of Time Trials. Sharp's Delphi Automotive Systems–backed car was 13th out, 70 minutes after Arie Luyendyk had been the first. Gil de Ferran's Dallara-Oldsmobile had the fastest four-lap average to that point at 224.406.

Sharp's pole-winning average was the fastest of the five 500s with the Indy Racing League's normally aspirated formula, and 2.566 mph better than Ray's 223.471 in 2000. Sharp had five IRL wins prior to taking his first pole at Indy, but he regarded it as the superior achievement. "I certainly would call it my greatest accomplishment in racing," Sharp said. "When you think about the emotions and anticipation, nervousness, all that goes into it, from a race driver's standpoint, I think qualifying for the Indianapolis 500 is probably the single hardest day you have all year. And so to be able to come out of it as we did feels like a tremendous accomplishment and, obviously, a tremendous weight off our shoulders."

Ray took two shots at Sharp trying to win the pole for the second straight year. The Team Menard driver, going out 26 minutes after Sharp, had an opening lap of 224.862 and didn't take a second one. "He didn't like the speed and he didn't like the setup," owner John Menard said. Nearly five hours later, with the shadows of Happy Hour descending across the front straight, Ray headed out for his second attempt. He ran three laps at over 225 and, with Pole Day's conclusion approaching, decided to put the Johns Manville Dallara-Oldsmobile into the field. The 224.512 final lap dropped his average to 225.194. It was not what Ray and the Menard team had worked for, but it did carry them into the middle of the front row. It was a disappointment, not a disaster.

Ray qualified on the front row for the fourth straight year. He also started second in 1998 and 1999. In Ray's rookie 500 of 1997, he started from 30th. That experience helped him keep 2001 in perspective. "I'd much rather start at the front rather than at the back," Ray said. "I remember back in '97, you see all the sand and haze. You can't breathe back there. That haze is all the pavement being thrown up on you. My eyes were burning and tearing up because of all the methanol. The air made it feel like I was being lifted up. I'll tell you, I never want to be back there ever again."

Ray accepted that Sharp's 226.037 was out of reach. "We never did find that magic sweet spot," Ray said. "I think there might

have been a little bit more in the car had we done a few more things. I don't really know that we could have done four 226s even if it was perfect. I'm pretty proud of my guys. I don't think we left a whole lot on the table. I really felt like we gave it our best shot.

"Team Kelley just stepped up. They found something different. They blew up one of the engines the day before or two days before trying to test it, and so they have a big-time hot qualifier (engine). They had about 30 pounds more of drag, if you look at all the downforce pieces and appendages on the race car. They had a lot more drag in the car, a lot more downforce. So for them to be more stuck to the ground and be faster, that's pretty impressive. They have something really big in the back."

Like Ray, John Menard was satisfied with second. "We wish we had the pole, but we're very happy with second," Menard said. "The front row is great, second is great. We were just a little ticked off and that isn't much when you're running those speeds. They (Sharp and the Kelley team) came up with more speed than we thought they would and we came up with less speed than we thought we would."

Robby Gordon had not been expected to challenge for the front row, based upon his practice speeds, but he ran four of his fastest laps of the month to take the third starting position. Gordon's average of 224.994 in A.J. Foyt's Dallara-Oldsmobile was better than any other lap he ran the entire month. The performance put Gordon on the front row for the first time in seven 500s. It was the fourth year in a row that a Foyt-owned car qualified on the front row.

Gordon had not been over 223.032 before MBNA Pole Day. He ran 224.524 in the morning practice, but was seventh in a high-speed session. He and Foyt decided to wait until the late afternoon to make their first attempt, and Gordon was the second out among a wave of cars using the same strategy. His opening lap was a stunning 225.990, which he followed with 225.366, 224.291, and 224.338. "I didn't think we would be able to put up that high of a number," Gordon said. "We waited for a little better condition. We probably missed our gearing just a little bit, because I never got on the rev limiter at all. I stayed flat through that first lap. I was going 233 when I entered Turn 1 and had a big loose condition. I adjusted the (sway) bars a little too much and went to a push and had to lift in Turn One. It took a few more laps to recover after that. The third lap was slow because of the push. I'm very happy where we qualified and pretty excited about being on the front row."

Mark Dismore, Sharp's teammate, was on the front row for 32 minutes before Gordon and Ray knocked him off. Dismore, whose first attempt was waved off after one lap at 221.197, averaged 224.964 to take the fourth starting position. "I've had a hard time getting around Turn 1," Dismore said. "What's a little disappointing is there's more left in the car than we showed. I just couldn't get through Turn One. I was turning the wheel (in Turn 1) the right direction half the time and the wrong direction the other half."

Gil de Ferran and Helio Castroneves took the pressure off Penske Racing before it had a chance to build. They qualified solidly in their first attempt, banishing the haunting history of 1995 when Penske failed to make the race. The organization had undergone a

Robby Gordon (41) turned in an outstanding qualifying run to earn a spot on the outside of the front row. Gordon races infrequently, and in a variety of vehicles, but usually does well at Indy. *Walt Kuhn*

complete renovation in the six years since the last 500 it entered, but owner Roger Penske wasn't taking anything for granted this time. He focused the team's attention on qualifying and did little race preparation in practice.

The week had gone smoothly for de Ferran, who peaked with a 225.620 in the MBNA Pole Day morning practice. He averaged 224.406 in his four-lap qualifying attempt, placing him in the middle of the second row. "It was a solid run," de Ferran said. "There were no heart-stopping moments. I knew what the car [Dallara-Oldsmobile] had and I let it do it. It's been a great week for us; not once was '95 mentioned. We were concentrating on getting in the show. We accomplished that and we're happy."

Castroneves had trouble with tricky Turn 1 in practice. He grazed its wall on Thursday and banged it with enough force on Friday to damage the right-front suspension. The Brazilian had to switch to his backup Dallara-Oldsmobile, which had run only 36 laps previously that week, for the remainder of Friday and Pole Day.

Castroneves's confidence was boosted from a 224.190 in the morning practice prior to qualifying. He averaged 224.142 on his first attempt, placing him 11th on the grid. Turn 1 nearly got him that time, too. "Since I've been here, Turn 1 has been my biggest nightmare," Castroneves said. "I was really close again, but I knew where I was going. I had a little wiggle in Turn 1. I asked, 'Should we wave off?' They said no way. I just told myself, 'Let's keep going. I don't have another chance.' I think it was a good run. It was a little disappointing. I was flat out and expected to go faster. It's the best we had."

It was crucial for the two Penske drivers to get into the race on their first attempt. They had to leave on Monday for a Championship Auto Racing Teams (CART) race in Japan, taking away the possibility of working on race setups in the second week of practice. Safely in, they used the practice time available on Sunday's second qualifying day to prepare for the race.

Arie Luyendyk was going for his fourth pole at Indianapolis, but his effort was thwarted by a down-on-power Oldsmobile. The Dutchman, the first to attempt a qualifying run, averaged 224.257 in Treadway-Hubbard Racing's G Force to take the outside starting position on the second row. "I know I'm in there, but I want to be up there," Luyendyk said. "The week had gone really smooth except a day like today when it really counts. On the backstraight, I heard a clunk. I felt it (the engine) this morning already. It didn't feel like it did yesterday. We thought about changing the motor this morning (following practice). We weren't sure. There were no signs on any of the data, so we decided to take this first run. I guess my instinct was right.

"I definitely went into Turn One a lot harder than I have all week because that's what you have to do, save the best for last," Luyendyk added. "It feels good to know that I'm still able to feel the car and work with the guys to set up the car even with feeling things that don't show up on the data. The next time I tell the guys to change the engine, they'll know to just do it."

Veterans Tony Stewart and Jimmy Vasser, driving Chip Ganassi Racing's G Force-Oldsmobiles, would have preferred to be closer to the front, but they were content with productive runs that put them in the race.

Stewart qualified in 7th position at 224.248, and Vasser was 12th at 223.455. "I had a good run," Stewart said. "It's not quite what we had been hoping for, but we're in. The first two laps weren't bad. The third and fourth were a little tighter (understeer), but this wasn't a situation where we were trying to go for the pole. I was taking the conservative approach to the qualifying run. All we wanted was to be in the first three rows."

Vasser suspected he did not have the horsepower of some of the other Oldsmobiles. "The car was fantastic," he said. "I just think we are a little down on power. It didn't have the straightaway speed. You're never satisfied if you're not on the pole. Obviously, we had higher expectations than that. You have to respect this place. You can't get greedy."

Jeff Ward abandoned an early qualifying attempt, pulling in after one warm-up lap. "We had zero downforce," Ward explained. "It made for a long day knowing the car wasn't quite perfect. We changed the balance to try to get some grip back."

Four and a half hours later, Ward averaged 224.222 to take eighth on the grid in Heritage Motorsports' G Force-Oldsmobile. Ward's first lap was a crowd-stirring 225.751, but each of the three that followed was slower. "We decided to come back late in the afternoon where we'd been good earlier in the week," Ward said. "We had a push on my first lap. It wasn't too bad, but I knew I had to back out of it. It just floated up the track and I downshifted between the short chute. It kept pushing in Turn One and I had to ease off. It was challenging in Turn One."

Robbie Buhl, in Dreyer & Reinbold Racing's G Force, was the fastest qualifier with the Infiniti engine, ninth on the grid at 224.213. "We had a tire vibration right from the get-go," Buhl said. "Normally a vibration goes away into the run, but this one picked up. We're just happy to be in the show solid."

we had a shot at the front row without the engine overheating, but I'm happy to be in the position I'm in."

The week leading to Pole Day had been a search for speed that had eluded and baffled Sam Hornish Jr. and Panther Racing. Hornish ran 263 laps through Thursday and his fastest was 220.235. "We were very frustrated after five days," Hornish said. "We finally found something that worked for us and made me feel comfortable in the car. We kept going to Dallara and asking, 'What else do you have to try on this car? We tried five different sets of suspensions.'"

Finally, on Friday, Hornish ran 222.380 in his Oldsmobile-powered car. "We knew we found something in the right direction and

Stock car racer and Indy 500 veteran Tony Stewart (33) returned to the Speedway in his quest to win the 500. He posted the seventh-best qualifying speed for a third-row starting spot. *Ron McQueeney*

Buddy Lazier's qualifying attempt began with much promise, laps of 225.403 and 224.495, before falling off to 223.904 and 222.973. Lazier averaged 224.190 in Hemelgarn Racing's Dallara-Oldsmobile, placing him 10th on the grid. Lazier lost speed when the Oldsmobile overheated during the final two laps. "It went up 50 degrees and we lost some power," he said. "The car was handling perfectly. My engineer (Ronnie Dawes) hit the setup perfectly. I think

fine-tuned it in Saturday's practice," said Hornish, who lapped at 224.873 in the session.

Hornish's qualifying run was a little erratic, but he averaged 223.333 to take the 13th starting position. Hornish led off with his fastest lap of the month, 224.942, then fell off to 220.764 from a handling problem on his second lap and concluded with 223.808 and 223.862. "I'm more relieved than I am happy," Hornish said.

Walker Racing was forced to wave off Sarah Fisher's first attempt when the headrest from her Dallara-Oldsmobile flew into the air intake during a 221.704 lap. "Since it (headrest) was in the back, it just about pulled my head off," Fisher said. The team regrouped and 90 minutes later Fisher qualified for the 15th starting spot at 222.548 average. "What we got on the run was all we had," Fisher said. "We even got a little more than we thought we would have. This year is harder compared to last year because the competition has been stepped up about 10 notches, but I'm definitely having a lot more fun this year."

At the 6 p.m. gun ending MBNA Pole Day, the field held 27 cars. They included those driven by Robby McGehee (14th), Scott Goodyear (16th), Jaques Lazier (17th), Jon Herb (18th), Al Unser Jr. (19th), Michael Andretti (24th), Eddie Cheever Jr. (25th), Roberto Guerrero (26th), and Buzz Calkins (27th).

Unser's 221.615 average would eventually become the final speed from Pole Day to make the 33-car field. Five of the eight drivers behind Unser did requalify for the 500 in the final two days of Time Trials, but the fact they had to run again showed the tremendous depth of the field.

The fastest car on MBNA Pole Day clearly belonged to Sharp. "Today is the first race, and I guess you can say we won that," Sharp said.

But the day did not end on an upbeat mood, especially for the Kelley and Penske teams. Late in the afternoon, news from England reached the track that Ilmor Engineering cofounder Paul Morgan had died in an airplane crash.

The Kelley and Penske teams had joined together to fund a development effort with Ilmor for their Oldsmobile engines, each paying $750,000. The Ilmor-built Oldsmobiles had taken three of the top five positions on Pole Day.

Ilmor had not been involved at the Speedway since 1996. It had built the Chevrolet powerplants that won Indy between 1988 and 1993 and the Mercedes-winning engine of 1994. Roger Penske had provided the capital for Ilmor to establish its operation in 1984, partnering with Morgan and designer Mario Illien. At the time of Morgan's death, they each owned 25 percent. The other 25 percent is owned by Mercedes. "It's just devastating," Penske said. "Mario was the designer, but Paul Morgan was the one that kept it together, so it's a tremendous loss."

Ilmor's first Oldsmobile had been on the dyno in December 2000. "They've bridged a huge gap from never even having an IRL engine on the dyno until December to where they are now," Sharp said. "These other engine builders are very strong in the IRL. They told us all along they thought they'd be here by Indy and if you'd asked me a couple of races ago, I probably would have raised an eyebrow, but they've really closed the gap amazingly." But Sharp put the role of his engine in perspective. "It's the package here, not just the motors, but a large part of that (pole) is the gains that Ilmor has made."

Tom Kelley had not known Morgan long, but it was evident they were developing a strong friendship. "Paul Morgan was the open-wheel racing fan in Ilmor," Kelley said. "I know they approached this as a business decision, but they really wanted to be here. I know

Ilmor put a lot of their own resources into this program. They wanted to do well. For them to put together a pole-winning engine in six months is phenomenal.

"It breaks my heart for Paul Morgan to miss this."

DAY-AT-A-GLANCE

Date: Saturday, May 12
Qualification Attempts: 35
Qualifiers: 27

POLE DAY QUALIFIERS

Car	Driver	Speed (mph)
8	Scott Sharp	226.037
2T	Greg Ray	225.194
41	Robby Gordon	224.994
28	Mark Dismore	224.964
66	Gil de Ferran	224.408
5T	Arie Luyendyk	224.257
33	Tony Stewart	224.248
35T	Jeff Ward	224.222
24	Robbie Buhl	224.213
91T	Buddy Lazier	224.190
68T	Helio Castroneves	224.142
44	Jimmy Vasser	223.455
4	Sam Hornish Jr.	223.333
10	Robby McGehee	222.607
15T	Sarah Fisher	222.548
52	Scott Goodyear	222.529
77	Jaques Lazier	222.145
6	Jon Herb	222.015
3	Al Unser Jr.	221.615
21	Felipe Giaffone	221.100
55T	Shigeaki Hattori	221.098
32	Didier André	220.985
88T	Airton Daré	220.966
39	Michael Andretti	220.747
51T	Eddie Cheever Jr.	220.513
7	Roberto Guerrero	220.054
12T	Buzz Calkins	220.039

Michael Andretti, Eddie Cheever Jr., and Buzz Calkins took major gambles by withdrawing, withdrawing cars that were in the field in order to qualify for a second time. When the second day of time trials had concluded, it was clear they had each made a prudent decision. Andretti, Cheever and Calkins increased their four-lap averages and moved from shaky to solid ground in the starting lineup.

Andretti qualified at 220.747 mph in the opening hour on MBNA Pole Day, a speed he considered safe. By that night, Andretti wasn't sure. "I didn't sleep well," he said. "It was a stressful time." Team Green had planned to use Sunday's midday practice to work on race setups for Andretti, who had to leave for a CART race in Japan that night and would not be able to return to the Speedway for at least a week. After nine cars, including the backups of Cheever and Calkins, exceeded 221 in the morning practice, team owner Barry Green decided to instead prepare Andretti's backup Dallara-Oldsmobile for a qualifying attempt.

Green had formed a technical partnership with Panther Racing for the 500. "Barry said, `Let's put Sam's (Hornish Jr.) setup on it exactly,' " Andretti said. "We blueprinted his car. It was definitely a better setup."

Andretti practiced for 22 laps. "We ran a 220 in the heat, which was good for me," Andretti said. They waited deep into Happy Hour. Andretti reached the front of the qualifying line with 18 minutes in the session remaining and Green notified Indy Racing League officials the team's qualified car was being withdrawn. "We were reluctant to do it, it's a bit risky," Green said, "but now we can go to Japan knowing we're safely in."

Andretti averaged 223.441. "The car stuck," he said. "It was really good. I didn't know how quick we would go. I sure didn't think 223. If we weren't quick enough, we were going to wave off the run and put someone else in the car to get it up to speed (for Bump Day). We still had plans B, C and D." None of those, of course, were preferable to Andretti getting into the show himself. "I'm getting too old for this," he said. "But at least now we know we're in for sure."

Cheever had been unhappy with his 220.513 on Pole Day. "It was definitely one of my worst first qualifying days," he said. "The only thing that could have been worse is we could have crashed."

The 1998 Indy winner had been forced into his backup Dallara-Infiniti by electrical problems. "We had a series of failures we could not find this morning," he said.

The Cheever-owned team installed new electrical components in the primary car and Cheever ran 223.183 in the morning practice on Sunday. It convinced him to requalify in Happy Hour. With eight minutes remaining, Cheever withdrew the backup and started an attempt that finished with a 222.152 average.

"The car's handling was good," Cheever said. "You can put that down as one of my happiest moments at Indy in a long time. I can't think of anything more humiliating than not qualifyng for the Indy 500. I actually do feel like I qualified on the pole."

Calkins had been the second to qualify on Pole Day, running 220.039. It turned out to be the slowest of the 27 cars that qualified. The team knew it was in trouble. After Calkins ran 222.760 in practice, they became the first to withdraw their qualified car.

"A lot of people thought we were crazy," team owner Brad Calkins said. "They said you never do that because too many things can happen and catch you out. But we had to take the chance."

Calkins requalified his Dallara-Oldsmobile at 222.467. "Feelingwise, it wasn't that much different than yesterday," he said. "The conditions are pretty great right now. Knowing the speed was there made the decision easier. It is a big risk [to requalify], but if you look at the weather you know it [Pole Day speed] was out of there. You have to be a little proactive. We knew we were going to get bumped."

Chip Ganassi had originally intended to bring his regular CART drivers Bruno Junqueira and Nicolas Minassian, both rookies, to

Indianapolis. Neither had any oval experience prior to 2001. Ganassi had a change of heart in late April and, looking for drivers with more oval experience, hired Tony Stewart and Jimmy Vasser for the 500. But after Stewart and Vasser qualified on Pole Day, Ganassi decided to put Junqueira and Minassian in backup cars.

"Stewart and Vasser had the cars set up," Ganassi explained. "Mike (Hull, team managing director) and I talked about it and figured we've got two cars, we've got two guys, we might as well give them some experience."

Junqueira and Minassian had passed Indy's Rookie Orientation program in mid-April, but that constituted their only laps on the famed 2.5-mile track prior to the second day of qualifications.

Open-wheel racing veteran Jimmy Vasser (44) qualified 12th-best for the 2001 Indy 500, giving him hope that he could break through for his first Indianapolis victory.
Dan Boyd

It didn't take long for them to get up to speed. Junqueira, driving a G Force-Oldsmobile that Vasser had run at 222.907, topped the morning practice with a dazzling 225.243 achieved on his 20th of 23 laps. Minassian ran 222.054 on his 21st of 35 laps in a car Stewart had lapped at 223.186 in practice. They were ready to qualify.

Ten minutes after the track opened for qualifications at noon, Junqueira and Minassian were both in the field. Junqueira had the fastest average of the day at 224.208; Minassian ranked third at 223.006.

"I have to thank Jimmy (Vasser) and Tony (Stewart) for giving me a great car," Junqueira said. "I went out on one outing this morning and did a 225. I said, 'This car is awesome. We can qualify on, like, the front row.' If I had the opportunity to win the pole, I would have tried harder."

Minassian also credited his veteran teammates for the work they did on the car. "Tony Stewart and Jimmy Vasser did a hell of a job this week," he said. "I just jumped in the car this morning and ran a few laps. You just have to get in and do it."

Jeret Schroeder and PDM Racing, stretched thin financially and in manpower, bounced back from two crashes that restricted their practice laps to qualify at 222.786.

Schroeder had been in one of 11 cars involved in a chain-reaction crash at Atlanta Motor Speedway the week before practice began at Indianapolis. PDM's Dallara-Oldsmobile was destroyed and Schroeder missed the opening three days of practice as a new car was put together.

After running 103 laps over two days, with a best of 220.856, Schroeder crashed hard in Turn 2 on Thursday. The Dallara was extensively damaged. PDM, which had insurance that carried a $50,000 deductible, took delivery of another new Dallara, received some parts help from John Menard in exchange for carrying a sponsor decal, and had the car on the track by MBNA Pole Day. Schroeder didn't find the speed to make a qualification attempt until the Sunday-morning practice, when he ran 222.327.

"I have no idea how they put the car back together so quickly," Schroeder said. "They gave me a car that was capable of 222. I finally had a car with good balance and that felt comfortable so that I could attack the corners and stand on it. I knew it was a solid, safe car."

Davey Hamilton had not been able to break the 220 barrier in practice until the Sunday-morning practice, when he ran 222.979. Hamilton, who crashed in the Sam Schmidt Motorsports' Dallara-Oldsmobile in the closing minutes on Friday, became a second-day qualifier by averaging 221.696.

Part of Hamilton's overnight improvement was additional horsepower supplied by an Ilmor-built Oldsmobile, loaned to Schmidt by Kelley Racing. "The Ilmor gave us the power," Hamilton said. "The car was as free (aerodynamically) as we've had it. Thank God we're in, and we're in with a decent speed."

Tyce Carlson, in Tri Star Motorsports/Immke Racing's Dallara-Oldsmobile, qualified at 220.480. The team had decided that the perfect conditions, in the 60s and with no wind, were too good to pass up. "We were flat, flawless all the way around," Carlson said. "We had to take a time. It might rain or be 90 degrees next Sunday."

It was a heartbreaking day for Eliseo Salazar. The Chilean had completed three laps with a high-222 average when an engine failure prevented him from qualifying. "I only had two corners to go," Salazar said. "I felt the motor going as I went into Turn Three, but I thought I could make it. I knew it was going to blow, but I once heard a story about how (Arie) Luyendyk was smoking on the last lap and got through and it blew on the cool-down lap. That was my hope, it would get one more corner." The engine erupted in smoke in Turn Four, forcing officials to turn on the yellow lights for oil on the track. Salazar's last lap was 191.966, dropping his four-lap average to 214, but it did not count. Under the rules, a qualification attempt cannot be completed under caution.

Salazar's previous two days had been rough, too. He crashed in A. J. Foyt's Dallara-Oldsmobile on Friday and Saturday in practice. The second crash was also caused by an engine failure. "This is just something unreal," Salazar said on Sunday.

Memo Gidley, in practice, and Stan Wattles, in qualifying, also crashed Sunday.

Stephan Gregoire waved off after three laps that averaged 218 in the day's other qualification attempt.

Indianapolis added a third qualification day, one more than in 2000. Salazar, Wattles, Gregoire, Gidley, and the other hopefuls would have another chance in a week on Bump Day.

Of the 32 cars in the field, Roberto Guerrero's 220.054 was slowest and Carlson's 220.480 was next. One spot remained before the bumping would begin.

DAY-AT-A-GLANCE

Date: Sunday, May 13
Qualification
Attempts: 11
Qualifiers: 8

DAY TWO QUALIFIERS

Car	Driver	Speed (mph)
44T	Bruno Junqueira	224.208
39T	Michael Andretti	223.441
33T	Nicolas Minassian	223.006
9T	Jeret Schroeder	222.786
12	Buzz Calkins	222.467
51	Eddie Cheever	222.152
99T	Davey Hamilton	221.696
60	Tyce Carlson	220.480

by Tim Tuttle

Billy Boat posted the fastest lap among the nonqualified drivers at 219.203 mph on the Opening Day of a short second week of practice. It was a productive 26-lap session in which Boat tried to balance saving tires and protecting his Dallara-Oldsmobile from harm with developing a setup capable of putting him into the field.

"What we're working for now is consistency," Boat said. "We think we found some things today that will help with that. The problem is you run out of tires. Obviously, you run the fastest with new tires, but you have to save tires for the race. Firestone brought a great tire here, but they are best when they are new. That's when you can really tell if you're making gains." Each driver had 25 sets of tires available for practice, qualifying, and the race this year at Indianapolis. Eight sets were considered optimum for the race.

Indy veteran Boat also was careful to keep his car off the wall, running just within the limit of the car. "Usually, that point becomes the qualifying effort," Boat said. "As a driver, you want to push it all the time, but you don't want to put yourself further back than you already are with a torn-up race car. You want to push it hard enough to know where you are at, but not hard enough to go over the edge.

"It can be frustrating and that's the whole challenge of Indianapolis. It can be taxing. We know we need a couple of more miles an hour to make the race. We've been struggling with mid- to corner-exit understeer. You can't qualify here if you're lifting off the throttle." Boat was fifth-fastest overall for the day. Greg Ray had the top lap at 222.266 and was also second in his backup at 221.085.

"We worked hard on race setup running with full tanks," Ray said. "We were looking for more balance in muggy, thick air like we had today. It makes the car a lot different in this type of air. We've been really conservative with our tire usage this month. With only 25 sets per driver, you've got to watch how you are using your tires."

Shigeaki Hattori ran a whopping 76 laps in his Dallara-Oldsmobile and was the second-ranked driver at 220.639. "We tried our race setup," the Japanese driver said. "I have a good feeling for what the car will do. It's pretty good in traffic. It's very consistent in any conditions."

Several drivers in the field prepared their backups to be ready if they were bumped on the final qualifying day. Brazilian Airton Dare was the day's third-fastest driver in his unqualified G Force-Oldsmobile at 220.369. "Basically, we are fine-tuning our setup and getting it prepared for Sunday if we have to use the primary car," Dare said. "The next three days will be very busy for the crew and me, but we are making big strides and making lots of progress."

McGehee ran 45 laps with a best of 219.128 and pronounced Cahill Racing's Dallara-Oldsmobile ready for the race. "Our race day setup is perfect," McGehee said. "The car is great. We're going to do everything else that is associated with Indy." McGehee didn't run another lap until Carburetion Day.

Rookie Cory Witherill was the second-fastest nonqualified driver at 215.860. He was 13th overall. Steve Knapp was third among the nonqualified group and 15th overall at 214.664.

Fashion model, motorsports enthusiast, and IRL spokesperson Elaine Irwin-Mellencamp, wife of singer John Mellencamp, helped promote the 2001 Indy 500 and the Indy Racing Northern Light Series. *Jim Haines*

DAY-AT-A-GLANCE

Date:	Wednesday, May 16
Drivers on Track:	22
Cars on Track:	21

TOP FIVE DRIVERS OF THE DAY

Car	Driver	Speed (mph)
2	Greg Ray	222.266
55	Shigeaki Hattori	220.639
88	Airton Dare	220.369
98	Billy Boat	219.203
10	Robby McGehee	219.128

by Tim Tuttle

Always a top contender in the 500, veteran Scott Goodyear put his Thermos Grill2Go Cheever Indy Racing Infiniti into the field in the 16th starting position.
Walt Kuhn

Raul Boesel had no intentions of driving at Indianapolis this year. Without what he considered a competitive opportunity lined up prior to May, the veteran of 12 Indy 500s decided against going from garage to garage in Gasoline Alley looking for one.

Boesel was in his native Brazil when he received a phone call from countryman Felipe Giaffone following the second day of qualifications. Giaffone knew that his 221.100-mile-per-hour four-lap average, sixth slowest in the 32-car field thus far, could be in trouble. "I asked Raul if he could come and help me out by qualifying another car," Giaffone said. "If I wasn't bumped, then Raul could drive it in the race. If I was, I would replace him. He agreed."

Two nights later, Boesel arrived at Indianapolis. He was fitted into a Treadway-Hubbard Racing G Force-Oldsmobile, originally intended as Arie Luyendyk's backup, the next day. And on Thursday, Boesel put his experience to work by running 50 laps with a best of 220.518. It was the third fastest of the day.

Boesel had not driven a race car since the previous 500, when he had been with the Treadway team. "Some other teams had called, but I wanted to make sure it was a good effort," Boesel said. "When Treadway called, I didn't think twice. It was a good day. We made good progress. Indianapolis is so special and every opportunity you have to run here is wonderful."

Team Menard's Greg Ray was fastest, for the sixth time in eight practice days, at 222.283. "We worked with a heavy, full race setup trying to find a good, balanced car and also on aerodynamic downforce," Ray said.

Billy Boat was fastest among the nonqualified drivers and second for the day at 220.866. After a three-hour and 37-minute delay in the 11 A.M. scheduled practice start, Boat spun exiting Turn Two only six minutes into the session. His Dallara-Oldsmobile made light contact to the inside wall with the left-rear wheel, but the Curb-Agajanian/Beck Motorsports team had it back out before the close of the session. "We have been struggling with exit understeer for some time," Boat explained about his early spin. "We made some adjustments, but we just went too far the other way."

Boat was happier at the end of the day. "I think we are making progress," he said. "We made a big change to the setup and we had more success. We've got something very good to work with and tweak. Conditions are constantly changing and we're working with them."

A. J. Foyt decided to add Donnie Beechler to his stable, a decision complicated by primary driver Eliseo Salazar's two crashes and failure to qualify the previous weekend. Foyt purchased a new Dallara for Salazar and put Beechler in Salazar's backup. Foyt's team needed Wednesday to prepare Salazar's car, which prevented Beechler from running. In Thursday's first outing in his new mount, Salazar completed 33 laps and was sixth fastest at 218.891; Beechler's top lap out of 27 was 218.224, 13th for the session.

"We're just shaking down a brand-new car and getting rid of some minor problems," Salazar said. "We had a fuel pickup problem and stuff like that. The weather is very hot and muggy. I don't think it was a day conducive to really find the setup for speed. We're just getting ready for the weekend."

Beechler used the session as a reorientation to the track and the car. "I haven't been in an [Indy] car since October and haven't been here since last year," he said. "We weren't planning on going fast, but I took some laps and A. J. slapped some [new] tires on. We clicked off a 218 and I stayed in the car and did some more laps. I'm fortunate because [teammates] Robby [Gordon] and Eliseo have already shaken down the cars. They are already set up. It makes my job easier."

DAY-AT-A-GLANCE

Date: Thursday, May 17
Drivers on Track: 26
Cars on Track: 26

TOP FIVE DRIVERS OF THE DAY

Car	Driver	Speed (mph)
2	Greg Ray	222.283
98	Billy Boat	220.866
5T	Raul Boesel	220.518
24	Robbie Buhl	220.222
52	Scott Goodyear	219.959

by Tim Tuttle

As the hours dwindled, drivers still looked for the speed that would put them into the 500. They lost the previous day's entire practice to rain, and only one full-day session remained before Bump Day. It was crunch time.

Indy veterans Steve Knapp, Jimmy Kite, Jim Guthrie and John Paul Jr. were on the outside and in a desperate quest to put together a car that would sustain four laps fast enough to make the field.

Knapp, who finished third and was Indy 500 Rookie of the Year in 1998, was driving for small-budgeted Brayton Racing. The team also entered rookie Memo Gidley and concentrated on his effort in the first week. Knapp didn't turn his first laps at speed until the eighth day of the event. His G Force-Oldsmobile had run only 107 laps, with a best of 219.720 mph, going into this session.

During the session, Knapp's situation deteriorated further. Knapp had a top lap of 217.865 when the G Force scraped the wall between Turns 1 and 2 in the closing minutes of the practice. The car wasn't damaged, but it wasn't going very fast, either.

"I don't know what happened," Knapp said. "We've had limited track time with this suspension. It felt good. It got to the bottom of the track, like it should. All of a sudden, it started to move. It started going up toward the wall. I let off and couldn't recover it and hit the wall. I got on the brakes before it could spin around and send me somewhere else."

Kite, a three-time starter in the 500, replaced rookie Brandon Erwin in McCormack Motorsports' G Force-Oldsmobile at the end of the opening week of practice. He had run only 84 laps, with a best of 220.004, prior to that practice. Kite continued to struggle, with a 217.804 as his fastest.

Guthrie ran 227 laps over the opening seven days of the event but couldn't crack the 220 barrier. Finally, the three-time 500 starter broke through with a 221.454 in Blueprint Racing's G Force Oldsmobile. The underfunded team, conserving its resources, sat out two practice days before resuming.

What had been a difficult day, with a best of 217.312, became a disaster with 35 minutes left in the session. Guthrie's G Force slapped the wall hard in Turn Four and damaged its right side extensively. The crash crushed the hopes of Guthrie and Blueprint of making the race.

"The car didn't turn," Guthrie said. "We're done. Done. The sponsorship potential is gone. We had to be in the show. We're only about $100,000 upside down and have a totaled car. This is worse than a broken leg."

Paul's opportunity with Zali Racing came together very late. The team didn't get Paul's G Force-Oldsmobile onto the track until May 17, when the seven-time 500 veteran ran seven shakedown laps. This session was his first at speed and Paul managed a 212.394 in 38 laps. The team lost more time in the afternoon when the engine had oil pressure problems. With a long way to go, Paul had only the practice time squeezed in around Bump Day qualifying to do it.

In only his second day in the car, Raul Boesel posted the day's fastest lap at 222.547. Impressively, the Brazilian needed only 15 laps to reach that speed in Treadway-Hubbard Racing's G Force-Oldsmobile. "The car is really solid," Boesel said. "I'm still coming up to speed myself, but I'm really comfortable in the car."

Billy Boat was second for the day at 222.177 and confident he could put four laps in that range together in qualifying. "I think the biggest thing that the team found is that we had some discrepancies when we were setting up our race car, actually on our setup pad itself," Boat said. "Once we discovered that, we seemed to have made the car more consistent, a happier race car to drive."

DAY-AT-A-GLANCE

Date:	Saturday, May 19
Drivers on Track:	35
Cars on Track:	37

TOP FIVE DRIVERS OF THE DAY

Car	Driver	Speed (mph)
5T	Raul Boesel	222.547
98	Billy Boat	222.177
8T	Scott Sharp	221.218
4T	Sam Hornish Jr.	221.059
14T	Donnie Beechler	221.03

by Tim Tuttle

Billy Boat wasn't going to sweat out Bump Day this year, not after what he'd been through in 2000. When the Speedway opened at noon for the third and final day of qualifications, Boat's Dallara-Oldsmobile was the first to roll out of the line. He put four laps together that averaged 221.528 mph and became the 33rd car in the field.

A buffer of six cars stood between Boat and the uncomfortable position of being on the bubble. He was "moderately optimistic" that the speed was secure. And, when the six-hour session was over, there were some moments of high anxiety. With 48 minutes remaining, Boat slid onto the bubble with cars still in the qualifying line. "To sit there and you say it's 48 minutes, but it seems like eternity because car after car was taking a shot at us," Boat said. Twelve drivers attempted to dislodge Boat. "Every time somebody went out and they'd click off a 221, it was like someone was punching you in the stomach," he added.

Shigeaki Hattori, trying to bump himself back into the field, gave Boat his most harrowing moment with 10 minutes remaining. Hattori averaged 221.467 in his Dallara-Oldsmobile, completing his 10 miles .0448 second slower.

In 2000, Boat sat in the opposite position when he bumped his way into the field in the final minute. "At least last year when I was in the race car I knew what I had to do," Boat said. "I was focused and I went out and did my job. This year, I'm sitting on a golf cart absolutely helpless, and somebody else is out there taking a shot at me. It (driving) is a much better feeling. At least you have some control when you're in that race car and you can say either I put the thing in or I didn't. When you're standing outside, you just look up at the sky and say, 'Help me out here.' Once again, we proved this is not an easy race to make. You don't walk into the Indianapolis Motor Speedway and sit in a race car and qualify for this race."

It was a typical, pressure-packed, make-or-break Bump Day, like so many in the past. With 23 qualifying attempts and six cars bumped—the most since 1993—it was dramatic.

Eliseo Salazar, Donnie Beechler, Raul Boesel, Cory Witherill, and Stephan Gregoire forced their way into the field. Roberto Guerrero, Tyce Carlson, Didier André, Felipe Giaffone and Shigeaki Hattori were knocked from it. Airton Daré had the distinction of bumping back in after being bumped out. Jimmy Kite, Memo Gidley, Richie Hearn and Casey Mears took their shots and missed.

Salazar had been sailing smoothly along toward a Pole Day effort he hoped would land him on the front row. The Chilean, who drove over 223 mph in practice, was thwarted twice that first qualifying weekend, both times by engine failures. The first put him in the wall in the Pole Day morning practice; the second sank an attempt on his final lap to put him solidly into the field.

Fifteen minutes into Bump Day, Salazar breezed to a four-lap average of 223.740 in A. J. Foyt's Dallara-Oldsmobile. The bad dream was over. "I don't want to lie," Salazar said. "I was really worried. This must be the 21st century version of Chinese water torture. It was a nightmare what happened last week, (losing the engine on) the last corner of the last lap. We knew we had the speed, but after last week, you don't believe anything until you see the checkered flag."

Beechler's opportunity to qualify was dependent upon Salazar, Foyt's full-season driver in the Indy Racing Northern Light Series. Beechler, the veteran from Springfield, Illinois, didn't have a ride at the start of the month. Foyt hired him prior to the second week of practice. "When he told me he wanted me for his third car, my heart started pumping," Beechler said.

Foyt was looking for a driver with the experience to get on the pace in a minimum of laps. Beechler proved to be an ideal selection. In 70 laps of practice, Beechler ran 222.622. Now, with Salazar in the show, it was Beechler's turn. He was next in line. Beechler opened with a 224.616, and his second lap was 225.206. "I thought to myself, 'We really don't need to run that fast. We weren't going for the pole.' Once we got up to speed, I took my time and feathered the throttle a little bit." Slowing slightly for the final two laps, Beechler's four-lap average of 224.449 was the fastest of Bump Day. "A.J. is amazing," Beechler said. "Don't ever think that he doesn't know what he's talking about when it comes to getting around that racetrack."

Boesel, another who didn't start practicing until the second week, delivered Felipe Giaffone's insurance policy less than 30 minutes into the session. The Brazilian, with 75 laps in practice prior to his qualifying attempt, put the Treadway-Hubbard Racing G Force-Oldsmobile into the show with a 221.879 average. "We knew this morning (in practice) we had the speed," said Boesel, who had done a 222.041. "We didn't change much. I took it a little conservative. It didn't take much to get comfortable in the car."

Boesel knocked out Airton Daré, who was prepared to respond. Daré bumped himself back in 45 minutes later, averaging 222.236 in TeamXtreme's G Force-Oldsmobile. The Brazilian had averaged 220.966 in his initial qualifying effort and, fearing it wouldn't keep him in the field, ran 142 laps in the second week of practice. "We were ready to be bumped," Daré said. "That half hour (out of the race) was the worst half hour of my career, for sure. I watched guys last year in my position and I thought, 'Man, that's got to be bad.' Now I know it's the worst feeling."

Daré's G Force had some mechanical problems in the practices leading up to Bump Day and were using the qualifying attempt as a trial run. "We had a gearbox problem last night and our guys did an engine change last night," Daré said. "We didn't know if we had fixed the gearbox problem. We thought we'd go out on this run and see how it felt, since we had two attempts left. But the car felt good, so we took it." Daré spoke about his subsequent run, "We started to pick up a little understeer on the third lap and then I had a big understeer on the fourth, so we had a little bit of a slowdown. I was pushing it to the limit, for sure. I tried to correct with the weight jacker, but it still pushed."

Daré's return to status as one of the 33-fastest qualified cars was the final attempt in nearly four hours. Those hours were spent by drivers and teams trying to either get their current mounts going faster in practice or making a deal in the garage for a more promising machine.

Two minutes into the final hour, rookie Cory Witherill rolled out of the qualifying line. In 501 laps in practice prior to the Bump Day session, Witherill's fastest lap had been 219.746. He made a dramatic jump in the midday practice, lapping at 222.006 in Indy Regency Racing's G Force-Oldsmobile. Witherill proved it was no fluke with a splendid four-lap qualifying average of 221.621 that put him in the field. It included his fastest lap of the month, 222.117.

Indy Regency had gained some horsepower on Friday when it switched to a Team Menard–built Oldsmobile, but it alone did not supply the extra speed. Witherill had the Menard Oldsmobile on his initial Bump Day qualifying attempt that averaged 220 and was waved off following three laps. The chassis setup had to be good, too.

"We put our heads together," Witherill said. "Today we did a lot of setups to our car. We made one minor (setup) change before our qualifying attempt and just jumped right there into the 222s. It's a dream come true. I've been wanting to be a part of the Indy 500 for so long. Five years ago when I started racing the Indy Lights series, I didn't think I would have this day right now." Witherill also credited the new engine. "The power was just awesome," he said. "I noticed the difference right off hand. It helped out a lot."

Like Witherill, Stephan Gregoire had also endured a difficult month. The Frenchman started as the primary driver for Dick Simon

Racing. Gregoire was unable to exceed 220 in Simon's Dallara or G Force chassis in practice. Simon, with Gregoire's approval, brought in Roberto Guerrero to give the team a different perspective. Guerrero qualified the Dallara-Oldsmobile on MBNA Pole Day, leaving Gregoire to concentrate on the G Force for the second weekend. When Gregoire couldn't get over 220 early in the second week of practice, he went looking for another ride.

Gregoire found it at Heritage Motorsports, moving into Jeff Ward's backup G Force-Oldsmobile on the Saturday prior to Bump Day. Gregoire ran 12 laps in the afternoon, topped by a 217.796, and burst into 223.541 in 10 laps of the Sunday-morning practice.

Buoyed by the fastest lap of the session, Gregoire tried to qualify in the opening 30 minutes and ran 222.993 on his initial lap. Surprisingly, Gregoire pulled into the pits, complaining the G Force was dangerously loose. After making an adjustment, Gregoire went back out 21 minutes later and completed three laps that averaged 220.690. The team waved off the attempt. "We made a change and the car pushed too much," Gregoire explained. Gregoire used the midday practice to fine-tune the setup. With 53 minutes remaining,

Having started and finished third in the 2000 Indy 500, Chilean Eliseo Salazar (14) struggled to qualify in the 28th position for the 2001 race in the Harrah's A. J. Foyt Racing Dallara-Oldsmobile.
Ron McQueeney

Raul Boesel qualified for his 13th Indianapolis 500 but turned his car for race day over to Felipe Giaffone. *Wlalt Kuhn*

Force-Oldsmobile, Kite completed four laps at 221.048. It didn't get him into the field.

Rookie Didier André had been in the field for a week, but he was bumped out by Daré. André would make two attempts in the final hour in Galles Racing's G Force-Oldsmobile. Andre waved off after a 220.012 lap in his first try and after a 221.195 on his second. "It's pretty tough not to make it," André said. "With the speed we had last week, I thought we were safe. I went 220 flat and we pulled in. I did a 221 flat and I had a big push and I knew that was the end."

Hattori, bumped by Witherill, also made two attempts to return to the field in his Dallara-Oldsmobile. The Japanese driver waved off the first after two laps that averaged 220.104. Hattori's second attempt of 221.467 barely missed knocking Boat out.

Rookie Memo Gidley had been unable to exceed 219 in Brayton Racing's G Force-Oldsmobile in practice. The team struck a deal with Kelley Racing for a Dallara-Oldsmobile on Bump Day. The car had not turned a lap before Sharp took it out in the midday practice and ran a 222.001 in 17 laps. Gidley moved into the seat, after only eight laps of practice and was forced into the qualifying line because time was running out.

Gidley's first attempt averaged 221.032 for three laps and the team waved it off. Gidley beat the gun ending qualifications by 10 seconds on his second attempt, but averaged a too-slow 221.198. "It was nice to get into a car and be able to bang on it and know that if you had just a few more laps to get it right, you could really do something," Gidley said. "When you're hanging on doing 218, you start to wonder how guys are getting those 223s. I mean, you know, but some doubt creeps in. But to go out and do 221.5 after eight laps of practice restores the faith I had in myself."

Rookie Casey Mears reached an agreement in the late afternoon on Bump Day with Walker Racing to drive its backup Dallara-Oldsmobile. Mears, the son of two-time 500 starter Roger and the nephew of four-time winner Rick, had entered Indy with Galles Racing, but had a fastest lap of 219.731 after more than 400 practice laps in its G Force-Oldsmobile. Mears also had crashed in practice, escaping without serious injury.

Mears didn't have time to practice in Walker's car. It had been set up by Sarah Fisher, who ran 217.851 the previous day working on race setups. Mears began his qualifying attempt with five minutes remaining. He had his three fastest laps of the month, all over 221,

Gregoire began his third and final attempt. He averaged 222.888, guaranteeing a spot in the field.

"It's such a relief," Gregoire said. "I've been worried all month. Was it the car? Was it me? Dick Simon has always been fast, especially with me. I was losing my confidence. Thanks so much to (Heritage Team Manager) Mitch Davis. He's a great engineer and gave me a great setup. Finally, I know it's not me." Gregoire would be the final driver to bump his way into the race. He was not the last to try.

Jimmy Kite had made an attempt early on Bump Day, waving off after three laps in the 219s. Kite had followed Gregoire's successful effort with another attempt, but waved off again after two laps that averaged 219.65. On his final attempt in McCormack Motorsports' G

but it was below what was needed to get into the race and the team waved it off to allow Gidley a chance. "If we'd have had a few more laps to make adjustments, I have no doubt he would have been in the field," team owner Derrick Walker said. "There was not much time to do anything."

Mears hadn't made the race, but it did rebuild some of his confidence. "For me, this is just awesome," Mears said. "When you're struggling, you can't but doubt yourself. I feel a whole lot better. It's nice for me inside to know that I could get the job done here."

Veteran Richie Hearn had been trying to land an opportunity all month. Finally, he found one on Bump Day with Tri Star/Immke Racing. Hearn replaced Tyce Carlson, who crashed the previous day and wasn't cleared to drive because of a sore back. Carlson's primary Dallara-Oldsmobile was knocked out of the field early on Bump Day.

Hearn was on the pace immediately, hitting 221.116 in the morning practice. Hearn's progress was halted in the midday practice when a fresh Oldsmobile, intended to be the engine used in qualifying, failed. The team was forced to put a high-mileage Oldsmobile with less horsepower into the Dallara.

Hearn ran one qualifying lap at 220.528 with 28 minutes remaining and the team waved it off. "We came close and it wasn't meant to be, but we proved that we could do it," Hearn said. "I'm glad I tried. I'd rather try and fail than not try at all. It just wasn't our day."

After Gregoire abandoned the Simon G Force-Oldsmobile, Guerrero worked with it to be prepared for being bumped. Guerrero, like Gregoire, could not get the G Force over 220. After being bumped earlier in the day, Guerrero took a shot in the final hour, but didn't come close. The Simon team waved off after Guerrero had an opening lap of 214.336. It was the second time in three years the Simon team failed to qualify for the 500. Prior to 1999, Simon had been in the field every year since 1983 as either a driver or owner. "There was something funny with the G Force right from the start," Guerrero said. "The first time I drove it, it wasn't quite right. We never got it going."

Unable to run competitive laps in Brayton Racing's G Force-Oldsmobile, Steve Knapp climbed into a Hemelgarn Racing Dallara-Oldsmobile on Bump Day. The car had been entered as a backup for Buddy Lazier, who had run 223.008 in it earlier in the month. Knapp, whose best lap in the Brayton car was 219.720, worked his way up to speed in the Hemelgarn Dallara and hit 219.393 by late afternoon.

Knapp missed his chance to make a qualifying attempt. Continuing to practice, Knapp spun exiting Turn Two with 80 minutes in the session remaining. The Dallara hit the outside wall. The damage wasn't severe, but there wasn't time to repair it. "I drove it hard into (Turn) One and it was good," Knapp said. "I got loose in (Turn) Two, which was strange because I hadn't been loose there all day." Knapp had qualified for the 2000 race without turning a lap prior to Bump Day. He had practiced 27 laps and put his car into the field, making it look easy. Knapp was trying to qualify for his fourth straight 500 this year. "I'd been here for three years before and things had worked out well," he said. "I talked to drivers then who were struggling and I didn't understand. Now I do."

After Gregoire bumped Giaffone in the final hour, Giaffone tried to get back into the field with 15 minutes remaining. He waved off following a 215.992 initial lap.

With the gun at 6 P.M. and Gidley's final-minute run too slow, Boat's place in the field was finally secure. The 33 fastest cars had been determined. The next day brought a change of drivers (allowed by Indy rules), however. Giaffone, Treadway-Hubbard Racing's full-season driver, was substituted for Boesel. It was a deal Boesel agreed to prior to joining the team. If Giaffone successfully qualified, Boesel would have driven a third Treadway-Hubbard car in the 500.

"I'm certainly disappointed because I really thought 221.100 (Giaffone's qualifying average from Pole Day) would be enough and I would have a chance to race," Boesel said. "Everything happens for a reason, I guess. I knew why the team called me and what the plan would be in this situation. All the appropriate arrangements were made up front. I wish the team the best and I hope I have the opportunity to work with the team again in the future."

Treadway-Hubbard Vice President Scott Cronk explained: "Our commitment is to Felipe and Hollywood for the 2001 season. We all really thought 221.100 would hold, so we didn't want to withdraw our qualified car. We knew, however, if we did get bumped, it would be late in the day. So, we did not want to risk not having the opportunity to go back out and qualify if time ran out or if we had a problem as we saw with some other guys last week. We did, in fact, have a mechanical problem with the 21T [Giaffone's backup] on Sunday and could never get the car up to speed. This was a well-thought-out plan to protect our interest in having Felipe and a Hollywood car in the race." Giaffone had mixed emotions. "It wasn't the way I wanted to get into the race," he said. "I have to thank Raul for his help. But I'm happy to get into the race. We needed to make sure we were in it no matter how we did it."

DAY-AT-A-GLANCE

Date: Sunday, May 20
Qualification Attempts: 23
Qualifiers: 7
Bumped: 6

BUMP DAY QUALIFIERS

Car	Driver	Speed (mph)
84	Donnie Beechler	224.449
14	Eliseo Salazar	223.740
35	Stephan Gregoire	222.888
88	Airton Dare	222.720
5T	Raul Boesel	221.879
16	Cory Witherill	221.621
98	Billy Boat	221.528

by Tim Tuttle

Scott Sharp (8) and the Kelley Racing Team beat Gil de Ferran (66) and Marlboro Team Penske in a preliminary round of the 25th annual pit stop contest as part of Coors Carb Day. Sharp and his team went on to win the competition.
Dan Boyd

Scott Sharp and Kelley Racing landed a solid one-two punch on Carburetion Day, taking a decisive victory in the final on-track activity prior to the race. Pole-sitter Sharp posted the fastest lap at 223.678 mph during the two-hour practice, which is used primarily to ensure that chassis and engines operate perfectly. Sharp and his crew also triumphed in the Coors Indy 500 Pit Stop Challenge.

Sharp ran 19 laps in the session in approximately the same late-morning time frame as Sunday's scheduled start. "Obviously, it's the last chance to run the car," Sharp said. "We wanted to confirm the race-starting setup was strong right out of the box. The car was real strong and we just didn't need to stay out any longer. That was probably the real advantage of running today. No one has had an opportunity to run in cool conditions. It gave you some data to be able to guess off for Sunday (Race Day)."

Gil de Ferran was second fastest at 222.757. The Penske Racing driver completed the most laps in the session, 43. "Overall, I'm very happy with the car," de Ferran said. "It's handling very well. I'm very comfortable with where we are at. We know what we have and we know what we have to do."

Buddy Lazier's 222.392 was third. "I felt the practice went quite well," the Hemelgarn Racing driver said. "We ran a speed that we were able to get a good feel for, gearwise. It's a pretty fast day out there, faster than I thought it would be. At this stage, we're not going to make too many changes.

"This is our race engine. We did a leak test to make sure there were no leaks and did setup verification. We did a fair amount of practice last week with our backup car and just wanted to make sure, verifying that all the work we did transferred over to this car."

Team Menard's Greg Ray ran the fourth-best lap of 222.372 and Heritage Motorsports' Jeff Ward was next at 222.039. "We ran on full tanks and worn tires," Ray explained. "We were just trying to confirm the gear ratios."

Ward had the top lap by a G Force chassis. "I'm really excited about this car," he said. "It looks good and it runs even better. Today was a great practice. Our speed was good and consistent. The car was easy to drive, which will make for great racing for the team on Sunday."

Several drivers did find problems with their cars: Eddie Cheever Jr.'s Dallara had braking problems and the team replaced its rear rotors; Jeret Schroeder's Dallara was limited to 12 laps from trouble with its gearbox; Cory Witherill's G Force caused a yellow for engine smoke, created by a loose oil-fitting.

Sharp's Kelley crew had four flawless and increasingly quicker pit stops to earn $42,500, including $5,000 donated to the American Red Cross, in the 11-car competition. "We really wanted this one," said Robert Perez, Sharp's chief mechanic. "These guys worked very, very hard. We started in November getting things orchestrated and getting guys in the right place on pit stops. I took a different role and became a conductor, so to speak."

The Perez-directed crew defeated Buddy Lazier and Hemelgarn Racing in the opening round 10.32 seconds to 11.91. Cars are timed from when they enter the pit box until they exit it and must complete a four-tire change and simulate fueling. In the second round, the Kelley No. 8 car eliminated Eliseo Salazar's A. J. Foyt Enterprises entry, 9.53 to 10.65. Sharp's team, gaining momentum, needed only 9.31 seconds in the semifinals and won easily over the Penske Racing car of Gil de Ferran, who stalled in the pit box.

The Penske team, a six-time champion of the pit stop competition at Indy, also had its other hope, driven by Helio Castroneves, stopped in the semis by Al Unser Jr. and Galles Racing. Galles triumphed, 9.47 to 9.74. "It's like anything else out here," a disappointed Roger Penske said. "You want to win the pole, you want to lead the most laps, and you want to win this."

Sharp's Kelley team had the fastest stop of the competition in the finals, 9.20. The Galles team (which had won six previous pit-stop competitions) had trouble changing the right-rear tire when a lug nut got away and had to be replaced by one from the crewman's belt. Unser's stop took 12.67. "I really didn't expect a 9.2," Perez said. "This is a dream come true. We've been ridiculed a bit on pit stops."

"I tell you to go out there and beat Rick Galles, he's the best there is in pit stops," owner Tom Kelley said. "He even beat Penske out there. I told the guys to go out there and give it the best they've got. It's a real pleasure to beat Galles Racing."

Roger Penske congratulated Kelley, just as he had when Sharp won the pole, and it was a proud moment for the automobile dealer from Ft. Wayne, Indiana. "I told Roger any time you shake my hand twice in one week, it has to be a great week for me," Kelley said.

Sharp was understandably proud of his team, too. "The whole Kelley team has been practicing night after night and it's great they can come out here and show what they've got," he said. "Obviously,

it is the guys. I have the easy job. To ask these guys to do it perfectly four times, they did the job."

Mark Dismore's Kelley team scored a first-round triumph over Michael Andretti's Team Green, 10.14 to 10.66. Unser's Galles crew eliminated Dismore, 10.13 to 10.24, in the second round.

De Ferran's team opened with a win over Arie Luyendyk's Treadway-Hubbard team, 11.10 to 11.63, and took a second-round victory over Greg Ray's Team Menard, 9.88 to 11.00.

Castroneves eliminated 2000 Indy pit stop champion Panther Racing and Sam Hornish Jr., 9.61 to 10.42, in the first round, and Buzz Calkins and the Bradley team, 9.46 to 27.18, in the second round.

The Menard, Foyt, and Bradley teams had first-round byes.

With the conclusion of the pit stop competition, the track was closed to competition. Directly ahead was the 85th running of the world's most famous race and all the riches and glory that go with winning it.

DAY-AT-A-GLANCE

Date:	Thursday, May 24
Drivers on Track:	34
Cars on Track:	34

TOP FIVE DRIVERS OF THE DAY

Car	Driver	Speed (mph)
8	Scott Sharp	223.678
66	Gil de Ferran	222.757
91	Buddy Lazier	222.392
2	Greg Ray	222.372
35	Jeff Ward	222.039

It's me. What's shakin'?... Oh, really? Did you turn in your lineup already?... Man, I won my league two years ago, but injuries are just killing me this season... Yeah, like I can predict a torn ACL and two concussions when I'm drafting... Me, too. I drew the thirteenth spot this year, so all the stars were gone. Anyway, that's not what I was calling about... Well, about tomorrow... It doesn't look good... No, I'm not chickening out, I just... Oh, please. I'm not the guy who squealed when he got a little blood on his shirt... Dude, it was a scratch... No, Dickinson was the one who was really hurtin'. Did you know he had knee surgery like a month later?... Yeah, you might be able to cover him now... Right. You can't even... No, I want to play, but... No she didn't. Well, yeah, she did, but only because she had other plans for us tomorrow. It's not like... Okay... Okay, you done?... Very funny... What do you mean? She's not the boss. I'm not the boss either. It's all about compromise, man... I tried. She didn't bite... I tried that, too... Yeah, yeah, yeah. I tried everything. It's not gonna happen, man... No, you don't have to call the whole thing off. Why would you do that?... Why?... Call Stewart... Patterson, then... I don't know. Surely you know somebody who can play... I didn't put you in this situation. Apparently, I'm not the only one who... I already tried that, man. She won't budge... Why would I do that? Have you ever even dealt with a woman before?... Well, it's no wonder. Man, you've got a lot to learn... Okay, whatever. You can yap all you want. It still doesn't change anything... Listen to me. Tomorrow is not gonna happen. I'll be back next week... Yes, I swear... I'll be there... Yes, I've already cleared it with her, thank you... Ha ha... Okay, let me know who wins... Yes, I'll be there next week... Okay. See you tomorrow. I mean next week... Yeah, yeah. Whatever... Take it easy... Later.

Make a long story short.

With a new Nokia 5100 Series wireless phone, you can send mobile messages from phone to phone. You can also send e-mail and choose from our Xpress-on™ color covers. So express yourself, in as few words as possible.

www.Nokia.com

Top off your fluids.

HELIO CASTRONEVES AND PENSKE RACING DOMINATE

By
Jonathan
Ingram

The Indianapolis 500 has rarely seen a winner like Helio Castroneves, the exuberant Brazilian rookie who won the 85th running of "The Greatest Spectacle in Racing." After the race, he climbed the fence above the Yard of Bricks to salute the crowd before heading to victory lane—where he celebrated by pouring the traditional milk over his head!

"Hey, I just want to express my feelings, and I think everybody liked that," said the unabashed newcomer.

One thing was familiar, at least, about this wacky, postrace happiness. Fifteen members of the crew from Penske Racing joined Castroneves on the fence. They were helping to celebrate the record 11th victory at Indy by team owner Roger Penske and—after Gil de Ferran took second—the team's first one-two result.

In many ways, a large part of the Penske contingent clambering up the wide-mesh barrier and then hanging on by one hand to wave and pump their fists in triumph in front of the crowd symbolized the opening of a new era at the Brickyard. After a five-year absence, several of the front-line entrants from CART returned to challenge the regulars in

Helio Castroneves (68) became the eighth rookie to win the Indianapolis 500—and the first ever to climb the fence near the hallowed yard of bricks to celebrate his epic victory. Castroneves piloted the Marlboro Team Penske Dallara-Oldsmobile/Firestone to victory ahead of teammate Gil de Ferran, who finished second.

It was a short-lived lead for MBNA Pole winner Scott Sharp (8), who leads Greg Ray (2) down the front straight to start the race. Sharp failed to negotiate the first corner and crashed, ending his day.

HELIO CASTRONEVES AND PENSKE RACING DOMINATE

By
Jonathan
Ingram

The Indianapolis 500 has rarely seen a winner like Helio Castroneves, the exuberant Brazilian rookie who won the 85th running of "The Greatest Spectacle in Racing." After the race, he climbed the fence above the Yard of Bricks to salute the crowd before heading to victory lane—where he celebrated by pouring the traditional milk over his head!

"Hey, I just want to express my feelings, and I think everybody liked that," said the unabashed newcomer.

One thing was familiar, at least, about this wacky, postrace happiness. Fifteen members of the crew from Penske Racing joined Castroneves on the fence. They were helping to celebrate the record 11th victory at Indy by team owner Roger Penske and—after Gil de Ferran took second—the team's first one-two result.

In many ways, a large part of the Penske contingent clambering up the wide-mesh barrier and then hanging on by one hand to wave and pump their fists in triumph in front of the crowd symbolized the opening of a new era at the Brickyard. After a five-year absence, several of the front-line entrants from CART returned to challenge the regulars in

Helio Castroneves (68) became the eighth rookie to win the Indianapolis 500—and the first ever to climb the fence near the hallowed yard of bricks to celebrate his epic victory. Castroneves piloted the Marlboro Team Penske Dallara-Oldsmobile/Firestone to victory ahead of teammate Gil de Ferran, who finished second.

It was a short-lived lead for MBNA Pole winner Scott Sharp (8), who leads Greg Ray (2) down the front straight to start the race. Sharp failed to negotiate the first corner and crashed, ending his day.

IRL for motor racing's greatest prize, including a $1.27 million payoff to the race winners. The new era began with an ultracompetitive race that proved to be a Super Bowl of open-wheel racing in America with teams squaring off in a bid to claim the Borg-Warner Trophy.

Even Penske himself got caught up in the moment in one of his greatest triumphs and most unique moments in Indy history. "I promised Helio I'd climb the fence, too," joked the urbane business-man/racer, "but I'm going to climb it tonight with him when nobody can see me."

Perhaps no one had missed competing at Indy more than Penske, if only because he failed to make the field with both of his cars in 1995, the last season before the CART teams elected to go elsewhere instead of participating at Indy.

"When I think about today's race, and the finish, one-two, it kind of takes away the pain that we had in 1995," said Penske. "And I can tell you walking back to the garage with Al Unser Jr. and Emerson Fittipaldi at that time after we didn't make the field and coming up to Victory Circle today is a big difference."

The presence of three CART team owners—Penske, Chip Ganassi (who began the revival of front-line CART team owners competing at Indy by winning with Juan Montoya in 2000) and Barry Green—affected the competitiveness of the race. Penske's one-two finish was the fourth closest in history with just 1.7373 seconds separating Castroneves from de Ferran. Michael Andretti, driving for Green in a partnership with IRL regular Panther Racing, added 16 laps to a total of 398 laps led at Indy before finishing third.

Ganassi's team occupied fourth through sixth, the latter position

held by former IRL champion Tony Stewart, who became the first driver to repeat a same-day Indy–NASCAR double by flying to Charlotte, North Carolina, for NASCAR's 600-mile race immediately after the Indianapolis 500.

Although the three CART teams finished with their cars in the top six positions, the overall statistics were divided among the IRL and CART drivers in terms of laps led. Greg Ray (40), Mark Dismore (29), Stewart (13) and Arie Luyendyk (1) combined to lead 83 of the 200 laps. Driving for IRL regular A. J. Foyt Enterprises, Robby Gordon held the lead for 22 laps. CART drivers Castroneves (52), de Ferran (27), and Andretti (16) led a total of 95 laps.

Scott Sharp's (8) dream came true when he won the MBNA Pole, but the start of the race was a nightmare. He crashed in Turn One, never reached Turn Two, and finished last.

After three weeks in the media spotlight and attracting a legion of fans, Sarah Fisher (15) had only a short run on race day. She crashed on Lap 8 and finished 31st after having started 15th.

Back where he belongs—racing in the Indianapolis 500—two-time winner Al Unser Jr., crashed out of the race on Lap 17 while trying to avoid contact when Sam Hornish Jr., spun in front of him.

final 30 laps of green-flag racing, but he concurred with the Indiana native about the IRL versus CART situation when it came to the track action.

"We were all mixing it up together," said Andretti. "The end result was guys on top from CART, but throughout the whole race there was a mixture there."

Penske said he would put quite a few IRL drivers in his cars. Mike Hull, who directed the Ganassi effort, was also highly complimentary of Stewart after his experience during the month of May with the former IRL champion. "Both series have guys of equal ability, guys who can prepare the cars, and guys who know how to call the races," said Hull after his

Following the postrace exuberance, olive branches were offered in both directions as IRL and CART drivers relished the aftermath of an opportunity to compete in the white heat that characterizes battles on the 2.5-mile circuit at 16th Street and Georgetown Road.

"It's a bunch of guys driving race cars," said Mark Dismore, who lost five laps with a transmission change midway into the race before returning to finish 16th. "I think everybody is way past the CART/IRL thing." Andretti complained about Dismore holding up his progress as he tried to advance from third versus the Penske onslaught in the

team's Jimmy Vasser, rookie Bruno Junqueira, and Stewart finished fourth through sixth. "Some of the IRL guys favored before the race fell out with mechanical problems."

That included defending IRL champion Buddy Lazier, whose Hemelgarn entry ran most of the race on seven cylinders, and Robby Gordon, whose Foyt Dallara had an engine go soft after the first 75 laps following a front-row start.

Castroneves ran the perfect race by being ready to take the lead when it counted. He was not to be denied, despite his first

Greg Ray (2) sweeps past Davey Hamilton (99) on the front straight. Ray led three times for 40 laps and finished 17th in the Johns Manville/ Menards' Dallara-Oldsmobile/Firestone.

The elusive dream of an Indy 500 victory once again slipped from the grasp of Robby Gordon (41), who started on the front row in the Team Conseco/Foyt Racing/Richard Childress Racing Dallara-Oldsmobile/Firestone.

appearance at Indy, where he cheerfully underwent some rookie hazing by whitewashing the walls after scrubbing them with his Firestone tires earlier in the month during practice. The Brazilian spent most of his practice time extracting as much knowledge as possible from his veteran Penske team, which, for the first time at Indy was directed by Tim Cindric.

Where he was once white with fear after nearly crashing at the intimidating Turn 1 during his rookie orientation in April, Castroneves focused his dark eyes on gaining new knowledge every lap of the race. "The best lap I ever did at Turn 1 was during the race," he said with his trademark, ardent enthusiasm. "All during the race I tried to learn something there in traffic or by adjusting the car.

"When I came over here for practice and also when I did the rookie test it's easy for you to get lost," continued Castroneves, "and I was getting a little frustrated with Turn One because, man, sometimes it wouldn't steer, sometimes understeer, then oversteer, until I reached the point that I was kissing the wall. And I said, 'OK, that's the limit.' So sometimes you don't want to find the limit this way. And I believe we passed the whole time to try to make sure that we understand the car and then the weather.

"Sometimes you stop for lunch, then when you go back to make a change the wind is blowing a different direction. So I was getting upset with myself because I understood that when the wind changes you have to change the way, as well, to drive in a car. And it's not all the ovals you do that. Basically it's this one here only."

In 2000, Montoya won for Ganassi by getting his G Force-Aurora into the lead from the front row and keeping it there by gobbling up lapped traffic on the restarts. This year, Castroneves won by setting up his Dallara with Olds engines built by Ilmor Engineering to run well in traffic, enabling him to stay close to the leaders. Unlike in years past, the leaders had no lapped traffic in front of them on restarts because at the outset of the 2000 season the IRL adopted the practice of putting the leader at the front of the field after pit stops and waving any other cars around to the back.

"When I prepared my car it was to be balanced in traffic all the time," said Castroneves, whose laps in the free air as the leader in the final 52 laps were not the race's fastest. On the other hand, his best lap of 219.385 miles per hour came while trailing in second place behind teammate de Ferran.

The second half of the race may have been characterized by Penske dominance, but the first half consisted of cool weather, crashes, and mechanical breakdowns.

For the second straight year—and only the fifth time in 85 runnings—the pole-winning driver finished last. This time, Kelley Racing's Scott Sharp didn't last past the first corner. "It snapped right out on me," said a regretful Sharp, the first to be caught by the cold weather and track temperatures that dropped 10 degrees just before the start. Front-row starters Gordon (who would take the lead) and de Ferran narrowly dodged the whirling Kelley Racing car on its way to the outside wall. "He was sliding down the wall and the car started to come down, so I accelerated hard to make it by him and ran over a couple of pieces of debris," said de Ferran. "Thankfully, nothing happened there."

Within 7 more laps, Sarah Fisher spun at Turn 2 after taking a low line and collided with the car of Scott Goodyear, who went to the

Mark Dismore (28) was one of the eight drivers who swapped the lead 14 times. Dismore led twice, pacing 29 laps in the Delphi Automotive Systems/Bryant Heating & Cooling car before finishing 16th.

hospital due to a cracked vertebra. Sam Hornish Jr., another sophomore, took out the entry of Al Unser Jr. with exactly the same type of mistake, this one at Turn Four on the subsequent restart.

Unser Jr., who won the 1992 race in similar conditions that sent drivers crashing into the walls, said the front tires were not getting enough heat in them on the windy, cloudy morning. "It's just a matter of not getting up to speed [on the cold tires]," said the two-time Indy winner. "There's not enough downforce when you're following other cars."

"I've been running on the white line all month," said Fisher of her low line at Turn 2. "It's just very cold and there's absolutely no grip out there."

For his part, Hornish did an excellent job of collecting his car at Turn Four and returned to competition after getting towed into the pits, losing four laps. Andretti also came down pit road during the yellow-flag period for fresh tires after running over some debris from Hornish's spin. That would put him out of sequence with the other leaders for the remainder of the first half of the race.

Once the drivers began to adapt to tires that were slow to come up to temperature, the IRL entrants began to shine. After Gordon led

the first 22 laps, Kelley Racing's Dismore, Team Menard's Ray and Andretti, primarily due to his out-of-sequence stops, exchanged the lead for the next 112 laps.

Dismore was the first to falter, adding to a dismal day for Kelley Racing, when his transmission balked just shy of halfway after leading twice for 29 laps.

The weather then became a significant factor once more when overcast conditions began to signal the onset of rain. Running in second place behind Ray on the restart after a caution for the stranded car of Jeff Ward, Andretti began to pressure the leader, fearing rain might end the race officially after the halfway mark at 100 laps. "If there was no threat of rain then I would have coasted behind him and tried to save fuel," said Andretti. "I saw the clouds coming. I was pushing him as hard as I could. We were able to push him into a mistake. He hit the wall coming off Turn Three and I was able to get back into the lead."

The rain indeed began to fall four laps after Andretti got into the lead, and a yellow flag flew for 11 laps due to moisture on the track. Barry Green's desire to put his driver back on the same fuel sequence as the other leaders brought Andretti into the pit.

For the first time, de Ferran went into the lead after 110 laps, albeit under the yellow for the rain. Once the sun broke through, he clicked off laps in the 218- and then 219-mile-per-hour range following the restart. De Ferran pushed his lead up to 2.07 seconds versus his Penske teammate and 8.19 seconds over Andretti. After the caution flew for the accident of Cory Witherill in Turn Four, on Lap 135 all the leaders came down pit road together for the first time in the race.

It was the perfect opportunity for those who had not yet run at the front to test their cars in the clean air as the leader by beating the competition out of the pits. It also turned out to be the turning point in the race. Ganassi short-fueled Stewart, and he was rolling out of the pits as de Ferran and then Castroneves left their boxes. When de Ferran spun his wheels, Castroneves darted to the outside lane in front of Stewart—already at maximum pit speed—and apparently took the lead.

As it happened, Castroneves and de Ferran's move to the outside lane in the pits balked Stewart, who then braked, getting hit in the rear by Andretti, whose front wing was damaged. The IRL ruled that Castroneves and de Ferran had to move behind Stewart. The drivers at the lower end of pit road, where the Penske team had set up shop, had been told during the drivers' meeting to stay in the inside

lane until they reached the blend line and to not block cars already rolling down the pit lane.

So the first three positions were rearranged under the yellow to put Stewart ahead of Castroneves and de Ferran. "Tony pulled up alongside me (during the yellow) and waved and I waved back," said de Ferran, who took the demotion to third place in stride and said the

Michael Andretti (39) returned to the Speedway and led three times for 16 laps but fell from the lead in the second half of the race and took third place in the Motorola/Archipelago Dallara-Oldsmobile/Firestone.

Gil de Ferran (66) led 27 laps but was beaten out of the pits by teammate Helio Castroneves after their final stop, and de Ferran never regained the lead. He finished second behind the rookie winner.

Robbie Buhl (24) was pleased with his starting spot on the outside of row three, but he had to settle for a 15th-place finish, just behind IRL points leader Sam Hornish, Jr.

rules had been made clear at the drivers' meeting. But Castroneves, when dropped to second behind Stewart, took exception.

"When Gil started spinning his wheels, I went around him," he said. "The other drivers on pit road have to expect that we are in a battle. I'm just trying to not hit my teammate."

Now relegated to third, de Ferran's car did not work well in dirty air. He was passed for third place by Robbie Buhl down the front straight and into Turn 1 on Lap 142. For his part, IRL regular Buhl was running another outstanding race at the Brickyard, this time under Infiniti power in his Dreyer & Reinbold Racing G Force.

The front-runners all moved up one position when Ganassi, who called Stewart's race himself, brought his leading driver into the pits from the lead after just 12 laps during the next yellow for the damaged radiator of Donnie Beechler, another IRL driver who suffered bad luck. Since Ganassi had short-fueled him on the previous stop, he decided to get more fuel in the Target-backed G Force of Stewart. Andretti, meanwhile, lost track position when he came in to have his damaged front wing replaced.

By staying on a regular pit schedule, Castroneves moved into the lead ahead of Buhl and de Ferran with 52 laps to go, and gained

valuable track position on Stewart and Andretti, who restarted 14th and 21st in line, respectively.

The order was then briefly fixed during a red-flag period called at Lap 155 when a second, heavier spurt of rain came across the Speedway and drivers were instructed to halt their cars in the pits, where they stayed 16 minutes, 34 seconds. That was just long enough for Stewart, suffering a cramp in his right leg, to get a massage from a trainer and then return to his Ganassi entry.

Following two laps of yellow, the race went green once again at Lap 158, with Buhl hectoring Castroneves' rear wing. On Lap 159, Buhl tried to use his Infiniti power to get past the Brazilian at Turn 1. But Castroneves maintained the inside line and stayed above the white line, thwarting that bid. He added one-tenth of a second to his lead for each of the next two laps before Buhl spun at the exit of Turn Two on Lap 166.

"We had a car that could have won," said Buhl, a two-time winner in the IRL who made a nice recovery to keep his car off the inside retaining wall. "The Infiniti power was great. We had the car geared right. We didn't miss a beat. We were running second at the time, and we didn't want to run second. We wanted to lead."

It was clear the lead was the place to be on this day. One more

"Iron Man" Tony Stewart (33) led the 500 twice for 13 laps and finished sixth, then hopped into a helicopter to begin the trek to Charlotte, North Carolina, where he raced in a 600-mile stock car race that night.

Two-time Indy 500 winner Arie Luyendyk (5) endures the frustration of mechanical gremlins as his crew works frantically to get him back into the race. He finished two laps off the pace in 13th.

Close, but not fast enough, Jimmy Vasser (44) posted a top-five finish in the Target Chip Ganassi Racing's G-Force-Oldsmobile/Firestone. He started 12th and finished fourth.

round of pit stops gave de Ferran one last chance to get out in front due to the eighth and final yellow for Buhl's spin. The remaining leaders, now including Ganassi's Junqueira (who had benefited by the wave around rule to get back on the lead lap), pitted en masse one last time.

This time Castroneves and de Ferran both had problems with sputtering engines as they left their pits. But the leader got out first after getting to his pit stall first. Stewart, meanwhile, was late coming down pit road after giving up track position on his previous stop when the other leaders stayed out. He emerged 12th in line and fifth on the lead lap behind teammate Junqueira from the final round of pit stops. The team took the time to adjust the front wing on Stewart's car, which cost him.

"I hurt us," said Stewart, who had stalled on his inaugural trip down pit road. "We took too much downforce off the car in the end and that cost us."

Other than not taking each other out, Penske issues no team orders. So on the final restart, de Ferran tried his best on the outside at Turn 1 as Castroneves again protected the inside line—without going below the white line. "I wasn't going to squeeze my teammate down into the grass," said de Ferran. "So I tried to go around the outside. My car began to push and I couldn't get back on the gas soon enough.

"I didn't have enough for him when he was leading. I felt I was faster when in front by myself than he was by himself," continued de Ferran. In fact, de Ferran set the race's fastest lap (219.774 miles per hour) on Lap 132 while leading. But getting passed by Buhl prior to the red flag had confirmed that de Ferran's car did not work well in traffic.

With Stewart also mired in traffic—along with teammate Jimmy Vasser who had spent the first half of the race trying to get his Target-backed G Force balanced—that left Andretti as the only other con-

tender. After a day of out-of-sync pit stops for a cut tire, followed by the damaged wing episode, Andretti was a long shot, but the leading contender for first, in his family's history of bad luck at Indy.

Although he pulled to within 1.8 seconds of the leaders before a failed attempt to get past Dismore, Andretti said his new sticker Firestone tires were the wrong choice instead of scuffs as all the teams came down pit road the final time. The team also adjusted the front wing that had been replaced. But that was not enough, especially in traffic.

"We put a half turn into the front wing and we probably needed a full turn," said Andretti. "Not having the front end stuck down hurt me in traffic. The front wing was my fault, the tires the team's (fault)." So Andretti came up empty at Indy again.

The Penske camp had a sense of emptiness, too. Paul Morgan, one of the co-founders of Ilmor Engineering, had died in a tragic private plane crash in England the day before qualifying opened. Team

owner Penske also made note of the fact that the fatal accident of Greg Moore in the final race of the 1999 CART season, had led to the hiring of Castroneves as the teammate to de Ferran.

Morgan had experienced victory at Indy on seven straight occasions with his company's engines from 1988 to 1994, but Moore, a Canadian who came of age during the years CART teams did not compete at Indy, never had the experience of racing an open-wheel car at the Brickyard after one IROC race appearance in 1999. At least the 2001 race was a portent that the best teams in open-wheel racing—and drivers—would continue to meet at 16th and Georgetown in the future.

Three weeks before the race, rookie Bruno Junqueira (50) did not even expect to attempt to qualify, but team owner Chip Ganassi helped him qualify in 20th and the Indy first-timer finished fifth.

A roadside assistance program that puts AAA to shame.

If you have car trouble on some deserted stretch of highway, the Pennzoil Pit Crew is who you want showing up to help. They'd have you back on the road in no time. Somewhere around 9.5 seconds.

PENNZOIL
RACING

DALLARA/OLDSMOBILE/FIRESTONE

HELIO CASTRONEVES

#68 Marlboro Team Penske
Entrant: Penske Racing
Crew Chief: Rick Rinaman

Helio Castroneves, a rookie this year at Indianapolis, showed his inexperience at moments during practice. But when the race started, Castroneves drove with the poise and patience of a veteran. The 26-year-old from Brazil fashioned a flawless performance to win the 85th running of the "500."

Castroneves, supported superbly by the well-organized Penske team, led the final 52 laps. His skill was tested as he fought off challenges from Robbie Buhl and Gil de Ferran to hold onto the lead.

The victory was the first for Castroneves on an oval. With its long straights and four distinct turns, 230-mph entry speeds into Turns 1 and 3, and low-banked corners, Indianapolis provided him with a unique challenge.

Castroneves struggled in Turn 1 in the final two days of practice before qualifying. His Dallara escaped damage from a slight brush the first time, but he slapped it a little harder and broke the right-side suspension the next day. Those experiences turned out to be valuable lessons that he put to use during the race.

"I believe we practiced the whole time to try to make sure that we understand the car and then the weather. Sometimes you stop for lunch, then when you go back to make a change, the wind is blowing a different direction." Castroneves said.

"So, I was getting upset with myself because I understood that when the wind changes, you have to change the way (line) to drive the car. And it's not (with) all the ovals you do that. Basically, it's this one here only, because normally Japan or the rest of the ovals, like Nazareth or Chicago, you change the car to make sure that you go fast."

Castroneves averaged 224.142 mph on his qualifying run in his Dallara-Oldsmobile and started 11th. He realized early in the race that his Dallara was well balanced through an entire fuel load and was at its peak performance over the final 15 gallons of the 35-gallon tank.

Castroneves climbed into the top five by Lap 64 and was up to second by Lap 117, behind de Ferran. When the caution came out on Lap 137, the leaders pitted. De Ferran's pit box was near pit-out, with Castroneves' pit box directly behind. Tony Stewart was pitted seven boxes behind. Owner Chip Ganassi decided to save time by not filling Stewart's fuel tank. He was coming down the outside lane in the pits when Castroneves shot out from his pit box, across the inside lane and directly in front of Stewart.

Castroneves' Dallara had hit the ground one second ahead of de Ferran's Dallara and his move to the outside gave him the momentum to pass. But it also forced Stewart to lock up his brakes.

Indy Racing League officials ruled that Castroneves' double-lane exit from the pit box was a rules violation. Officials also said de Ferran would not have beaten Stewart to the exit line without Castroneves' interference. Under caution, they ordered Castroneves and de Ferran to move behind Stewart.

Castroneves said he moved to the outside to avoid running into de Ferran. "When I dropped the car, Gil was still waiting to finish the fuel," he said. "So, as soon as I started to engage first and leave the pits, he (de Ferran) started spinning the wheels. But I was already in the movement, so I didn't want to hit him in the back and even (hit) the mechanic. So, I tried to avoid him and I did not see

who was coming behind. So, sometimes in a situation like that, the guys coming behind, they should know that the guys leaving the pit, there's nothing we can do about it because we're in a battle on the pit lane."

Stewart's run at the front lasted only 12 laps. The Ganassi team's decision to short-fill his fuel tanks in order to get into the lead forced him into two more pit stops. Castroneves and de Ferran made it on one. When Stewart pitted on Lap 149, Castroneves went into the lead, with Buhl in second. Buhl challenged Castroneves inside and outside going into Turns 1 and 3 for many laps. Then, Buhl spun exiting Turn 2 on Lap 166.

It brought out the race's final caution. Castroneves and de Ferran pitted on Lap 168 and returned to the track running 1–2. De Ferran attacked Castroneves on the outside on the Lap 171 restart, drawing alongside in Turn 1. Castroneves held him off and wasn't seriously threatened again. "If you are leading, it's very difficult when you don't have somebody in front of you to go fast," Castroneves said. "I was consistent all the way, all four corners. When Gil pulled right beside me, I knew he wouldn't lift off. I knew he was going for it. But my car was working very well in the low line."

Castroneves' car worked better and better as the fuel load went down. Handling in traffic was a problem for many drivers, but not for Castroneves. "My car was getting faster and faster and faster by myself or behind somebody," he said. "And that's what I just kept thinking, do the same line, do the same thing to make sure. Don't change what you're doing right now, because what you're doing so far is working."

Castroneves became the second straight rookie and only third since 1927 to win at Indianapolis. Like 2000 Indy winner Juan Montoya, Castroneves is a veteran of the CART series. Castroneves' victory celebrations in CART had been to climb a chain-link fence to share the moment and salute the fans. Castroneves saw no reason to change his trademark performance. He climbed the outside fence and was joined by the Penske crew.

2001 INDY 500 PERFORMANCE PROFILE

Starting Position:	11
Qualifying Average:	224.142 mph
Qualifying Speed Rank:	13
Best Practice Speed:	224.716 mph (5/12)
Total Practice Laps:	458
Finishing Position:	1
Laps Completed:	200
Highest Position 2001 Race:	1
Fastest Race Lap:	123 (219.389 mph)
2001 Prize Money:	$1,270,475
Indy 500 Career Earnings:	$1,270,475
Career Indy 500 Starts:	1
Career Best Finish:	1st 2001

GIL de FERRAN

Gil de Ferran put forth a formidable effort as he challenged and then chased Helio Castroneves to the checkered flag. De Ferran's second place was a disappointment, softened by finishing behind his teammate and contributing to the first 1–2 at the 500 for Penske Racing.

"Ultimately, I wish I was first and Helio second, but I think when you step back for a moment and think about what this means for the team, it's just incredible," de Ferran said. It was de Ferran's second Indy 500 and it almost ended the way the first had in 1995, when his car was damaged in Turn 1 on the opening lap.

Starting from fifth position, de Ferran narrowly escaped the spinning car of pole sitter Scott Sharp. "I thought, 'Oh, no, not again,' " de Ferran said. "But he (Sharp) was sliding down from the wall, so I really accelerated hard to make it by him and ran over a couple of pieces of debris. Thankfully, nothing happened there."

De Ferran emerged in third place and was still running there, through two rounds of pit stops, until Lap 85, when he moved into second. Through his track position and good pit stops and strategy by the Penske team, de Ferran moved into the lead on Lap 110 and held it to Lap 136.

Under caution, de Ferran and second-running Castroneves pitted. In one of the key moments of the race, Castroneves edged de Ferran exiting the pits. "I thought I had him," de Ferran said, "but he just beat me. I didn't want to pull all the way out into the fast lane and when I hesitated briefly, my engine kind of coughed a little bit and he got by. That could have made a difference in the race."

Tony Stewart, working on a different pit strategy, was the leader, followed by Castroneves and de Ferran. On Lap 142, Robbie Buhl dropped de Ferran to fourth by passing him on the inside in Turn 3. After Stewart pitted on Lap 149, de Ferran was in third and in place for his second near-miss of the race. "Buhl spun off (exiting Turn 2) right in front of me and, boy, I tell you I had no idea where I was going," de Ferran said. "All I saw was smoke. I'm on the brakes. I didn't want to tear everything up and lose control. I drove straight. As soon as the smoke cleared, I saw him (Buhl) kind of veering off to the left. I got on the power again to try to clear the accident and stayed high."

De Ferran and Castroneves both made their final pit stops under the ensuing caution. Castroneves, by a nose, beat his teammate out. De Ferran's final strong attempt to reclaim the lead came on the Lap 171 restart. "I thought it was a great opportunity on that restart," he said. "I got on it (throttle) hard. He (Castroneves) went to the inside, so I said, 'OK, here we go.' And I decided to go to the outside, but you can't pinch a car down in the grass. I went out and turned in and it started to push, push, push. So, I really couldn't get back on the power and that was it. I couldn't get on the gas as hard as I wanted to. I guess I stayed high and that was it really." De Ferran was 1.73 seconds behind at the checkered flag. "It may have looked easy at the end, but it was a very tight and competitive race," de Ferran said.

Practice and qualifying went smoothly for de Ferran. He had the sixth-fastest lap in practice at 225.620 mph and qualified at 224.406. De Ferran's 219.769 was the fastest leading lap and second fastest of the race.

The Brazilian, a CART regular since 1995, was racing at Indy for only the second time. De Ferran was the CART champion in 2000.

2001 INDY 500 PERFORMANCE PROFILE

Starting Position:	5
Qualifying Average:	224.406 mph
Qualifying Speed Rank:	6
Best Practice Speed:	225.620 mph (5/12)
Total Practice Laps:	464
Finishing Position:	2
Laps Completed:	200
Highest Position 2001 Race:	2
Fastest Race Lap:	132 (219.769 mph)
2001 Prize Money:	$482,775
Indy 500 Career Earnings:	$632,228
Career Indy 500 Starts:	2
Career Best Finish:	2nd 2001

DALLARA/OLDSMOBILE/FIRESTONE

MICHAEL ANDRETTI

#39 Motorola/Archipelago
Entrant: Team Green
Crew Chief: Simon Morley

Michael Andretti's return to Indy was a roller coaster ride that carried him to third place, his second-best finish in 12 500s. Andretti had not competed at Indy since 1995 and made it clear before the race that his only joy would come from winning. Andretti's feeling wasn't altered in the aftermath of his determined charge from 21st on the grid.

"Yes, I'm disappointed," Andretti said. "You know, third is nice and great and stuff, but that's not why we were here."

Andretti avoided serious trouble twice early in the race. He dodged the out-of-control car of Sarah Fisher on Lap 8 and Sam Hornish Jr.'s spin on Lap 17.

Andretti's Dallara-Oldsmobile didn't escape entirely unscathed. It ran over some debris and a tire sensor told Andretti the left-rear tire was losing pressure. Andretti pitted on Lap 20 under caution, putting him at the back of the field. Following a Lap 21 restart, Andretti began carving his way forward during a stretch of 69 straight green-flag laps. He was out of pit-stop sequence with the leaders, allowing him to stay out longer and take the lead from Laps 48 to 52 before making his second pit stop. Andretti emerged in eighth, evidence of his competitive speed.

"We had a pretty good race car," Andretti said. "It was as good as anybody's." Still out of sequence with the leaders, Andretti took the lead again from Laps 81 to 84 before making his third pit stop at the end of Lap 84. He reentered the race in sixth. Andretti moved up to second on Lap 92 after several cars pitted under a caution that started on Lap 90.

With Greg Ray leading, Andretti began to pressure him following the green flag. Ray slid high in Turn 3, touching the outside wall, and Andretti moved into the lead on Lap 103. Rain was approaching the Speedway and, with the race past the halfway point and an official result assured, Andretti wanted to be in front in case it arrived and ended the race. "If there wasn't a threat of rain coming, I would have just coasted behind him," Andretti said. "But I saw those clouds coming in, so I pushed him as hard as I could and he made a mistake."

Rain caused a caution on Lap 107, but the race continued. Team Green decided to bring Andretti into the pits at the end of Lap 109. Andretti dropped to third for the Lap 119 restart. Andretti ran behind leader Gil de Ferran and Helio Castroneves for the next 18 laps before all three pitted under caution on Lap 136.

Exiting the pits, Andretti was behind Tony Stewart on the outside lane when Castroneves darted from his pit in front of Stewart. Stewart braked heavily and Andretti, despite slamming on his brakes, rammed Stewart with his Dallara's nose. "I just happened to get the worst of it," Andretti said. "It broke my [left front] wing." Andretti's wing began to tear apart in the wind force of 225-mile-per-hour race conditions and he slipped back to fifth. A caution on Lap 149 allowed Andretti to pit and replace the front wing. "That was the lucky part of the race for us," he said. "Otherwise, we were going to be in big trouble."

Andretti fell back to eighth and had five lapped cars between him and the lead. He made his final pit stop on Lap 168 and was in third for the final restart with 30 laps remaining. "We were back up front again," Andretti said. "At the last pit stop we made two mistakes: one was mine, one was the team's. They put stickers (unused tires) on and I asked for more front wing. The combination of the two made me really loose. I really couldn't fight there in the end. The car was as loose as it had been all day, which is a shame, because if it would have been as good as it was midrace or even early in the race, we had something for them (Castroneves and de Ferran), I really think. It was quite disappointing."

2001 INDY 500 PERFORMANCE PROFILE

Starting Position:	21
Qualifying Average:	223.441 mph
Qualifying Speed Rank:	16
Best Practice Speed:	223.566 mph (5/13)
Total Practice Laps:	391
Finishing Position:	3
Laps Completed:	200
Highest Position 2001 Race:	1
Fastest Race Lap:	100 (218.962 mph)
2001 Prize Money:	$346,225
Indy 500 Career Earnings:	$2,634,146
Career Indy 500 Starts:	12
Career Best Finish:	2nd 1991

JIMMY VASSER

#44 Target Chip Ganassi Racing
Entrant: Chip Ganassi Racing Teams
Crew Chief: Barry Wanser

Starting from 12th position, Jimmy Vasser drove a steady, savvy, and unspectacular race to finish fourth. It left him far from satisfied. "You come here to win and it's disappointing when you don't," Vasser said. "We had some problems. We lost fourth gear and it really hurt us on the restarts. We were just too far back there at the end to make much of a charge."

Vasser never had the outright speed to challenge for the lead, but consistently climbed toward the front. Vasser's high-water mark came on Lap 166 when he hit third. Vasser lost three positions on his final pit stop on Lap 168, and regained two of them by Lap 177. Vasser was 14 seconds behind winner Helio Castroneves at the checkered flag. The veteran, driving in his sixth 500, was sixth by the 100-lap mark and fourth with 150 laps in the books. Vasser moved up to third by going past the spinning Robbie Buhl on Lap 166. Vasser's fast lap of 217.265 mph ranked him 13th among drivers in the race.

Less than a month prior to the opening of practice for the 500, Vasser had not expected to be at Indy. He was driving for Patrick Racing in CART, and the team did not enter Indy. But Chip Ganassi, who had released Vasser at the end of the 2000 season, decided he needed more experience than he had in rookies Bruno Junqueira and Nicolas Minassian and hired Vasser and Tony Stewart for the 500.

Vasser had driven for Ganassi from 1995 to 2000. "Jimmy was the first guy that came to mind," Ganassi said. "He can climb in these cars today (May 7) and get the most out of it by this afternoon. He's familiar with our program, our structure, our personnel, and he understands the goal, and that is to win the race."

It was an opportunity with tremendous appeal for Vasser. "You know, it seems a little funny to come back and don the red Target uniform after what's gone on," he said. "In its simplicity, I'm stepping into, I think, one of the cars that has the best chance to win this race and I very badly would like to win the Indianapolis 500. I have to thank Chip for having the confidence in me to come and do a job."

Vasser ran up to 222.587 mph on his second day of practice and topped out at 224.394 in the MBNA Pole Day morning practice. Vasser qualified at 223.455 on Pole Day, placing him 12th on the grid. "The car was fantastic," Vasser said. "It was the best it has been all week long. I just think we were a little down on power. It just didn't have the speed, the straightaway speed. You're never satisfied if you're not on the pole. Obviously, we had higher expectations than that, but you have to respect this place. You can't get greedy."

Vasser also finished fourth in the 500 in 1994, with Hayhoe Racing. The 35-year-old led for 20 laps in the 1995 race when he crashed on Lap 171. Although it was a severe disappointment at the time, Vasser later credited that run at the front for energizing his career. Vasser won the 1996 CART championship, was third in 1997, and second in 1998. After missing four straight 500s, Vasser returned in 2000 and finished seventh.

Vasser's career at Indy began in 1992. He was a second-day qualifier, but was knocked out on Bump Day. Vasser used a backup car to get back into the

field and became the fastest rookie qualifier in the process. Vasser crashed in the race, conducted in extremely cold conditions, and broke his right leg. Vasser returned to the 500 in 1993 to finish 13th, completing 198 laps in an effort that solidified his career.

2001 INDY 500 PERFORMANCE PROFILE

Starting Position:	12
Qualifying Average:	223.455 mph
Qualifying Speed Rank:	15
Best Practice Speed:	224.394 mph (5/12)
Total Practice Laps:	351
Finishing Position:	4
Laps Completed:	200
Highest Position 2000 Race:	3
Fastest Race Lap:	51 (217.265 mph)
2001 Prize Money:	$233,325
Indy 500 Career Earnings:	$1,256,852
Career Indy 500 Starts:	6
Career Best Finish:	4th 1994, 2001

5

BRUNO JUNQUERIA

#50 Target
Chip Ganassi Racing
Entrant: Chip Ganassi Racing Teams
Crew Chief: Steve Gough

After going a lap down in the early portion of the 500, Bruno Junqueira rebounded to capture a fine fifth place. He was the second-highest finishing rookie behind winner Helio Castroneves. "Normally, I'm only happy if I win a race, but I'm really happy with a fifth-place finish," Junqueira said. "This is my second oval race and first 500-miler. I have never experienced a race like this before. This was a big experience."

The 25-year-old from Brazil had no previous oval race experience except for a CART event on the .946-mile track at Nazareth, PA. Junqueira did only 217 laps at Indy before starting the race, 40 in official practice and 177 in completing Indy's Rookie Orientation Program in mid-April. "The first half of the race I was just learning and I learned a lot," Junqueira said. "This was a long, hard race. You have to be 100 percent just to finish. I wasn't supposed to even be here, so I'm really very happy with fifth."

Although Junqueira had been fastest at 219.978 in the ROP, team owner Chip Ganassi decided to replace him and regular CART teammate Nicolas Minassian with Indy veterans Jimmy Vasser and Tony Stewart. When Vasser and Stewart qualified solidly in the field on MBNA Pole Day, Ganassi made an on-the-spot decision to put Junqueira and Minassian into backup cars. Junqueira did 23 laps of practice on the second day of qualifying and then posted the fastest four-lap average of the day at 224.208 to put it into the field. Junqueira was unable to practice in the second week because of CART's race in Japan. His other 17 laps were on Coors Carb Day.

"I knew I had one shot," Junqueira said. "I thought I was supposed to concentrate on the Japan race, then Chip gave me this opportunity. It's the biggest race ever in my life. All the drivers in the world dream of racing here. It was a big surprise when Chip called me to race.

"I have to thank Jimmy and Tony for giving me a great car. I went out on one outing (in practice) and did a 225(.243). I said, 'This car is awesome.' If I had the opportunity to win the pole, I would've tried harder. I knew I had to do laps of 222 to be safe and when I saw three laps of 224 (in qualifying), I slowed down on the fourth to be safe."

Junqueira went down a lap on the 48th lap. Running stronger, Junqueira moved up to ninth at 100 laps. He made his third pit stop out of sequence with the leaders on Lap 107 and fell back to 15th. Junqueira climbed up to 10th by Lap 130, but was still a lap down.

When a caution period began on Lap 134, the leaders pitted. Junqueira stayed out, returned to the lead lap and was in seventh position. The Ganassi team gambled on a caution being needed before Junqueira would have to pit again and it worked. The yellow came out on Lap 148. Junqueira was able to make his pit stop and settle back on the same sequence as the leaders. Junqueira made his final pit stop with the leaders under caution on Lap 168 and emerged in fourth position, his highest of the race. Junqueira was overtaken by teammate Vasser on Lap 176 and maintained fifth to the checkered flag.

Junqueira arrived in North America with outstanding road-racing credentials from South America and Europe. Junqueira was the European Formula 3000 champion in 2000. He also won the South American Formula 3 title in 1997 and several karting titles in Brazil. Junqueira was a test driver for the Williams Formula 1 team in 1999 and 2000.

2001 INDY 500 PERFORMANCE PROFILE

Starting Position:	20
Qualifying Average:	224.208 mph
Qualifying Speed Rank:	11
Best Practice Speed:	225.243 mph (5/13)
Total Practice Laps:	40
Finishing Position:	5
Laps Completed:	200
Highest Position 2001 Race:	4
Fastest Race Lap:	97 (215.781 mph)
2001 Prize Money:	$255,825
Indy 500 Career Earnings:	$255,825
Career Indy 500 Starts:	1
Career Best Finish:	5th 2001

6

TONY STEWART

#33 Target Chip Ganassi Racing
Entrant: Chip Ganassi Racing Teams
Crew Chief: Simon Hodgson

Tony Stewart was a bona fide contender until a trouble-filled final pit stop thwarted his chances of winning. The versatile driver from Columbus, Ind., brought his G Force-Oldsmobile home sixth, the final car on the lead lap.

Stewart led Laps 137 to 148 before making his next-to-last stop under caution. He had been hoping for an extended green-flag period, optimally to the checkered flag, which likely would have allowed him to regain the lead following the final round of stops by the leaders. But when the next caution period began on Lap 166, Stewart came with the leaders rather than face the prospect of a green-flag stop in another 12 to 14 laps. The situation forced Stewart into making a strategic decision to adjust his car's aerodynamic performance.

"It seems like if we could get ahead of the Penske cars (of Helio Castroneves and Gil de Ferran), we could hold them off," Stewart explained. "We were just fast enough to keep them from making a run on us, but if they got ahead of us, there wasn't any way we were really going to get by."

That had been the case during Stewart's 12-lap stretch in the lead. Knowing it would take two stops to the checkered flag, Stewart surrendered the lead with his pit stop on Lap 149 and dropped back to fifth position. Stewart's advantage, if the flag stayed green, was that he needed only one stop while the cars in front of him needed two. It was a scenario that meant a commanding lead.

"I was hoping to make a tire change on that last stop and get another set of tires that we had been saving for the end, but the way the yellow fell didn't work for us," Stewart said. "We did need that last caution."

Stewart's car needed less fuel than those of leaders Castroneves and de Ferran, both of whom had last pitted on Lap 136, when they came in on Lap 168. Stewart decided to forsake tires and took on fuel only. He also ordered the Chip Ganassi Racing crew to take away downforce. Stewart was ready to go three or four seconds ahead of Castroneves and de Ferran, but he stalled exiting the pit box. By the time Stewart restarted, he emerged in fifth.

"I hurt us," Stewart said. "We took too much downforce off the car in the end and that cost us. We were fairly reasonable in traffic as long as we had the downforce on it, but as soon as we took the downforce off, which was my call, we couldn't pass anybody."

Stewart started seventh and stretched his fuel, thanks to several cautions, to take the lead on Lap 46. He pitted on the next lap and fell to 14th. Stewart climbed up to fourth before making his second pit stop on Lap 80. Taking advantage of cautions, Stewart pitted early twice, on Laps 94 and 108. He was up to fourth by Lap 120 and stayed there until pitting on Lap 136.

Stewart, needing slightly less fuel because of superior mileage, got out of his pit box and into the outside fast lane at the maximum 80-mile per-hour speed before third-running Michael Andretti. Castroneves' stop was a little slower than Stewart's. Castroneves was pitted farther toward pit-out and darted from his pit box directly to the outside lane, forcing Stewart to slam on his brakes. Officials ruled Castroneves' move illegal and ordered Stewart to the front on Lap 137.

Stewart was the Indy 500's Rookie of the Year in 1996 and drove in it four straight years through 1999. He switched to racing full time in NASCAR's Winston Cup Series in 1999.

Chip Ganassi recruited Stewart in April to join his Indy effort in 2001. Stewart almost immediately reacclimated himself to the Indy-style car, running 225.004 mph in his third practice day. Stewart's lap of 226.996 was fastest of the month in practice. Stewart qualified in seventh position at 224.248.

2001 INDY 500 PERFORMANCE PROFILE

Starting Position:	7
Qualifying Average:	224.248 mph
Qualifying Speed Rank:	8
Best Practice Speed:	226.996 mph (5/12)
Total Practice Laps:	365
Finishing Position:	6
Laps Completed:	200
Highest Position 2001 Race:	1
Fastest Race Lap:	123 (217.512 mph)
2001 Prize Money:	$218,850
Indy 500 Career Earnings:	$1,192,873
Career Indy 500 Starts:	5
Career Best Finish:	5th 1997

ELISEO SALAZAR

#14 Harrah's A. J. Foyt Racing
Entrant: A. J. Foyt Enterprises
Crew Chief: Bill Spencer

After persevering through an agonizing period in practice and qualifying, Eliseo Salazar advanced steadily in an uneventful drive from 28th starting position to seventh place. Salazar was, considering the trials and tribulations of what had preceded the 500-mile race, relieved to reach the checkered flag in a relatively good position. "I'm happy because of what a terrible month we had," he said.

The Chilean's Dallara-Oldsmobile experienced handling problems in the heavy traffic in the early going and he went down a lap. Salazar was in 23rd position at the 80-lap mark. He consistently gained spots from there, up to ninth with 150 laps completed and into seventh with 10 laps to go. Salazar ran his fastest 10-lap segment from laps 171–180, averaging 213.165 mph. "We kept adjusting the car and got it to work better," Salazar said.

Salazar had arrived at Indianapolis with high hopes for his second-straight 500 with legendary owner A. J. Foyt. He qualified third and finished third in 2000. In the week of practice prior to Pole Day, Salazar seemed headed for a solid qualifying effort. He ran 222.166 mph on Tuesday, and Foyt's penchant for saving something for qualifying put forth the possibility that Salazar might have a front-row car.

The first sign of trouble for Salazar was late on Thursday when his Oldsmobile cut loose a trail of smoke on the front straight. But the car was not damaged, and Foyt had plenty of engines.

Salazar raised his top speed to 223.162 on Friday. Then, disaster struck: Salazar's Dallara hit the outside wall between Turns 1 and 2, continued adjacent to it and made contact again in Turn 2. The car had heavy right-side damage. With the exception of a bruise to the right side of his face and a sore right leg, Salazar wasn't injured and was cleared to drive.

In the MBNA Pole Day morning practice, Salazar's engine failed as he entered Turn One. The oil seeping onto the rear tires prevented Salazar from saving his Dallara from harm. It spun and whacked the outside wall with the left side, extensively damaged again. "The engine blew about 50 yards before going into (Turn) 1," Salazar said. "In a way, I'm lucky because it blew when I was so close to the wall. It wasn't that bad of an impact. It's unbelievable, that Turn 1. Two days in a row. I'm still limping from yesterday."

Salazar was cleared to drive, but two crashes in two days had left him without a car for Pole Day qualifying. After practicing the next day at 223.428, Salazar made his initial qualifying attempt. He had completed three laps at an average of 222.865 when the engine failed for the third time in four days.

"I only had two corners to go," Salazar said. "I felt the motor going as I went into Turn 3, but I thought I could make it. I had to fight to keep it off the wall in Turn 4. I don't know how, but I did it. I say I don't believe in luck, but this month, I'm not sure. I came into the race second in the (Indy Racing League) points and thought that I had a good run for the pole. Now I have to fight for my life just to make the race."

The second week, like the race, didn't have the drama of the first, to Salazar's relief. On Bump Day, the third and final qualifying session, Salazar made the race with a 223.740 average. "I don't want to lie," Salazar said. "I was really worried. This must be the twenty-first-century version of Chinese water torture. It was a nightmare what happened last week. We knew we had the speed, but after last week you don't believe anything until you see the checkered flag."

Salazar's seventh was his fourth top-seven in six starts in the 500. In addition to his third in 2000, Salazar was fourth in his rookie 1995 race and sixth in 1996.

2001 INDY 500 PERFORMANCE PROFILE

Starting Position:	28
Qualifying Average:	223.740 mph
Qualifying Speed Rank:	14
Best Practice Speed:	224.251 mph (5/20)
Total Practice Laps:	320
Finishing Position:	7
Laps Completed:	199
Highest Position 2001 Race:	7
Fastest Race Lap:	132 (218.378 mph)
2001 Prize Money:	$356,300
Indy 500 Career Earnings:	$1,665,270
Career Indy 500 Starts:	6
Career Best Finish:	3rd 2000

AIRTON DARÉ

G FORCE/OLDSMOBILE/FIRESTONE

#88 1-800-Bar None TeamXtreme
Entrant: TeamXtreme Racing
Crew Chief: Derrick Stepan

Airton Daré and TeamXtreme never found the sweet spot in the Brazilian's G Force-Oldsmobile Oldsmobile during the 500, but he kept it off the walls and finished eighth. It was a run that contrasted sharply with his rookie 500 in 2000, when Daré had a more competitive car that didn't make it to the checkered flag. Daré started 30th and ran as high as third in 2000 before an engine failure took him out after completing 126 laps.

"After the run we had last year, we expected better than eighth," Daré said. "But if you think of the conditions we had this year—we got bumped on the last day and had to requalify—eighth isn't so bad. Handling was the problem of the race. We didn't get a good feel."

Daré fought a front end that wanted to head for the outside wall in the turns for almost the entire race. "The car had a lot understeer, a lot of push," he said. "You can't make big changes here. You have to go step by step."

The 23-year-old ran through debris from early accidents twice, forcing him to pit on Laps 2 and 20 for fresh tires. "The first two stops, we didn't change anything because we ran into debris and I didn't have a good feel for the car," Daré said.

The fuel added on Daré's early stops allowed him to rise to sixth by Lap 50, but he went a lap down when making a stop during a green-flag pit sequence on Lap 52. In full-green conditions, Daré had averaged only 207.853 mph during Laps 31–40 and 209.803 during Laps 41–50, both segments well off the pace of the leaders.

"On the third stop, we made a full turn (of the front wing)," Daré said. The adjustment didn't solve the problem, and his pace remained the same over the next 32 laps, all run under green. Daré's fastest 10-lap segment was 209.677, during Laps 71–80. He made his fourth pit stop on Lap 84, from 11th position. "We made another full turn (of the front wing)," he said.

The team, with no track position to lose, decided to bring Daré in under caution under Lap 90 in the hopes that it would pay off in getting his lap back down the road. Daré emerged in 16th following the stop, which included a half-turn of the front wing. He climbed to 13th by his next stop on Lap 116. The team added another half-turn. "We put three full turns into the front wing, which is a lot," he said.

Daré's G Force finally had a decent balance. He averaged 211.108 in a green-flag segment during Laps 121–130. The team didn't adjust the chassis on the next stop on Lap 135. Daré kept advancing and was up to eighth by Lap 183. "Toward the end of the race, we picked up an oversteer (loose)," He said. "There was no way we could catch (seventh-running Eliseo) Salazar, so we leaned out the fuel and just brought it home."

Daré's fastest race lap of 214.628 ranked him 21st among the drivers.

Daré and TeamXtreme never found the speed they wanted in practice or qualifying. His fastest lap in practice prior to MBNA Pole Day was 221.573. On Pole Day, Daré became the 13th qualifier at 220.996. It turned out to be 23rd among 27 qualifiers. The team decided against withdrawing the qualified car in favor of an attempt in another car on the second day of qualifying.

Daré was bumped out of the field in the early afternoon on Bump Day, but the team had its second car ready for a qualifying attempt 44 minutes later. Daré put four laps together that averaged 222.236. "That half-hour was the worst of my career, for sure," he said. "Finally, we got a good car. We had a gearbox problem last night and today, and our guys did an engine change last night. We didn't know if we had fixed the (gearbox) problem. We thought we'd go out on this run and see how it felt, since we had two attempts left. But the car felt good, so we took it."

2001 INDY 500 PERFORMANCE PROFILE

Starting Position:	30
Qualifying Average:	222.236 mph
Qualifying Speed Rank:	25
Best Practice Speed:	223.458 mph (5/13)
Total Practice Laps:	523
Finishing Position:	8
Laps Completed:	199
Highest Position 2001 Race:	6
Fastest Race Lap:	160 (214.628 mph)
2001 Prize Money:	$320,325
Indy 500 Career Earnings:	$582,575
Career Indy 500 Starts:	2
Career Best Finish:	8th 2001

BILLY BOAT

#98 Curb Records
Entrant: Curb-Agajanian/Beck Motorsports
Crew Chief: Tom Bose

Starting from the 32nd position, Billy Boat was upwardly mobile throughout the 500. He reached his highest point, ninth, 16 laps from the checkered flag and finished there.

"I think overall the Curb Records team has to be pretty satisfied with a top-10 finish, having gained some 23 positions," Boat said. "We weren't great all day, but we were pretty steady. My team really helped me during the race with great pit stops. We never made any mistakes, and I really think that's what contributed to our good finish.

"We would've liked to have been up higher, but when you start in the back, it's awfully hard to stay on the lead lap, and once we got a lap down we were pretty much just racing everybody on that lap."

The 35-year-old from Phoenix, AZ, advanced to 13th by Lap 70 before going a lap down during a sequence of green-flag pit stops on Lap 75. Boat never regained the lead lap. However, he did continue to move through the field, to 11th by Lap 120 and to 10th after 150 laps. Boat's Dallara-Oldsmobile had its fastest 10-lap segment during Laps 171–180 at 210.424 mph and backed it up with a 209.860 during Laps 181–190. The team improved the handling of the car with a front-wing adjustment on the Lap 75 pit stop.

Boat had driven an A. J. Foyt–owned car in his previous four 500s and was offered one of Foyt's cars in 2001. Boat had plunged into team ownership earlier in the year, in partnership with Team Manager Greg Beck, Mike Curb and Cary Agajanian, and decided to stick with his operation for the 500. One of the goals of the 500 was to earn enough money to complete the IRL season. "I'm very happy because this finish is going to enable us to keep this team going over the next races and hopefully finish out the rest of the season," Boat said. The team did run the remaining IRL races, and Boat finished fourth in the championship.

Boat barely squeezed out enough speed to make the race. He was stuck in the 219-mile-per-hour range during the opening week of practice. In the Pole Day morning practice, Boat broke out with a 222.261, but he could not repeat it in a midday qualifying attempt. Boat ran laps of 219.663 and 218.770 and waved it off.

On the second day of qualifications, Boat had a 222.075 in midday practice, but the team wasn't confident in the car's consistency and ability to put four fast laps together and decided against making an attempt.

They took the second week of practice to prepare for Bump Day. Boat finally found the speed he was searching for in Saturday's practice with a 222.177. In the Bump Day morning practice, Boat ran a 221.580. More importantly, he liked the consistent handling of the car over several laps.

Boat was the first to attempt a qualification run and he averaged 221.528. All four laps were in the mid-221s. "We're pretty happy," Boat said immediately following his attempt. "It's pretty much all we had. We'll just wait it out now. Consistent right now, that is all we could ask for. I never thought it would be this hard. We were flat-out for four laps. That's all I could do. I'm moderately optimistic. Bump Day is a crazy day. A lot of things can happen."

Boat's run filled the 33-car field. Six cars bumped their way into the race.

With 48 minutes remaining, Boat was on the bubble. Twelve more cars made qualification attempts. They all failed. Even though Boat posted the slowest speed in the field, he would be racing in the 85th 500.

"It's not the way we wanted to get into the race," Boat said, "but we'll take it. It's one of those things where it's do or die for this race. We really had to put that Curb Records car in the race and to be so close to not doing it is scary. That's the thing about Indianapolis in that last hour: there's no guarantee that anybody can't run quick."

2001 INDY 500 PERFORMANCE PROFILE

Starting Position:	32
Qualifying Average:	221.528 mph
Qualifying Speed Rank:	33
Best Practice Speed:	222.261 mph (5/12)
Total Practice Laps:	430
Finishing Position:	9
Laps Completed:	199
Highest Position 2000 Race:	9
Fastest Race Lap:	100 (215.770 mph)
2001 Prize Money:	$337,325
Indy 500 Career Earnings:	$1,608,425
Career Indy 500 Starts:	5
Career Best Finish:	3rd 1999

FELIPE GIAFFONE

#21 Hollywood
Entrant: Treadway-Hubbard Racing
Crew Chief: Phil McRobert

Felipe Giaffone needed a backup plan to get into the 500, but he showed he belonged with a solid 10th-place finish. The Brazilian rookie, whose car was qualified by veteran Raul Boesel, gained 23 positions after starting 33rd. It certainly was a notable effort.

"It's a pretty good finish, but it's been a tough month," Giaffone said. "The team did a great job with race strategy. The car was pretty good, and we ran pretty quick all day. I think we could have finished a little better, but we got a big plastic bag stuck under the car for the last 10 or 15 laps of the race and it hurt the car's handling. We might have been able to pick up a position or two."

Giaffone, fearing he had punctured a tire running through debris from Scott Sharp's opening-lap crash, pitted on the second lap for tires and topped off his fuel. The 26-year-old made another early stop on Lap 11 to look for possible damage from Sarah Fisher's incident and filled up the fuel cell again.

With the speed to stay on the lead lap, Giaffone was up to 19th by Lap 40. When the leaders began making pit stops under green, Giaffone's early pit stop allowed him to reach second position by Lap 50. Giaffone pitted his G Force-Oldsmobile on Lap 52 and emerged in 16th, the top-running car a lap down.

Giaffone was up to seventh by Lap 83, but was unable to regain his lost lap the rest of the distance. "Physically, the race was not bad for me," Giaffone said. "I didn't have any trouble with the length of the race. I'm a little sore in the right leg, so I think I have to work on my throttle pedal."

Giaffone enjoyed the huge crowd and the pageantry before the race, but was able to put it out of his mind once the race began. "It's pretty cool to see all the fans and all the pre-race activities," he said. "So many people, it's just amazing. But once you get racing, it's just like any other race. The hard part is the two or three weeks before the race. That is the toughest part and it definitely wears on you mentally."

Giaffone, with a productive opening week of practice, peaked in the MBNA Pole Day morning session at 222.490 mph. He qualified with a 221.100 average, the 15th car in the field. By the end of the day, he was in the 20th starting position, ahead of seven cars in the field with slower averages. It appeared Giaffone's speed was safe.

By the close of the next day's second qualifying session, Giaffone and the Treadway-Hubbard team realized they could be in jeopardy on Bump Day. Of the 32 cars qualified, only five cars had slower speeds.

Giaffone called friend Raul Boesel in Brazil and asked him to come and qualify another Treadway-Hubbard car. Giaffone and the team made a deal with Boesel that if he qualified and Giaffone's car stayed in the field, Boesel would race the third team entry. The team did not want to risk withdrawing Giaffone's car prior to it being bumped.

Boesel had no trouble getting up to speed and qualified at 221.879 early on Bump Day. Giaffone was bumped in the final hour, the final car to be knocked out of the field.

Giaffone tried to qualify a backup car with 13 minutes remaining in an effort to keep Boesel in the race, but waved off after an opening lap of 215.992. A mechanical problem was later discovered in the G Force.

Giaffone replaced Boesel the following day, the final driver to get into the field. "It definitely was not the way I wanted to get into the race," Giaffone said.

2001 INDY 500 PERFORMANCE PROFILE

Starting Position:	33
Qualifying Average:	221.879 mph*
Qualifying Speed Rank:	29 (Boesel)*
Best Practice Speed:	222.490 mph (5/12)
Total Practice Laps:	524
Finishing Position:	10
Laps Completed:	199
Highest Position 2001 Race:	2
Fastest Race Lap:	103 (215.988 mph)
2001 Prize Money:	$211,575
Indy 500 Career Earnings:	$211,575
Career Indy 500 Starts:	1
Career Best Finish:	10th 2001

11

ROBBY McGEHEE

#10 Cure Autism Now
Entrant: Cahill Racing
Crew Chief: Kevin Hertle

Robby McGehee walked away proudly after a long, tough 500 miles at Indianapolis. McGehee's 11th-place finish was not his best in the famed race, but it provided a feeling of worthwhile accomplishment. "Given our circumstances, we did pretty good," McGehee said. "We came a long way from the beginning of the month."

McGehee's Dallara-Oldsmobile Oldsmobile got caught up in a 10-car crash on April 28th in the previous race at Atlanta Motor Speedway. The incident virtually destroyed Cahill Racing's only car, and the magnitude of it made finding replacement parts difficult. "The tub was repairable," team owner Larry Cahill said, "but we couldn't get uprights and a bell housing." The delay in repairs caused McGehee to miss the opening three days of practice. He had only two full days of practice prior to MBNA Pole Day and entered it with a top lap of 220.651 mph.

McGehee's first qualifying attempt, early on Pole Day, was waved off after laps of 220.745, 220.934 and 220.166. The team did extensive running in the midday practice and decided to make a second attempt in the final hour. McGehee ran his fastest lap of the month at 222.896 and averaged 222.607 to qualify solidly in the field.

"We're happy," McGehee said. "We were going to take anything over 221.5. I was really surprised how fast we went. The car was loose and free. On our first attempt, we used an engine with 500 miles on it. We changed to a motor with 300 miles on it. It was huge power, and I've got to thank (engine builder) Comptech.

"The car was also better. We pulled it together with our engineer's (Damon Chandler) experience, the team's experience, and my experience." The team, operating on a tight budget, ran only 77 more laps in practice. It sat out three entire sessions.

Starting from 14th, McGehee steadily maintained his position despite a car plagued by either understeer or oversteer. McGehee made his five pit stops in sequence with the leaders. By stretching his fuel mileage, McGehee climbed to fifth before making his initial stop on Lap 46. Although he was running 12th, McGehee went a lap down on Lap 73. McGehee did not lose another lap for the rest of the race.

McGehee was running 13th with 100 laps completed. A long final pit stop on Lap 167 dropped him to 14th, but he moved up to 11th at the checkered flag.

"Our car was not handling good enough to win," McGehee said. "It was real pushy (understeer) at the start of most fuel runs, and when I tried to correct it with the weight jacker (an in-car adjustment device), it went loose. After the first pit stop, I think I spooked myself when it went loose in traffic. We never were able to find a car with good balance, especially in traffic.

"If we hadn't had so many weather (rain) interruptions, we might have been able to tune the car better."

McGehee was the 1999 Indy 500 Rookie of the Year after finishing fifth with Conti Racing. McGehee was a contender to win in 2000 with Treadway Racing before an engine problem halfway through the race forced him to fall back. The

28-year-old from St. Louis, MO, suffered a compound fracture of his left leg in the Indy Racing Northern Light Series race at Texas in June 2001, and made a remarkable recovery to only miss two races. McGehee returned to his best finish of 2001 with a fourth at Nashville. McGehee's highest Indy Racing finish was second at Texas in June 2000.

2001 INDY 500 PERFORMANCE PROFILE

Starting Position:	14
Qualifying Average	222.607 mph
Qualifying Speed Rank:	21
Best Practice Speed:	220.651 mph (5/10)
Total Practice Laps:	287
Finishing Position:	11
Laps Completed:	199
Highest Position 2001 Race:	5
Fastest Race Lap:	163 (214.536 mph)
2001 Prize Money:	$286,025
Indy 500 Career Earnings:	$815,175
Career Indy 500 Starts:	3
Career Best Finish:	5th 1999

BUZZ CALKINS

#12 Bradley Food Marts/Sav-O-Mat
Entrant: Bradley Motorsports
Crew Chief: Todd Tapply

Buzz Calkins drove in his sixth-straight Indy 500 and completed the most laps of his career, 198, as he finished 12th. It was the fourth-straight year Calkins was running at the checkered flag, but that fact didn't leave him with a feeling of satisfaction.

"We brought it home in one piece, but overall I'm very disappointed," Calkins said. "I thought our car was better than where we finished. Overall, I thought the car was pretty good. We never got any breaks with the cautions. I think we just got stuck out on some pit strategy somewhat. We should have made some stops when we didn't and shouldn't have made some when we did. You need to get some breaks when you start where we started and we never did."

Calkins started 24th and quickly began passing cars. He was 17th by Lap 8, and only two of those had been run under green. Calkins was 14th at Lap 18, with only three laps under green. When a long green-flag stint began on Lap 22, he rocketed up to 12th by Lap 30 and to 10th by Lap 40.

Calkins made his initial pit stop on Lap 42 and continued with a solid, steady pace. He averaged 210.722 during Laps 61–70, his top 10-lap speed of the race. But it wasn't fast enough to hold off flying leader Mark Dismore, who put Calkins down one circuit on Lap 66.

Following the second pit stop on Lap 73, Calkins' Dallara had trouble adjusting to the changing track conditions. "I think we were chasing the car kind of the whole time and when the weather changed (to colder, cloud and rain-threatening conditions) we lost a little bit," Calkins said. "We did a lot to try to adjust. I was struggling to get the balance in the second half of the race. The track went to push and we never caught up to it."

Calkins' four final pit stops were under caution and without problems. He stayed one lap down until lap 190, when Helio Castroneves put him a second lap down. Calkins was running 11th at 110 laps and 13th at 190 and his consistency brought him home in 12th.

The 30-year-old from Denver, Colorado, was the second qualifier on Pole Day with an average of 220.039. By the end of the day, the Bradley Motorsports' team knew it was in trouble. Calkins was the slowest car in the 27-car field.

Calkins had run 47 laps in his backup Dallara-Oldsmobile. In the morning practice of the second qualifying day, Calkins clicked off his fastest practice lap of the month, 222.533. The team decided to withdraw the qualified car, a calculated risk, in an effort to improve its speed.

The team waited until 81 minutes remained in the session. Calkins did four laps that averaged 222.467 and included his fastest lap of the month, 222.760. It proved to be a speed that easily kept him in the field, which Calkins' MBNA Pole Day speed would not have.

"It was a little unexpected change of plans," Calkins said. "It's amazing because we had a relatively easy week. We had been running well all week. But, sure enough on Saturday (Pole Day) we lost a mile and a half per hour from what we had been running all week. I think you have to be proactive. We knew we were going to get bumped.

"Knowing that the speed was there made the decision easier. Looking back on the decision (to take the Pole Day speed), it was probably pretty foolish. But there have been so many instances where you've seen teams wave off runs they should've taken in hopes to move up the grid when they shouldn't have been so greedy, so we took it. We knew we had another car if we needed it."

Calkins and the Bradley team have been regulars in the Indy Racing League since it began in 1996. Calkins won the IRL's opening race at Walt Disney World Speedway.

2001 INDY 500 PERFORMANCE PROFILE

Starting Position:	24
Qualifying Average:	222.467 mph
Qualifying Speed Rank:	18
Best Practice Speed:	222.533 mph (5/13)
Total Practice Laps:	479
Finishing Position:	12
Laps Completed:	198
Highest Position 2001 Race:	10
Fastest Race Lap:	65 (214.061 mph)
2001 Prize Money:	$286,025
Indy 500 Career Earnings:	$1,306,078
Career Indy 500 Starts:	6
Career Best Finish:	10th 1998

13

ARIE LUYENDYK

#5 Meijer
Entrant: Treadway-Hubbard Racing
Crew Chief: Skip Faul

Two-time Indy 500 champion Arie Luyendyk returned from a self-imposed one-year hiatus to finish 13th. He liked being back, but the race didn't bring him any pleasure at all. "I'm glad I was here," Luyendyk said. "This is still a great event and a fun event, but it's only fun if you are competitive and we really weren't competitive."

The 47-year-old put his 16 years of experience at Indianapolis to use in trying to solve persistent handling problems on his G Force-Oldsmobile and never succeeded. "The car was a handful in traffic," Luyendyk said. "I got slapped around. I couldn't get close to anybody in traffic. The car was pushing. On the pit stops, we put wing in, we took wing out, and the car would push, push, push. I tried a different line and it would get loose. Boom, I'm stuck. On my own, I was happy with the car. I could do 215s or 216s, but I was never able to turn a big lap like the really fast guys were doing."

Luyendyk qualified in sixth position and nearly was knocked out on the first lap. "I missed Scott's (Sharp) driveshaft by inches," he said. "If he had come off the (Turn 1) wall hard, I would have been in trouble."

Although he led Lap 47, Luyendyk knew the car needed work to be a contender. He fell back to eighth, 22.975 seconds behind leader Greg Ray, at the 40-lap mark, but moved into the lead by staying out longer prior to his first pit stop on Lap 48. "I could tell right from the start when those guys pulled away from me that I didn't have the car," Luyendyk said.

When Luyendyk stalled exiting his initial pit stop, he went down a lap. "I had a big problem with the clutch and the guys had to give me a big push to get out of the pits," he said. "That hurt us, sure, but I just didn't have the car to come back from it."

By the 100-lap mark, Luyendyk was two laps down and all hopes of a third Indy 500 victory were gone. "We had a lot of bad things happen today," Luyendyk said. "We also had an oil pressure problem. It was one of those long days you can have here sometimes. I don't like to end it on this note. I'll be back (in 2002)."

Luyendyk announced his retirement from Indy car racing prior to the 1999 500 and worked as a television commentator at Indianapolis in 2000.

During the broadcast, however, he realized how much he missed racing at Indy and decided to make a comeback.

Reunited with engineer Tim Wardrop, whom he teamed with in his 1997 triumph, Luyendyk ran 223.986 on the third day of practice. The Flying Dutchman had hoped to capture his fourth pole, but his qualifying average of 224.257 fell short because of an engine that didn't maintain its optimum horsepower. It included his fastest of the month, 224.812, on his opening lap.

"I definitely went into Turn 1 a lot harder than I have all week because that's what you have to do, save the best for last," Luyendyk said. "On the back straight, I heard a clunk (on the third lap). I felt it this morning (in practice), but we weren't sure. There were no signs on any of the data, so we decided to still take this first run.

"I know I'm in there (the race), but I want to be up there."

Luyendyk also believes he made a mistake in his preparations for the race. "I don't think we did enough running on full tanks," he said.

2001 INDY 500 PERFORMANCE PROFILE

Starting Position:	6
Qualifying Average:	224.257 mph
Qualifying Speed Rank:	7
Best Practice Speed:	223.986 mph (5/8)
Total Practice Laps:	417
Finishing Position:	13
Laps Completed:	198
Highest Position 2001 Race:	1
Fastest Race Lap:	131 (216.232 mph)
2001 Prize Money:	$182,275
Indy 500 Career Earnings:	$5,772,046
Career Indy 500 Starts:	16
Career Best Finish:	1st 1990, 1997

14

DALLARA/OLDSMOBILE/FIRESTONE

SAM HORNISH JR.

#4 Pennzoil Panther Dallara
Entrant: Panther Racing
Crew Chief: Kevin Blanch

Sam Hornish Jr. drove a very fast car to a frustrating Indy 500 finish. He found himself in that ironic situation after he spun on a Lap 17 restart. Hornish's Dallara-Oldsmobile avoided contact with the walls, and other cars luckily missed him. The only damage to the car was four flat tires, and after a pit stop, Hornish was able to rejoin the race. The damage to his aspirations of winning was terminal, however. He resumed five laps down.

It did not deter Hornish from driving hard. The second-year Indy car driver from Defiance, Ohio, ran the race's fastest lap at 219.829 mph on Lap 125, and he managed to regain one of the lost laps. For his effort, Hornish finished 14th. "We had a real fast car," Hornish said. "It's kind of rough on the nerves passing the same race cars all day long and not getting anywhere. We were pretty loose all day long, but it was a good run."

Hornish started 13th and was running 11th for the restart. He got a good jump on Jimmy Vasser's G Force-Oldsmobile and went low exiting Turn 4 to pass him. His tires weren't up to full temperature and the back end of his Dallara came around. Hornish did a half-spin and briefly went backward down the front straight before the car spun around and stopped. Cars missed him on both sides. "Things were going good before the spin," Hornish said. "I thought I could go low on the cold tires, but the car was loose and snapped around on me. It was a tough lesson to learn."

Hornish posted some impressive 10-lap speeds under green. He averaged 215.331 during Laps 51–60 and 214.026 during Laps 171–180.

In the opening days of practice, Hornish and Panther Racing engineer Andy Brown had trouble finding a comfortable and competitive car. Hornish's best lap was 220.235. But on the Friday prior to Pole Day, Hornish jumped to 222.380. In the MBNA Pole Day morning practice, Hornish roared to a 224.873. "We were very frustrated after five days," Hornish said. "We finally found something that worked for us, that made me feel comfortable in the car. We kept going to Dallara and asking them, 'What else do you have to try on this car?' We tried five different sets of suspensions. On Friday, we knew we found something in the right direction and we fine-tuned it from there."

Hornish qualified in his first attempt at 223.333. His first lap of 224.942 was his fastest of the month. Hornish's speed fell off considerably to 220.764 on his second qualifling lap from a loose condition in Turn 1, but he adjusted the car and closed the attempt with laps of 223.808 and 223.862. "It's easier getting into the first 500 than the second 500," Hornish said. "It's harder because you are expected to. If we could have found the right setup sooner, we could have gone faster, but it feels good to be in the race."

It was Hornish's second 500. Driving for underbudgeted PDM Racing in 2000, he qualified an impressive 14th. He completed 153 laps before spinning out of the race and finished 24th.

The rest of Hornish's 2001 Indy Racing League campaign was remarkable. He won at Phoenix, Homestead-Miami and the second Texas race; took four second-place finishes and three thirds for 10 podiums in 13 races, and won the IRL championship. At age 22, Hornish became the youngest champion of a major open-wheel series in American history.

2001 INDY 500 PERFORMANCE PROFILE

Starting position:	13
Qualifying Average:	223.333 mph
Qualifying Speed Rank:	17
Best Practice Speed:	224.873 mph (5/12)
Total Practice Laps:	534
Finishing Position:	14
Laps Completed:	196
Highest Position 2001 Race:	11
Fastest Race Lap:	125 (219.829 mph)
2001 Prize Money:	$308,825
Indy 500 Career Earnings:	$577,075
Career Indy 500 Starts:	2
Career Best Finish:	14th 2001

15

ROBBIE BUHL

#24 Team Purex
Entrant: Dreyer & Reinbold Racing
Crew Chief: Brad Brewer

Robbie Buhl wasn't content to settle for second. He had leader Helio Castroneves in his sights as they began Lap 166 and decided to press the throttle a little harder in Turn 2 in an attempt to overtake him. "I flat-footed it," Buhl said. "If we'd have gotten by, we'd have stayed in front."

It was a gutsy but overly optimistic move. The back end snapped out, and Buhl's best effort to straighten it out failed. Buhl went into a three-quarter spin exiting the corner and slid softly into the inside wall on the back straight.

"I didn't spin because I was trying to stay in second," Buhl said. "I didn't spin because I was trying to hold on—I spun trying to go for the lead. I don't have any regrets about that. That's why we were there, to get in the lead and win the Indy 500. You have to calculate the risk against the reward. That was a risk worth taking. There was a slower car (Robby Gordon, almost a lap down) in front of Castroneves. I thought Castroneves might get held up off the corner and I could get a run on him and take the lead."

Buhl's contact didn't cause any damage and after a tow to the pits to replace four tires, he resumed to finish 15th. "I'm frustrated," Buhl said. "The guys gave me a car to win. We had the gear package right. We didn't miss a beat all day. The plan was to get in front and stay in front."

Buhl gradually moved to the front. He was sixth at 60 laps and fourth after passing Castroneves on a Lap 96 restart and climbed to third by Lap 104. Buhl was in second when he pitted under caution on Lap 116 and, because the other leaders stayed out, fell back to eighth. Buhl was running fifth for the Lap 139 restart. He passed Gil de Ferran on the inside in Turn 3 on Lap 142 to take fourth. Three laps later, Buhl climbed to third by passing Michael Andretti. By the Lap 158 restart, Buhl was second to Castroneves. Buhl made several attempts to overtake Castroneves going into Turn 3 and charged that the Penske Racing driver blocked him.

"Castroneves blocked me all over the place," Buhl said. "But that's not why I spun. I'm not making excuses."

In addition to trying to add power, Buhl also went down a gear to add acceleration off Turn 2 on the fateful Lap 166 spin. "The car got loose and I couldn't hold onto it," he said.

Buhl's practice laps and qualifying went smoothly. He had a top practice lap of 223.326 on the Friday prior to Pole Day. Buhl qualified in his first attempt. His laps of 223.596, 224.667, 224.605 and 223.989 were his four fastest of the month.

Buhl's primary car had been destroyed in a 10-car crash at Atlanta on April 28. "We were able to salvage the dash and two mirrors from it," Buhl said. "It had the next version of G Force suspension on it, and we didn't have another one for the backup car. The car we qualified is built identically to the one we lost at Atlanta. We knew the new suspension would be a better car for this track. We didn't get out with it until last night Friday. The guys pulled an all-nighter to get it ready. There is a special bond that is at three o'clock in the morning."

2001 INDY 500 PERFORMANCE PROFILE

Starting Position:	9
Qualifying Average:	224.213 mph
Qualifying Speed Rank:	10
Best Practice Speed:	223.326 mph (5/11)
Total Practice Laps:	304
Finishing Position:	15
Laps Completed:	196
Highest Position 2001 Race:	2
Fastest Race Lap:	165 (218.447 mph)
2001 Prize Money:	$300,325
Indy 500 Career Earnings:	$1,469,228
Career Indy 500 Starts:	6
Career Best Finish:	6th 1999

MARK DISMORE

DALLARA/OLDSMOBILE/FIRESTONE

**#28 Delphi Automotive Systems/Bryant
Heating & Cooling
Entrant: Kelley Racing
Crew Chief: Glenn Scott**

Mark Dismore experienced the elation of leading the Indy 500 for the first time in his career in 2001. It was not achieved through any fuel-saving or pit-sequence strategy. Dismore started near the front and had the speed to get into the top position. But on Lap 93, Dismore's hopes of winning were replaced with disappointment when the gearbox on his Dallara-Oldsmobile failed.

"We had the car to beat," Dismore said. "There wasn't anybody we couldn't deal with and we had a 50-cent part in the gearbox break.

"My heart is broken for (owner) Tom Kelley and the Delphi/Bryant crew."

The 44-year-old from Greenfield, Indiana, started fourth and held that position through his first pit stop on Lap 42. The combination of fast laps and a quick stop put him up to third behind Michael Andretti and Felipe Giaffone, who both had made early pit stops under caution.

When Andretti and Giaffone had to pit under green a few laps later, Dismore went into the lead on Lap 53. Dismore pulled away from Ray, to an 8.2-second advantage with 70 laps completed.

Dismore stayed in front through Lap 74, when he pitted for the second time. Dismore emerged in sixth and, as the race continued under green conditions and other leaders made pit stops, moved into second position on Lap 81 and into the lead on Lap 85.

When the caution slowed the race on Lap 91, Dismore surrendered the lead to pit. He resumed in fourth when the car slowed on the back straight and then rolled to a stop on the warm-up lane entrance in Turn 3.

Dismore had led 29 laps. A part in the gearbox called the cow pin had broken, disabling first and fifth gears. "That's my story," Dismore said. "It was some little inexpensive part that broke."

The Dallara-Oldsmobile was towed to the pits, where the Kelley team impressively changed the gearbox. Even though the race went green on Lap 96, Dismore lost only five laps.

Knocked down to 24th position, Dismore ran competitively the remainder of the race and didn't lose another lap. He finished 16th, five laps down.

Dismore was impressive in practice and qualifications. He led the third day of practice at 224.823 mph before devoting attention to race setup the rest of the week.

With the qualifying setup back on the car, Dismore ran 224.592 in the MBNA Pole Day morning practice.

But on his first qualifying attempt, Dismore waved off after a 221.197 initial lap. "We rolled out to qualify and the track temperature was about 20 degrees hotter than this morning," he said. "It really took the car away from me in Turn 1."

Dismore made his second attempt nearly four hours later. He started with his two fastest laps of the month, 225.119 and 225.316, and followed with 224.654 and 224.768 for a 224.964 average for fourth on the grid.

Dismore's fourth was his best qualifying effort at Indianapolis.

2001 INDY 500 PERFORMANCE PROFILE

Starting Position:	4
Qualifying Average:	224.964 mph
Qualifying Speed Rank:	4
Best Practice Speed:	224.823 mph (5/8)
Total Practice Laps:	514
Finishing Position:	16
Laps Completed:	195
Highest Position 2001 Race:	1
Fastest Race Lap:	73 (218.521 mph)
2001 Prize Money:	$287,375
Career Indy 500 Earnings:	$1,346,728
Career Indy 500 Starts:	6
Career Best Finish:	11th 2000

DALLARA/OLDSMOBILE/FIRESTONE

GREG RAY

#2 Johns Manville/Menards
Entrant: Team Menard
Crew Chief: Gary Neal

When the race progressed past 100 laps, with storm clouds approaching, Greg Ray was trying to hold onto the lead. Michael Andretti was making it tough on Ray. "We were right where we wanted to be," Ray said. "We thought the rain was going to end things early, so we wanted to do everything we could to stay in the front.

"The car was pushing, so I was adjusting the weight-jacker. It was working for us, but I didn't know where the limit was. The car bottomed out and bounced three times coming off Turn 3 and it went out to the wall."

Ray's Dallara-Oldsmobile did not hit the outside wall hard, but it was enough to bend the right-front suspension. It forced Ray into a long pit stop that put him eight laps down and he finished 17th.

The rain did arrive eventually, but did not stop the race from going the distance. "Looking at it now, we guessed wrong, but everyone out there was guessing about what to do," Ray said.

The 34-year-old from Plano, TX, started from the middle of the front row. He passed Robby Gordon for the lead on the inside in Turn 1 following a Lap 23 restart and opened up a 6-second lead over Gil de Ferran before making his first pit stop on Lap 45. Ray regained the lead on Lap 75 and surrendered it for his second pit stop on Lap 80. After other cars made their pit stops, Ray cycled back up front on Lap 92. He fell to eighth after slapping the wall on Lap 103.

Struggling with the Dallara's handling, Ray was off the pace in Turn 1 on Lap 107. Jon Herb hit the back of Ray's car and crashed, but Ray was able to continue. The caution came out, but the Menard team kept Ray out and he moved up to fifth as other cars pitted.

It also began raining lightly, but the sun emerged and the team brought Ray in for his extended pit stop on Lap 118. "We still were seventh before the yellow for the rain, thinking it might be over," Ray said. "But the sun came out and we had to repair the car. We went back out, but there wasn't much point to it then. Driving race cars, period, is fun, but winning is a lot more fun. I've got mixed emotions."

Ray led a total of 40 laps. It was the fourth straight year Ray led the 500.

In practice, Ray was fastest in four of the six full-day sessions. He had his fastest lap of the month, 226.108 mph, in the MBNA Pole Day morning practice.

On Ray's initial qualifying attempt, he ran 224.862 and aborted. "I wasn't happy with the car," Ray said.

Ray made his second qualifying attempt five hours later and averaged 225.194 for second position on the grid. "I feel good," he said. "I think we got the most out of our car. We never did find that magic sweet spot. I was flat for 15 of the 16 turns. I went straight toward the wall in Turn One on the fourth lap (the slowest of the four at 224.512) and

had to lift. We didn't nail the setup just right. We threw everything at it but the kitchen sink. We do have good cars, good engines, a good team. We just couldn't find the balance in the car."

Ray qualified on the front row for the fourth straight year, including three from the second position.

2001 INDY 500 PERFORMANCE PROFILE

Starting Position:	2
Qualifying Average:	225.194 mph
Qualifying Speed Rank:	2
Best Practice Speed:	226.108 mph (5/19)
Total Practice Laps:	455
Finishing Position:	17
Laps Completed:	192
Highest Position 2001 Race:	1
Fastest Race Lap:	99 (218.808 mph)
2001 Prize Money:	$335,325
Indy 500 Career Earnings:	$1,275,575
Career Indy 500 Starts:	5
Career Best Finish:	17th 2001

BUDDY LAZIER

**#91 Tae-Bo/Coors Light/Life
Fitness/Delta Faucet
Entrant: Hemelgarn Racing
Crew Chief: Dennis LaCava**

With a motor that was down on power from the start, Buddy Lazier endured a hapless 500 to finish 18th. It was his worst showing in the 500 since joining Hemelgarn Racing in 1996.

"I just think that we ran 500 miles on seven cylinders," Lazier said. "We ran the whole race dead in the water. Our motor was junk. We were going down the straightaway 201 [mph], 202, when we were normally running 220. We just felt like we threw our race way. It was just a miserable day."

Lazier had started from 10th position and radioed to the Hemelgarn crew during an early caution period that the Oldsmobile Oldsmobile was not performing at full strength. When a second caution came out, Lazier pitted on the ninth lap. The team hoped it was an electrical problem and changed several components.

Lazier returned to the track several times and the engine continued to run sluggishly, forcing him back into the pits. He had four stops in the opening 18 laps. It was eventually determined that a fuel injector had broken, rendering one cylinder useless.

"We came in three or four times on that first yellow," Lazier said. "The guys realized that we couldn't fix it."

Lazier's fastest lap of 207.881 was the slowest in the field with the exception of four drivers who crashed in the opening laps. He finished eight laps down.

"It's incredible the motor ran 500 miles like that," Lazier said.

The 1996 Indy 500 winner had completed 998 of 1000 laps in his previous five 500s with Hemelgarn. Lazier had been runner-up to Juan Montoya in 2000 and to Eddie Cheever Jr. in 1998.

Lazier's practice and qualifying provided every indication that he would be a strong challenger to win the 500 in 2001. Lazier ran a 223.315 lap on the third practice day, then switched to full-tank running to prepare for the race.

In the MBNA Pole Day morning practice, the Hemelgarn team put the qualifying setup back on and Lazier ran 223.920.

Lazier qualified at 224.190 on his first attempt to take 10th spot on the grid. He had an initial lap of 225.403 and followed it with 224.495, but dropped down to 223.904 and 222.973 on the final two laps. "The engine overheated and we lost power," he said. "The temperature went up 50 degrees over the last two laps. The car was handling perfectly. I couldn't have asked for a better car. I'm happy to be in the position I'm in."

Lazier closed out his preparation for the race in fine form, running third at 222.392 on Carburetion Day. The team had done 29 laps with the engine that would be used for the race without a hint of trouble. "We did a leak test to make sure there were no leaks and did setup verification," he said.

Following the 500, Lazier went on to an outstanding Indy Racing season. The driver from Vail, CO, became the first to win four races in a single IRL season. Lazier finished second in the 2000 season championship after winning it the previous year.

At the conclusion of 2001, Lazier held IRL records for consecutive laps led (187), most laps led in a single race (224), both at Richmond in 2001, most races led with 24, consecutive races started (54, tied with Eddie Cheever Jr.), and most races started (55, tied with Cheever).

2001 INDY 500 PERFORMANCE PROFILE

Starting Position:	10
Qualifying Average:	224.190 mph
Qualifying Speed Rank:	12
Best Practice Speed:	223.920 mph (5/12)
Total Practice Laps:	381
Finishing Position:	18
Laps Completed:	192
Highest Position 2001 Race:	9
Fastest Race Lap:	71 (207.881 mph)
2001 Prize Money:	$262,325
Indy 500 Career Earnings:	$3,725,201
Career Indy 500 Starts:	9
Career Best Finish:	1st 1996

G FORCE/INFINITI/FIRESTONE

CORY WITHERILL

#16 Radio Shack
Entrant: Indy Regency Racing
Crew Chief: Mark Walpot

In his first Indianapolis 500, Cory Witherill escaped unharmed from a spin en route to a 19th-place finish. For the rookie from Santa Monica, California, it was quite a ride. "I wanted a top 10, but I'm excited, I'll take a 19th," Witherill said. "Just making the field at Indy is a positive thing. Finishing the whole race and finishing 19th is a great thing."

Witherill admits he had some luck on his side to reach the checkered flag. When a right rear tire lost air pressure, Witherill's G Force-Oldsmobile did a quarter-spin exiting Turn 4 and slid across the track on Lap 134. Four cars dodged Witherill, who stopped near the pit entrance without hitting anything. "The tire went down low and the car spun around Turn 4 and I did whatever I could to stay from hitting the wall," he said. "Any spin where you stay out of the wall is all luck."

Witherill had started 31st. He was up to 20th after 30 laps, but went a lap down and slid to 23rd at the 40-lap mark. Witherill ran as high as 12th before making his second pit stop on Lap 50.

After 100 laps, Witherill had gone two laps down and was running 21st. Witherill remained two laps down and was in 18th when he spun. Witherill lost seven more laps before rejoining the race and eventually finished 13 laps down.

"I tried to stay out of trouble and ran well," Witherill said. "The car was good until the red flag (for rain, on Lap 155). Then, it was nervous (with oversteer). I tried to work with it, but it was just nervous. They (crew) said just to finish out the race, be smart and do the best I can."

Witherill, a Navajo, had a following of Native Americans cheering him at the race and more on television. "I knew I had a lot of people here supporting me," he said. "It just made me feel good, coming here and seeing it."

Brought along slowly by veteran Team Manager Sal Incandella, Witherill did not attempt a qualification run until Bump Day. He had taken warm-up laps on the second qualifying day, but didn't take the green.

Witherill made his first official attempt early on Bump Day, but waved off after three laps that averaged 220.086 mph. After a practice lap at 222.006 late in the afternoon, Witherill bumped his way into the field 37 minutes later by averaging 221.621. The team's effort had been boosted by acquiring a Team Menard-built Oldsmobile a few days before Bump Day.

"The power was just awesome," Witherill said. "Today we did a lot of setups to our car. We made one minor change before our qualifying attempt and just jumped right there in the 222s. It's a dream come true. I've been wanting to be a part of the Indy 500 for so long. Five years ago when I started racing the Indy Lights series, I didn't think I would have this day right now."

Witherill also took pride in representing Native Americans in the 500. "It's an amazing feeling to accomplish that," he said. "It's kind of great to see the Native American starting to get off in a high professional level of worldwide attention. It means a lot."

The 500 was Witherill's second Indy car race. He raced in off-road, Shelby Pro Series, and Formula 2000 before moving into Indy Lights in 1998.

2001 INDY 500 PERFORMANCE PROFILE

Starting Position:	31
Qualifying Average:	221.621 mph
Qualifying Speed Rank:	31
Best Practice Speed:	222.006 mph (5/20)
Total Practice Laps:	549
Finishing Position:	19
Laps Completed:	187
Highest Position 2001 Race:	12
Fastest Race Lap:	102 (211.949 mph)
2001 Prize Money:	$159,575
Indy 500 Career Earnings:	$159,575
Career Indy 500 Starts:	1
Career Best Finish:	19th 2001

DALLARA/OLDSMOBILE/FIRESTONE

JERET SCHROEDER

**#9 Purity Products
Entrant: PDM Racing
Crew Chief: Paul Murphy**

Jeret Schroeder's Indy 500 was like a two-act play, complete with an intermission. When the gearbox on Schroeder's Dallara failed just past the halfway point, PDM Racing repaired it in 21 minutes in the pits. Schroeder resumed racing, ran stronger than he had previously and finished 20th. "It was a good day turned bad and then turned good again," Schroeder said. "But it could have been a lot worse."

Schroeder started from 23rd position, but was forced to pit on the third lap after running through debris from a wreck. The team discovered Schroeder's Dallara had cut its right-front tire. "We don't have any pressure sensors, so we had to check it out," Schroeder said. "It turned out to be a good thing we did."

Schroeder fell back to 32nd. He made steady progress, up to eighth before making a green-flag pit stop on Lap 46. Schroeder dropped to 24th and went a lap down. He had gone a second lap down and was running 22nd at 100 laps. By then, Schroeder had lost sixth gear and was having trouble staying in either fourth or fifth gear. Rather than waiting for the deteriorating gearbox to fail completely, Schroeder pitted on Lap 103.

The track went under caution from Laps 107–118 and the fast work by the PDM crew got Schroeder back onto the track on Lap 116. Schroeder was 14 laps down, in 23rd place. Schroeder gained only three positions after the gearbox was repaired, but that wasn't indicative of his improved competitiveness. Schroeder gained one of his lost laps, finishing 13 laps down.

"After the crew changed the gearbox, I had all my gears," Schroeder said. "It felt a little different than what we started with, but it was OK. Fifth and sixth gears were a little shorter than what we started with. We needed a taller sixth gear, I think.

"PDM Racing gave me a good handling car. It came off the corners great in the draft. At the end of the race, I had a really good, well-balanced car and we were running as fast as the leaders. I wish we could have had the car we had at the end of the race all day."

The month of May at Indianapolis presented many trials and tribulations for Schroeder. He missed the opening three days of practice as PDM built a new Dallara. The team's previous Dallara had been destroyed when Schroeder was involved in a multi-car crash in Atlanta on April 28.

After running 103 laps with a best of 220.856 mph over two days of practice, Schroeder crashed hard exiting Turn 2. The car was demolished. PDM took delivery of another new Dallara, and Schroeder resumed running in practice on MBNA Pole Day. Schroeder ran 219.434 in 55 laps and the team decided against making a qualification attempt.

Schroeder jumped to 222.327 in the morning practice of the second day of qualifications. He was the first to make an attempt and qualified solidly at 222.786. "It's a major relief," Schroeder said. "Last

night, the crew worked real hard to get the car ready. The car had good balance, so I knew I could attack the corners at speed. I had confidence PDM would give me a good car to do this. I looked down and I saw 223 (.224, on his first lap). The car had a little push in three corners, but nothing significant. I knew we would be OK."

2001 INDY 500 PERFORMANCE PROFILE

Starting Position:	23
Qualifying Average:	222.786 mph
Qualifying Speed Rank:	20
Best Practice Speed:	222.327 mph (5/21)
Total Practice Laps:	251
Finishing Position:	20
Laps Completed:	187
Highest Position 2001 Race:	8
Fastest Race Lap:	113 (214.766 mph)
2001 Prize Money:	$256,325
Indy 500 Career Earnings:	$711,575
Career Indy 500 Starts:	3
Career Best Finish:	14th 2000

DALLARA/OLDSMOBILE/FIRESTONE

ROBBY GORDON

#41 Team Conseco
Entrant: A.J. Foyt/Richard Childress Racing
Crew Chief: Dave Milby

Robby Gordon had a promising beginning and premature ending in the Indy 500. Gordon broke fast out of the gate, leading the opening 22 laps, and was in position to challenge for a top finishing spot before engine problems eliminated him. "Some days the racing gods are with you and some days they aren't," Gordon said. "We gave it our best shot. I'm a little disappointed."

Gordon charged into the lead in the first turn from his third position on the grid, going around the outside of Greg Ray and past the crashing Scott Sharp. Ray passed Gordon in Turn 1 on a Lap 23 restart. Gordon remained in second until making his first pit stop on Lap 41. Gordon was delayed for 22 seconds from leaving the pit box by a jammed fuel nozzle. When the rest of the leaders had completed the round of stops, Gordon had dropped to 10th.

Gordon continued to run in the top 10 through the second round of pit stops. He was in seventh when the track went yellow on Lap 90. Gordon made his third stop under caution on Lap 91. At 100 laps, Gordon was in eighth, still on the lead lap.

Maintaining a pace that kept him on the lead lap, Gordon was in sixth, 20.25 seconds behind leader Helio Castroneves, under caution with 50 laps remaining. Gordon began losing power. Team owner A.J. Foyt saw the oil temperature rising on his telemetry. "A.J. told me on the radio with about 50 to go that we would have to nurse it home," Gordon said. "He even gave me some encouragement, saying, `I know that's not the way that you and I would race, but that's what we're going to have to do.'"

When the race was red flagged on Lap 155, Foyt decided to take the car to the garage to attempt to remedy the trouble, but the effort failed. The race resumed on Lap 158, and Gordon was given a drive-through penalty for the team working on the car during the red flag. He dropped to eighth position. He was running seventh, on the lead lap, when the engine failed on Lap 185. "We were just counting our chickens, going `one more lap, one more lap, " Gordon said. "I had a pace that I thought I could cruise and the motor just let go. Unfortunately, we came up 15 laps short."

The 32-year-old from Orange, California, showed he had the speed early, hitting 223.032 mph in his third day of practice. Gordon improved to 224.524 in the MBNA Pole Day morning practice. Foyt decided to wait for the late afternoon shadows on the front straight for his first qualifying attempt. Gordon ran laps of 225.990, 225.366, 224.291 and 224.338 for a 224.994 average to qualify on the front row for the first time in his seven-race Indy career.

"I thought we had a real shot of getting the pole," Gordon said. "We waited until weather conditions were ideal. I stayed full throttle on my first lap and entered Turn 1 at 233 mph. It went big loose on me.

I adjusted the car and it went to push and I had to do a light lift in Turn 1 on the second lap. I went back to where it was on the first lap and the car was good for the final two laps. I never hit the rev limiter, so we had too tall a gear. I am excited to be on the front row."

Before the engine failure, Gordon was in position for his fifth top-six finish in seven starts at Indianapolis. He was fourth in 1999, fifth in 1994 and 1995, and sixth in 2000.

2001 INDY 500 PERFORMANCE PROFILE

Starting Position:	3
Qualifying Average:	224.994 mph
Qualifying Speed Rank:	3
Best Practice Speed:	224.524 mph (5/18)
Total Practice Laps:	238
Finishing Position:	21
Laps Completed:	184
Highest Position 2001 Race:	1
Fastest Race Lap:	56 (218.161 mph)
2001 Prize Money:	$173,225
Indy 500 Career Earnings:	$1,7446,558
Career Indy 500 Starts:	7
Career Best Finish:	4th 1999

G FORCE/OLDSMOBILE/FIRESTONE

JAQUES LAZIER

#77 Classmates.com/Jonathan Byrd's Cafeteria
Entrant: Jonathan Byrd/TeamXtreme
Crew Chief: Tommy O'Brien

Starting from 17th position, Jaques Lazier vaulted up to 12th in the early stages of the Indianapolis 500. As he approached a restart on the 22nd lap, Lazier could not get the gearbox to engage. "All of the gears were just dead," he said. "Finally I found first and fifth gear. I knew I couldn't complete the race without a gearbox switch and, luckily, we had one in the pits with us."

Lazier pulled into the Jonathan Byrd/TeamXtreme pit box and the crew changed the gearbox in six and a half minutes. Lazier was 11 laps down when he returned to the race. With his promising beginning ruined, Lazier continued racing to the checkered flag and finished 22nd.

"It's a shame because all aspects of the car, before the gearbox problem, were performing well," Lazier said. "We had some understeer problems, but they were a quick fix."

The handling of Lazier's G Force-Oldsmobile changed dramatically following the first stop. "The second lap after that happened, the car went loose all day," he explained. "It stayed that way until the end, when we had a car I could drive."

Lazier showed good speed early in practice. He hit 221.289 mph on the third day and 223.310, fifth fastest for the session, on the fourth day. "I'll tell you what, today we did a lot of fine tuning and it resulted in a great speed," Lazier said. "We've been consistent from the first time we hit the track. Right now, we are just trimming the car out."

Lazier and the team spent the remainder of the week working on race setups. Back in qualifying trim, Lazier ran 223.018 in the MBNA Pole Day morning practice.

The eighth car out in qualifying, Lazier ran consistent laps of 222.988, 222.571, 222.000 and 221.032 to take 17th spot on the grid.

"We've definitely met our expectations with a 222 lap average," Lazier said. "The G Force was flawless except for a little push in Turn 1 on that last lap. We had planned on taking around a 221.5, but I stepped it up a little bit. I adjusted the car through the run. That thing was a bull out there.

"I'm just extremely happy. We know we've done a phenomenal job. I'm so proud of the entire team. We just put this (effort) together three weeks ago."

Lazier had driven for Truscelli Team Racing in his rookie year at Indy in 2000 and finished 13th. He joined forces with TeamXtreme for the 2000 season finale of the Indy Racing League at Texas and the 2001 500 was his first race of the season.

Lazier, younger brother of 1996 Indy 500 winner Buddy Lazier, enjoyed a breakthrough IRL season in 2001. He sat on the pole at Richmond and earned his first podium with a third at Kentucky with Sam Schmidt Motorsports. Hired by Team Menard for the final three races, Lazier started on the pole and won at Chicagoland Speedway.

Lazier qualified for the 1999 Indy 500, but was bumped from the field. He drove in his first IRL race two weeks later at Texas. Prior to Indy-style racing, Lazier competed in motocross, the International Karting Federation, SCCA Formula Ford, the American IndyCar Series and Indy Lights. In 1996, Lazier won the prestigious Mark Donohue Award.

Before deciding upon racing as his primary athletic endeavor, Lazier also played hockey, soccer and lacrosse. He earned a business degree from Chapman University in Orange, California.

2001 INDY 500 PERFORMANCE PROFILE

Starting Position:	17
Qualifying Average:	222.145 mph
Qualifying Speed Rank:	27
Best Practice Speed:	223.310 mph (5/9)
Total Practice Laps:	329
Finishing Position:	22
Laps Completed:	183
Highest Position 2001 Race:	12
Fastest Race Lap:	49 (212.841 mph)
2001 Prize Money:	$161,325
Indy 500 Career Earnings:	$451,575
Career Indy 500 Starts:	2
Career Best Finish:	13th 2000

DALLARA/OLDSMOBILE/FIRESTONE

DAVEY HAMILTON

#99 Sam Schmidt Motorsports
Racing Special
Entrant: Sam Schmidt Motorsports
Crew Chief: Mark Kilgo

The two-time Indy Racing Northern Light Series runner-up weathered through a difficult month of May at Indianapolis. It was punctuated by a practice crash, credible qualifying effort, and a steady drive in the race. Running seventh with 18 laps remaining, Davey Hamilton's engine failed and he fell to a 23rd-place finish. "It was a heartbreaker," Hamilton said. "It was a good feeling to be seventh. I want to win, of course, but I would have taken it."

The veteran from Eagle, Idaho, had started 26th and battled back from going a lap down early in the race. "It's a long day starting back where we did," Hamilton said. "We were consistently moving forward. We were pretty good by ourselves. We didn't have the fastest car, but were stable all day. The only real problems we had were in dirty air, and I don't think anyone was good in those conditions."

Hamilton took advantage of an early caution to pit on Lap 14. He had climbed to fourth by his second stop under green, on Lap 55. Hamilton went a lap down and fell to 20th.

From that point, Hamilton began a steady ascent. He was 15th at the 100-lap mark and 13th after 150 laps. Hamilton regained his lost lap by staying out under caution when the leaders pitted on Lap 166. He was eighth for the Lap 171 restart. "We got back on the lead lap and I passed Robby Gordon for seventh," Hamilton said. "He put me in the grass big time in Turn 3, but I made it through and we were running seventh. We had 17 or 18 laps to go and the motor broke."

Hamilton struggled finding speed in the week of practice leading to the opening qualifying weekend. His fastest lap in six days was 219.658 mph. Hamilton's problems took a turn for the worse on Friday, when he crashed exiting Turn 2 with 12 minutes remaining in the session. Hamilton was not seriously hurt, but the Dallara was badly damaged. Cleared to drive, Hamilton resumed practice in the team's other Dallara on MBNA Pole Day and ran 40 laps with a best of 219.845. His team, Sam Schmidt Motorsports, decided against making a qualification attempt.

Hamilton received a boost in horsepower the next day and it provided a jump in speed. The team had been using a standard Ilmor Engineering-built Oldsmobile. Kelley Racing loaned the Schmidt team one of its Ilmor Olds for qualifying. The Kelley and Penske teams had paid Ilmor $750,000 each for additional development and that technology had not been a part of Schmidt's engine deal.

Hamilton roared to a 222.979 in the morning practice on the second qualifying day. He was fourth out and averaged 221.696 to qualify for the 26th position on the grid. "The car is as free (aerodynamically) as we've had it," Hamilton said. "The Ilmor gave us the power. Thank God we're in and we're in with a decent speed. It's so calm (in terms of wind) that my car didn't really change at all in the

four laps. I was able to run flat out."

Hamilton did not have the use of the Kelley Ilmor Olds for the race. He drove a standard Ilmor version in it.

By qualifying for the 500, Hamilton continued to be the only driver to compete in every Indy Racing League race. This year's 500 was Hamilton's 47th straight IRL race. It ended at 48 when Hamilton suffered severe leg and foot injuries in a crash at Texas in the next race, forcing him to miss the remainder of the season.

2001 INDY 500 PERFORMANCE PROFILE

Starting Position:	26
Qualifying Average:	221.696 mph
Qualifying Speed Rank:	30
Best Practice Speed:	222.979 mph (5/13)
Total Practice Laps:	556
Finishing Position:	23
Laps Completed:	182
Highest Position 2001 Race:	4
Fastest Race Lap:	49 (213.538 mph)
2001 Prize Money:	$280,325
Indy 500 Career Earnings:	$1,416,978
Career Indy 500 Starts:	6
Career Best Finish:	4th 1998

JEFF WARD

#35 Aerosmith/Menards
Entrant: Heritage Motorsports
Crew Chief: Tim Whiting

In Jeff Ward's previous four starts at Indianapolis, he finished second in 1999, third in 1997, and fourth in 2000. Ward's stirring performance in the opening half of this year's 500 put him on track to add to those lofty accomplishments and, perhaps, even improving on them. Before an input drive shaft failed, Ward showed the strength to win.

"The car was perfect at the start of the race," Ward said. "I was running the car flat out and I was catching the leaders. This was the best package I've ever had at Indy. This car could have won the race."

Ward's G Force, powered by a Menard-built Oldsmobile, moved up from eighth on the grid to fourth after 70 laps. He was 11.8 seconds behind leader Mark Dismore. During a second round of green-flag pit stops, Ward ran in second on Lap 79 and continued in fourth after service. On Lap 85, Ward passed Greg Ray for third. "I was right on (second-running Gil) de Ferran," Ward said. "The car was quick all day."

On Lap 89, Ward slowed in Turn 1. He was able to limp around to the pits, where the Heritage Motorsports crew determined a $50 seal had broken and clogged the input drive shaft. "When that wheel shaft O-ring gave out, I just couldn't believe it," Ward said. "But once you have to come into the pits and watch other cars go by, you realize quickly you're not in contention anymore."

The team took the car back to the garage and repaired the shaft. Ward returned and ran to the checkered flag, finishing 32 laps down in 24th position. "We ran 219 after we came back, but I didn't have any motivation to run that hard to the finish since we were so many laps down," Ward said. "I'm confident we could have run at the front all day if the seal hadn't failed."

Ward was driving for a new team in Heritage (owned by Jim Rathmann Jr. and John Mecom III), but was working with team manager/engineer Mitch Davis for the fourth time at Indianapolis. Davis had prepared Ward's second- and third-place cars at Indy. They were a potent combination from the start in 2001, too. Ward ran 223.716 mph for third fastest on the third day of practice.

In the morning practice on MBNA Pole Day, Ward ripped off a 224.061. Ward halted his first qualifying attempt after the initial warm-up lap and waved off his second after a first lap of 219.370. Both came early on Pole Day. "We had zero downforce on our first lap out (in qualifying) this morning," Ward said. "When the track heated up, it got loose. It had no grip, so we didn't take the green. We changed the balance to try to get some grip back (on the next attempt). We went too far and didn't have the speed. We decided to come back late in the afternoon, where we'd been good earlier in the week."

Nearly four hours later, Ward streaked to an opening lap of 225.751 and followed with a 225.023. He fell off to 223.424 and 222.715 on the final two laps and averaged 224.222 to take eighth starting position. "I'm a little disappointed at how it dropped off a little bit, but we are happy to be in it," Ward said. "It made for a long day knowing the car wasn't quite perfect. The first lap was good, but then it was pushing a bit, so I eased off. It wasn't too bad, but I knew I had to back out of it. For whatever reason, the car just floated up the track. I even had to downshift in the short chute (between Turns 1 and 2)."

2001 INDY 500 PERFORMANCE PROFILE

Starting Position:	8
Qualifying Average:	224.222 mph
Qualifying Speed Rank:	9
Best Practice Speed:	225.061 mph (5/20)
Total Practice Laps:	353
Finishing Position:	24
Laps Completed:	168
Highest Position 2001 Race:	2
Fastest Race Lap:	95 (219.373 mph)
2001 Prize Money:	$248,325
Indy 500 Career Earnings:	$1,848,775
Career Indy 500 Starts:	5
Career Best Finish:	2nd 1999

DALLARA/OLDSMOBILE/FIRESTONE

DONNIE BEECHLER

#84 Harrah's
Entrant: A.J. Foyt Enterprises
Crew Chief: Craig Baranouski

Donnie Beechler's Dallara/Oldsmobile did not make it to the checkered flag, but he enjoyed racing it for as long as it lasted. "We had an awesome car," he said. "The car was the best I ever have driven. When things feel as good as they did, it's just so easy to drive."

Beechler rocketed up from 27th on the grid to seventh, on the lead lap, when smoke began to pour out of his engine on the 148th lap. "I was as fast as (winner) Helio (Castroneves) and really felt I had a terrific chance to win the race," Beechler said.

Beechler's crew initially believed a radiator leak overheated the engine. But after they replaced it, they discovered a broken fitting that caused oil to seep out.

"We found out that it was an oil fitting underneath, so it was hard to get to," Beechler explained. "By the time we found it and fixed it, the damage had already been done. We went back out (on Lap 185) and stayed out as long as we could. We didn't make it to the end, but we made it to Lap 198."

Beechler completed 160 laps and finished 25th. He went from 27th to 14th in the opening 30 laps and gained two more positions in the next 10. He went a lap down after making his initial pit stop on Lap 44, but returned to the lead lap as a round of green-flag pit stops was completed.

Beechler was up to eighth by Lap 70, 34.7 seconds behind leader Mark Dismore. Beechler went a lap down again after his second pit stop on Lap 76. Although running strongly, a caution period that began on Lap 90 trapped him a lap down.

Beechler put together a dazzling string of fast laps, averaging 217.741 mph for Laps 121–130. Beechler ran 219.528 on Lap 131, ranking him third among drivers for fastest lap of the race.

Beechler pitted under green on Lap 132 from eighth position, less than a second off the lead lap. When the caution came out two laps later, Beechler's rapid pace paid off with a return to the lead lap. He was in front of the pace car that picked up leader Gil de Ferran and circled around to the back of the field.

As the race resumed on Lap 139, Beechler was eighth and only 11.6 seconds off the lead. He passed Michael Andretti for seventh on Lap 147, but was forced to pit on the lead lap.

The veteran Sprint and Midget car driver from Springfield, IL, had arrived at Indianapolis without a ride. Owner A.J. Foyt decided to put Beechler in a third entry for the second week of practice and try to have Beechler qualify on Bump Day.

Beechler had only two days and 62 laps of practice before Bump Day. He ran eight more laps in the morning practice, then qualified in his first attempt at 224.449. It ranked fifth among qualifying speeds.

"I didn't even think I was going to drive here," Beechler said. "I just came here looking to see if I could find something. A.J. came along and said he wanted me for his third car. My heart started pumping."

Although he did not finish, Beechler clearly enjoyed this month of May at Indianapolis. "I met a lot of great guys on A.J.'s team," Beechler said. "A.J. was very kind to give me a chance. Dick Simon's crew was great on pit stops, so I gained a lot of new friends. You know, there is a lot more to racing than just finishing the race."

2001 INDY 500 PERFORMANCE PROFILE

Starting Position:	27
Qualifying Average:	224.449 mph
Qualifying Speed Rank:	5
Best Practice Speed:	222.622 mph (5/20)
Total Practice Laps:	89
Finishing Position:	25
Laps Completed:	160
Highest Position 2001 Race:	7
Fastest Race Lap:	131 (219.528 mph)
2001 Prize Money:	$730,625
Career Indy 500 Starts:	4
Career Best Finish:	12th 2000

DALLARA/OLDSMOBILE/FIRESTONE

EDDIE CHEEVER JR.

#51 Excite@Home Indy Race Car
Entrant: Cheever Indy Racing
Crew Chief: Owen Snyder

For Eddie Cheever Jr., the Indy 500 continued a pattern that began with practice and qualifying. The month of May had its bright moments, but they were supplanted by setbacks. Cheever made a solid run that held the prospect of a top-10 finish before electrical problems just past the halfway point, eliminated him.

"It's very frustrating," Cheever said. "It has not been a very good month for us, much less a good race. We did a lot of work and the car was good. It's very disappointing because we were running well and everyone has worked a lot of long nights for a long time. But this is racing and you have to take the good with the bad. Right now, we just have a big chunk of bad."

Cheever's Dallara/Infiniti had climbed impressively from 25th starting position to 13th by Lap 30, only 15 seconds behind leader Greg Ray. Cheever was running 10th before making his first pit stop on Lap 39.

The 1998 Indy 500 champion went a lap down, but as green-flag stops continued, Cheever returned to the lead lap. He was 12th before making his second stop on Lap 70. Cheever went a lap down and fell to 22nd.

With the race continuing under green, Cheever—who had pitted earlier on both his stops than most of the leaders—began to cycle forward and was back up to 12th at 90 laps. But Cheever's car had developed a loose condition and had been unable to stay on the lead lap. Cheever made his third pit stop, under caution, on Lap 91. Cheever's stop was delayed for about 15 seconds by a mishandled lug nut that went under the car.

Cheever was 18th and one lap down when the race resumed on Lap 96. His engine quit 12 laps later and he pulled into the pits. The team could not fix the problem and Cheever's race had reached its conclusion. He finished 26th.

"You have to remember that this Infiniti 35A engine is just three months old," Cheever said. "The guys on the team and at Infiniti have put a lot of effort into this. We had very good power."

Cheever posted his fastest lap of 223.981 in practice on the Friday prior to MBNA Pole Day. "We got lost two days ago with some wrong settings, but we made some progress today," he said. "I think that the front row is definitely possible."

The owner/driver's team regrouped overnight and Cheever ran 223.183 in the morning practice of the second qualifying day. Cheever withdrew the qualified car and requalified with a four-lap average of 222.152 for the 25th starting position. It was the second lowest of his 12-year career at Indianapolis.

"It was a nightmare, a horrible week," Cheever said. "It was good until Thursday, then we started having an electrical problem. We

thought we found something this morning, but I think it crept its way back in.

"I'm just elated. You can put that run down as one of my happiest moments at Indy in a long time. I can't think of anything more humiliating than not qualifying for the Indianapolis 500. That was everything I had."

2001 INDY 500 PERFORMANCE PROFILE

Starting Position:	25
Qualifying Average:	222.152 mph
Qualifying Speed Rank:	26
Best Practice Speed:	223.981 mph (5/11)
Total Practice Laps:	554
Finishing Position:	26
Laps Completed:	108
Highest Position 2001 Race:	10
Fastest Race Lap:	68 (216.273 mph)
2001 Prize Money:	$247,325
Indy 500 Career Earnings:	$3,810,277
Career Indy 500 Starts:	12
Career Best Finish:	1st 1998

27

DALLARA/OLDSMOBILE/FIRESTONE

JON HERB

#6 Epson
Entrant: Tri Star Motorsports
Crew Chief: Bill Curry

Jon Herb adopted a conservative plan for his rookie Indy 500, designed to gain maximum experience by reaching the checkered flag. Herb was just past halfway to his goal when came around Turn 1 and encountered Greg Ray's off-the-pace Dallara. With no time to react, Herb's Dallara hit Ray from behind and glanced off into the outside wall. The car's right side was heavily damaged, but Herb climbed out unharmed.

"The car was working fine," Herb said. "We weren't going to have to make any changes. We were just running the pace we wanted early, wanted to stay out of trouble and save the car for the end. Then, after the halfway point, I saw the rain coming in and we decided to pick it up a little bit.

"I made a clean move inside Davey Hamilton in Turn 1 and then came upon Greg Ray. He was moving really slow. I didn't have anywhere to go and ran into him. It put us into the wall. It's too bad because we had plenty left in that car to put us up front."

Herb had started 18th and was running 16th when Tri Star Motorsports' team manager Larry Curry decided to give up some track position for a pit-stop strategy out of sequence with the leaders. Herb made his first stop on Lap 14 and fell to 25th.

Gaining confidence, Herb averaged 206.362 mph for Laps 21–40 and 211.116 for Laps 41–50 and was running in sixth before making his second pit stop, under green, on Lap 54. Herb fell a lap down and to 22nd position after the stop.

Herb climbed back to 10th before making his second stop on Lap 87. It was troublesome, taking a minute more than his previous two stops, and Herb went another lap down. Herb was running in 20th position on Lap 107 when he rammed Ray, who had brushed the wall exiting Turn 3 a few laps previously and was trying to regain the handling of his car.

The 26-year-old Herb had a solid month in preparation for the race. He drove in only three Indy Racing events prior to Indy and ran fewer than 250 miles in competition. Herb also took 80 laps at Indianapolis during the Rookie Orientation Program.

Running on a limited budget, Herb ran only 135 laps, with a best of 220.359 mph, before making his initial qualifying attempt on Pole Day. Herb put it into the field, running 222.407, 222.328, 221.695 and 221.730 for a 222.015 average.

"It feels pretty good," Herb said. "I never really doubted we'd get in the show. It just took longer to get up to speed than we expected. Turn 1 was a little hairy going in at 230, or whatever our straightaway speeds were. It wasn't turning very good, but I kept it off the wall and we're in the show. It's another day at the track for me and I did what I was supposed to do. I'm satisfied with where we came from. I'm proud

of the job we did with what we had."

Herb did not start racing until 1997 and his experience prior to Indy Racing included FF2000, USAC Midgets and ARCA stock cars.

Herb recognized that some at Indianapolis doubted he had the experience or talent to qualify for the 500. "There's been a lot of people in the IRL who said, `This guy won't make the show,'" Herb said after qualifying. "I guess I'm still sort of unknown, though. This is a team sport and that's the only reason we did what we did today."

2001 INDY 500 PERFORMANCE PROFILE

Starting Position:	18
Qualifying Average:	222.015 mph
Qualifying Speed Rank:	28
Best Practice Speed:	220.359 mph (5/11)
Total Practice Laps:	180
Finishing Position:	27
Laps Completed:	104
Highest Position 2001 Race:	6
Fastest Race Lap:	56 (215.988 mph)
2001 Prize Money:	$245,575
Indy 500 Career Earnings:	$245,575
Career Indy 500 Starts:	1
Career Best Finish:	27th 2001

G FORCE/OLDSMOBILE/FIRESTONE

STEPHAN GREGOIRE

#36 Delco Remy/Menards
Entrant: Heritage
Motorsports
Crew Chief: John Palinca

Stephan Gregoire never had a chance to really get going in this year's Indy 500, falling out after completing 86 laps. The back end of Gregoire's G Force-Oldsmobile was sliding around almost from the start and it proved not to be a setup problem. "We had an oil filter break," Gregoire said. "It was putting oil all over the engine. I was loose in (Turns) One and Two and it was the oil."

The Frenchman was black flagged when heavy smoke began to pour out. "The IRL wanted us to stop, which is understandable," Gregoire said. "We might have gained four to eight positions if we had fixed it and gone out, but the car was in one piece and there wasn't much to be gained, so we decided to stop.

"It's disappointing, but the team did a good job and they got me in the show."

Gregoire qualified in 28th position. He stopped early under caution on Lap 14 hoping the yellows would fall his way later, but the early signs of the oil leak forced him to stop again on Lap 30. Gregoire went a lap down.

Unable to fix the problem and hoping it would not worsen, the team sent Gregoire back out and he ran well enough to not lose another lap until his next pit stop on Lap 64. Gregoire averaged 212.461 mph for Laps 51–60 and advanced to 23rd position before the third pit stop.

Gregoire was two laps down and running 24th when he was forced to drop out of the race.

The 32-year-old arrived in Indianapolis as the regular driver for Dick Simon Racing. Gregoire finished eighth in the 500 in 2000 with Simon, but struggled in practice this year.

Simon's team had Dallara and G Force chassis. Gregoire concentrated on the Dallara, but had an uncompetitive top speed of 214.284 through four days of practice.

Gregoire hit a low point following Thursday's fifth day, with a 204.863 best in 26 laps in the G Force-Oldsmobile. "We've tried for five days to find some speed," Gregoire said.

"I have asked Dick Simon a lot of questions and for a lot of help, but right now I just can't explain why we can't find the speed."

The next morning, the team announced it had hired Roberto Guerrero to assist Gregoire in setting up the car.

Guerrero ran 221.646 in the Friday practice in the Dallara. In only three laps with the same setup, Gregoire had a 218.855, but was still having problems.

The team decided to qualify Guerrero on MBNA Pole Day in the Dallara. He put it into the field at 220.054, but was later bumped.

Gregoire began working on the G Force-Oldsmobile and had a 219.510 during practice of the second qualifying day. But when

Gregoire fell back to 210.164 early the next week, he left Simon and joined Heritage Motorsports.

Driving Jeff Ward's backup G Force-Oldsmobile, Gregoire's initial session was the final full day of practice. He ran 17 laps, with a best of 217.796. In the Bump Day morning practice, Gregoire topped the charts at 223.541.

Gregoire averaged a robust 222.888 to make the race. "It's hard to explain everything I went through this month," Gregoire said, "but I will sleep well tonight. Thanks so much to Mitch Davis. He's a great engineer and gave me a great setup. Finally, I know it's not me."

2001 INDY 500 PERFORMANCE PROFILE

Starting Position:	29
Qualifying Average:	222.888 mph
Qualifying Speed Rank:	19
Best Practice Speed:	223.541 mp (5/20)
Total Practice Laps:	238
Finishing Position:	28
Laps Completed:	86
Highest Position 2001 Race:	23
Fastest Race Lap:	60 (213.985 mph)
2001 Prize Money:	$154,325
Career Indy 500 Starts:	6
Career Best Finish:	8th 2000

NICOLAS MINASSIAN

G FORCE/OLDSMOBILE/FIRESTONE

#49 Target
Entrant: Chip
Ganassi Racing Teams
Crew Chief: Grant Weaver

Nicolas Minassian did not expect to compete at Indianapolis this year. He completed the Rookie Orientation Program in mid-April, but team owner Chip Ganassi decided the Frenchman did not have enough oval experience and scratched him from the lineup.

Ganassi had a change of heart on MBNA Pole Day after Tony Stewart and Jimmy Vasser qualified the primary Target efforts solidly. Ganassi gave Minassian one of Stewart's G Force-Oldsmobile back-ups, and with minimal practice, Minassian put it into the field on the second day of qualifications.

It was an exhilarating experience to qualify, but Minassian's 500 did not go as smoothly. His learning curve was cut short by gearbox problems, knocking him out after completing 74 laps. Minassian finished 29th.

"I learned quite a bit, but I wish I learned more," Minassian said. "The engine died in the pits at our first stop, so we knew we were having gearbox problems. It took me two laps to get into fourth or fifth gear and up to speed. I knew the next time I came in, it would be a problem. At the end of the second stint, I was improving my lap times.

"I was just taking my time and didn't want to make a mistake. After the second stop, the gearbox was gone."

Minassian was running 16th before he pitted for the first time on Lap 42. He stalled pulling out of the pit box and the crew had to push the car back. Minassian's ordeal in the pit lane lasted more than two minutes, and he went four laps down.

Minassian made his second stop on Lap 79 and pulled out without problems. But as he tried to accelerate, Minassian could not find any gears. He coasted into the pits.

The 28-year-old had never driven on ovals prior to 2001. Minassian had spent his entire career in Europe, including three seasons in the Formula 3000 championship. Ganassi hired Minassian for CART's Champ Car series and originally planned to run him at Indianapolis.

Then, Ganassi changed his mind. Minassian was on the way to his Indianapolis residence when team manager Mike Hull called late on Pole Day and told him to return to the team's garage.

"As I was going home in the car with my wife, I said, `I have to go back to the track,' " Minassian said. "I was a bit scared. I didn't know what was going to happen. When I arrived, I was told, `We have to find everything, all your stuff, because you're going to qualify tomorrow.' "

Minassian got into a car set up by Stewart, who had run 223.186 in it earlier in the week. Minassian did 35 practice laps, with a best of 222.054 mph in the morning practice on the second qualifying day.

One short practice was all Minassian needed. He was second out in qualifying and put four laps together that averaged 223.006. It put Minassian in 22nd position on the grid.

"It just came as a surprise (to be qualifying), but it's a good one," Minassian said. "It's exciting. They gave me a good car. I just had to jump in the car."

2001 INDY 500 PERFORMANCE PROFILE

Starting Position:	22
Qualifying Average:	223.006 mph
Qualifying Speed Rank:	18
Best Practice Speed:	222.054 mph
Total Practice Laps:	62
Finishing Position:	29
Laps Completed:	74
Highest Position 2001 Race:	16
Fastest Race Lap:	41 (212.174 mph)
2001 Prize Money:	$149,575
Indy 500 Career Earnings:	$149,575
Career Indy 500 Starts:	1
Career Best Finish:	29th 2001

AL UNSER JR.

Al Unser Jr. tried to squeeze past a spinning Sam Hornish Jr. on the outside exiting Turn 4 in the Indianapolis 500. He didn't make it. Unser's G Force-Oldsmobile missed Hornish, but its right-front tagged the merciless concrete. The two-time 500 champion was out after completing only 16 laps, his fewest in 14 races at Indianapolis and thus his worst result. "I got taken out," Unser said. "We just came off that restart and Sam Hornish spun in front of me and then he went up towards the wall. I tried to sneak through. I was already committed. I was wanting him to stay low. But I didn't get through.

"It's the Indy 500. It's the greatest spectacle in racing. It's extremely disappointing."

The 39-year-old from Albuquerque, New Mexico, started from 19th position, but never really had the opportunity to race. Of the 16 laps Unser completed, 14 were run under caution. "I thought we had a good race car," Unser said. "We just never got going with all the restarts and yellow flags. We didn't get going enough to even get a feel for the tires."

Unser, never known for his blazing speeds in practice or qualifying, had a productive, consistent month of May in preparation for the race. He steadily worked up to speed, running 220.630 mph on the third day of practice and 222.023 on the sixth. "We've had kind of an uneventful month," Unser said. "We've just been going along trying to develop our race car and we feel like we learned quite a lot as the week has gone on."

On MBNA Pole Day, Unser was the third to qualify into the field. He averaged 221.615 mph. "We missed it (car setup) by a little bit," he said. "The run was OK. We had a push on the front end too much, so we lost some speed. It didn't stick as well as I'd like.

"What can I say? We're in the show and it's a long race. I'll be in the middle of the pack and I wish we were up a little further. I don't think we have a big worry of being bumped. We can start thinking of the race. What wins this race is a good, consistent race car, good pit stops and a hell of a lot of luck."

Unser's qualifying speed ended up 32nd in the field, one position above the bubble. The final hour of Bump Day was a nervous time for Unser. "It was the longest hour of my life," he said.

Unser's luck in the race was all bad. He was running 15th when he clipped the wall avoiding Hornish.

"Tony George (Indianapolis Motor Speedway President) already gave me a call and wanted to know if I was all right," Unser said an hour after the crash. "He was checking on me. He said, `I'm sorry you have to wait 364 days now.' Unfortunately, that's what I have to do."

Unser, son of four-time Indy winner Al Unser and nephew of three-time winner Bobby Unser, won the 500 for the first time in 1992 driving for owner Rick Galles. He won in 1994 driving for owner Roger Penske.

After winning the Super Vee championship in 1981 and the Can-Am title in 1982 with Galles, Unser moved into Indy-style racing in CART in 1983. In addition to his two Indy wins, Unser won 29 races in CART from 1984 through 1995. Unser was the CART champion in 1990 and 1994.

2001 INDY 500 PERFORMANCE PROFILE

Starting Position:	19
Qualifying Average:	221.615 mph
Qualifying Speed Rank:	32
Best Practice Speed:	222.023 mph (5/11)
Total Practice Laps:	456
Finishing Position:	30
Laps Completed:	16
Highest Position 2001 Race:	15
Fastest Race Lap:	7 (200.356 mph)
2001 Prize Money:	$255,825
Indy 500 Career Earnings:	$4,776,535
Career Indy 500 Starts:	14
Career Best Finish:	1st 1992, 1994

SARAH FISHER

DALLARA/OLDSMOBILE/FIRESTONE

#15 Kroger Special
Entrant: Walker Racing
Crew Chief: Ron Catt

Sarah Fisher prepared diligently for the Indy 500, running 522 laps in practice. Fisher's efforts with Walker Racing paid off handsomely on MBNA Pole Day when she qualified for the 15th starting position, but they were wasted in the race. On a cold day with cold tires following a restart, Fisher's Dallara-Oldsmobile snapped around exiting Turn 2 and hit the outside wall.

Fisher's second 500 lasted only seven and a half laps and she finished 31st. Fisher wasn't injured, but tears as she rode away on a golf cart from the infield's Clarian Emergency Medical Center were evidence of the pain inside.

"It was really, really slick out there," Fisher explained. This is the loosest I've been here at Indy. I was hanging on for dear life. There's absolutely no grip. There's absolutely no tire pressure ([which builds from heat]) out there. I tried to hang on to it as long as I could and finally it just came around on me."

Fisher's Dallara initially hit the wall with its back end. Scott Goodyear's Dallara-Infiniti had gone to the outside and made nose-to-nose contact with Fisher. She went slightly airborne and the Dallara's front tires lifted and skidded upon the top of the concrete wall before sliding off and stopping.

Fisher was able to climb out of the car herself. "I'm fine," she said. "I'm 20 years old and I can take hits like that."

Fisher had arrived in Indianapolis with high hopes. She finished second—the best ever for a woman in a major race—at Homestead-Miami Speedway in April, and she had appeared ready to build on a solid rookie campaign at Indianapolis in 2000.

The speed came more quickly in 2001 than it had in the previous year. Fisher ran 220.414 mph on the third day of practice, 220.944 on the fourth, and 220.297 on the fifth. Over those three days, Fisher did complete a whopping 270 laps in her primary car and 282 total.

After running 38 laps in her primary car and 35 in the backup in Friday's sixth day of practice, with a best of 220.521 in the primary, Fisher peaked in the MBNA Pole Day morning practice with a lap of 223.279.

Fisher waved off her first attempt after one lap of 221.704. Her headrest had flown off and become lodged in the air intake. "Since it was in the back, it just about pulled my head off," Fisher said.

She returned an hour and a half later and qualified with four fast and consistent laps: 222.197, 222.630, 222.789 and 222.575. Fisher's average was 222.548.

"We've been working really hard all week," Fisher said. "For our team and what we've prepared for and the budget we've had to work with, this was the best we could do. I've been stressed out all week, but the team is really behind me. They are like a second family to me."

Fisher became the third woman to race in the 500 in 2000, following the footsteps of Janet Guthrie and Lyn St. James. A few days before her sophomore 500, Fisher talked about the difference from her rookie season.

"I feel much more confident in the race car," she said. "I'm a lot more excited about Indy, too, because last year, there was so much more pressure and so much emphasis on us media-wise and fan-wise that I really couldn't stop and enjoy the tradition of Indy.

"This year it's a lot different because I'm able to step back and really see, wow, I'm still only 20 years old and racing at this awesome race. It is the greatest spectacle in racing and to be a part of that is awesome."

2001 INDY 500 PERFORMANCE PROFILE

Starting Position:	15
Qualifying Average:	222.548 mph
Qualifying Speed Rank:	22
Best Practice Speed:	223.279 mph (5/12)
Total Practice Laps:	522
Finishing Position:	31
Laps Completed:	7
Highest Position 2001 Race:	13
Fastest Race Lap:	7 (197.650 mph)
2001 Prize Money:	$247,325
Indy 500 Career Earnings:	$413,075
Career Indy 500 Starts:	2
Career Best Finish:	31st 2000, 2001

DALLARA/INFINITI/FIRESTONE

SCOTT GOODYEAR

#52 Thermos® Grill2G TM
Entrant: Cheever Indy Racing
Crew Chief: Dane Harte

Scott Goodyear was the only driver seriously injured in the 2001 Indianapolis 500. The Canadian fractured his lower back in a collision with Sarah Fisher and the outside wall exiting Turn 2. Goodyear spent three nights in Indianapolis's Methodist Hospital with the compression fracture of the L1 vertebra before being released. He did not require surgery.

Goodyear was eliminated on the eighth lap when Fisher spun into his path. "I was very pleased with how the car was running," he said. "The car was sliding a little bit through the turns at the beginning, so I was just waiting for the tire temperatures to come up. Unfortunately, when the No. 15 car (Fisher) spun in front of me, I had nowhere to go except into the wall."

Goodyear's 32nd-place finish was the worst of his 11 races at Indianapolis.

The 41-year-old had decided to concentrate on the 500 rather than compete in the full Indy Racing League season. He joined Cheever Indy Racing to race the 500 and serve as a test driver for the Infiniti program.

Goodyear ran 571 laps in practice, the most of any driver. He had the fourth fastest lap of Opening Day, 220.084 mph. "I'm starting to settle in with these guys," Goodyear said. "We turned a good lap, but there is more left in the car."

In Tuesday's third session, Goodyear had clocked his fastest practice lap of the month at 222.132. He ran 57 laps despite losing a transmission in the morning.

"We got some good running in," Goodyear said. "We went through a lot of things with shocks and springs and bars. We found some things that worked very well for us and we ran throughout the heat of the day, which I think was also beneficial. There's more speed in the car.

"We decided not to run in Happy Hour just to keep some tires and some miles for the heat of the day tomorrow, when the race will be and when qualifying for us will be. We have yet to use a fresh set of sticker tires."

Goodyear was not able to run 222 over the next three days. In Friday's sixth practice, he was disappointed with a 221.677. "We are not as quick as I would like to be, which is disturbing because at the beginning of the week I had anticipated that we had a shot at the front row," Goodyear said.

Goodyear did make some gains on MBNA Pole Day, qualifying 16th at 222.529 on his second attempt.

The team waved off his first attempt on his first timed lap. "We got a low battery voltage signal on the car and decided to call off our run," Goodyear said.

Goodyear's successful second attempt was nearly six hours later. He posted laps of 222.354, 222.815 (his fastest of the month), 222.508 and 222.438.

"We're not where we thought we would be when we unloaded the trailers," Goodyear said. "We (teammate and owner Eddie Cheever) were second and fourth early in the week, then eighth and tenth later in the week. Then we fell out of the top 10, unfortunately. We took a run at it just to get into the field."

Goodyear, who was treated with a back brace, rest and rehabilitation, did not race for the remainder of 2001, but made a full recovery from his injury.

2001 INDY 500 PERFORMANCE PROFILE

Starting Position:	16
Qualifying Average:	222.529 mph
Qualifying Speed Rank:	23
Best Practice Speed:	222.132 mph (5/8)
Total Practice Laps:	571
Finishing Position:	32
Laps Completed:	7
Highest Position 2001 Race:	16
Fastest Race Lap:	7 (201.776 mph)
2001 Prize Money:	$143,325
Indy 500 Career Earnings:	$3,000,990
Career Indy 500 Starts:	11
Career Best Finish:	2nd 1992, 1997

33

DALLARA/OLDSMOBILE/FIRESTONE

SCOTT SHARP

#8 Delphi Automotive Systems
Entrant: Kelley Racing
Crew Chief: Robert Perez

Scott Sharp climbed to the top of the mountain in qualifying, winning the MBNA Pole for the 85th Indy 500. He fell hard in the race, crashing in the first corner of the first lap. "You can't really put into words how disappointing it is," Sharp said. "It's hard to figure out why it has to happen. We all talked about how there were 800 corners here and you don't want to throw it away on the first one. I made a mistake and did."

The veteran Indy car driver accelerated into the lead at the green flag. He was fully aware of the cool conditions. "Obviously, we all know the track temperature was about 15 degrees cooler than Carb Day," Sharp explained. "I lifted a lot more in Turn 1 than some of the practice starts we had done, but, unfortunately, it just snapped right out from under me. I thought I could almost catch it, but obviously I wasn't able to."

Sharp's left-front tire went below the white line in Turn 1 and the back end swung to the outside. He tried to correct it, but the front tires went into the grass and all hope of saving it was lost. Sharp went up the track and hit the wall with the Dallara-Oldsmobile's right side.

"I obviously got a good start as I pulled through the green," Sharp said. "I backed off a lot more, thinking it was enough. As I looked at the (video) tapes, I had two guys right behind me carrying similar pace but, for some reason, mine just got loose and theirs didn't.

"I was the inside starter (in the three-wide formation), so I had to run a low line through there. I had run on the white line in other places on the track a lot during the month without having any trouble."

Sharp and Kelley Racing had enjoyed an impressive month prior to the race. He ran 226.137 mph mph on the fourth day of practice, then began concentrating on race setups.

On MBNA Pole Day, Sharp put together laps of 225.783, 226.020, 226.423, and 225.923 for a 226.037 mile-per-hour average.

"I certainly would call it my greatest accomplishment so far in racing," Sharp said. "When you think about the emotions and anticipation, anxiety, nervousness, all that goes into today, from a race driver's standpoint, I think qualifying for the Indy 500 is the hardest single day you have all year. And so to be able to come out of it as we did feels like a tremendous accomplishment and, obviously, a tremendous weight off our shoulders.

"Honestly when I got up this morning, I didn't know where we'd sit. We didn't spend a lot of time on low downforce (qualifying setup) in practice. I felt the best we could finish would be the pole and the worst we would finish was probably sixth or seventh and it just was going to be how we could put our four laps together. This was the first race and you can say we won that."

Sharp was also fastest in the final practice on Coors Carb Day and his team won the Coors Indy 500 Pit Stop Challenge the same day.

It had been a glorious month for Sharp and the team until he went into Turn 1 on the first lap.

"I feel so bad for the people that worked so hard, Delphi and the whole team," Sharp said. "It's pretty tough. I'm a perfectionist. I demand that for myself. I wasn't very happy with myself.

"That's the whole story of Indy——the high highs and the low lows. Unfortunately, we experienced both this month. This is a place that I love, but it sure hasn't been kind to me."

2001 INDY 500 PERFORMANCE PROFILE

Starting Position:	1
Qualifying Average:	226.037 mph
Qualifying Speed Rank:	1
Best Practice Speed:	226.137 mph (5/9)
Total Practice Laps:	303
Finishing Position:	33
Laps Completed:	0
Highest Position 2001 Race:	33
Fastest Race Lap:	None
2001 Prize Money:	$427,325
Indy 500 Career Earnings:	$1,718,344
Career Indy 500 Starts:	7
Career Best Finish:	10th 1996, 2000

Who do you trust with your heart?

Heart disease can be complicated by other serious health problems. It's often necessary to treat more than the cardiovascular system. Which means the cardiovascular facility you select should also offer more.

The IU School of Medicine and its world-renowned Krannert Institute of Cardiology have aligned with the clinical leadership of Methodist Heart Institute to form The Clarian Cardiovascular Center. This is the core, but only the beginning of care.

The Clarian Cardiovascular Center offers comprehensive care in a full service hospital environment – "a heart hospital within a hospital." Patients here have immediate access to medical care from a complete group of specialists who are down the hall – not across town, or even further.

Now, there are choices all around you. And complicated medical conditions add weight to the question: who do *you* trust with *your* heart? The answer is here.

THE CLARIAN
CARDIOVASCULAR CENTER

♡ THE HOSPITAL FOR ALL YOUR *heart* NEEDS

KRANNERT INSTITUTE OF CARDIOLOGY

INDIANA UNIVERSITY SCHOOL OF MEDICINE

Clarian Health
Methodist · IU · Riley

Methodist Heart Institute

Methodist Specialty Physicians

**To access the physicians and resources of
The Clarian Cardiovascular Center, call (317) 916-3525
or toll-free (800) 265-3220**

Doing Our Part To Keep America Moving...

Delco Remy

The Pennzoil Copper World Indy 200, held at Phoenix International Raceway's Desert Mile, was the opening event for the sixth season of Indy Racing League competition. It also marked the opening act for Indy Racing's brightest new star—Sam Hornish Jr.—and the revitalization of the Panther Racing team.

Hornish took over the Pennzoil Panther Racing seat formerly held by Scott Goodyear. Pundits began debating the wisdom of this selection as soon as it was announced. When the checkered flag fell on the event, Hornish dispelled any doubts about his speed or competitiveness. Right from the start, Hornish stamped his authority on

the event and proved his prowess with top-shelf equipment. He was passed twice during the race, but he remained composed and came back to claim the lead and victory by 1.38 seconds over second-place A. J. Foyt Racing's Eliseo Salazar.

A new twist to this year's event combined the immensely popular Copper World Classic for short-track machinery with the cars from Indy to create the Pennzoil Copper World 200. With this opportunity, Davey Hamilton entered in all four divisions, adding midgets, Silver Bullet cars, and supermodifieds to his schedule.

In addition to series regulars, the Penske team entered its first-ever IRL race, using the event as a test for a future appearance by Helio Castroneves and Gil de Ferran at the Indianapolis Motor Speedway.

After the first day of practice, Hornish sat on top of the speed chart with a practice lap of 173.451 mph. In qualifying on Saturday, Hornish put together a 176.801 lap as the sixth car out. Greg Ray bettered his time with a lap at 177.663, but Hornish's run proved good enough for the outside spot on the front row.

From the green flag, Hornish got the drop on Ray and moved past the Texan on the outside in Turn 1. He built a lead of more than five seconds over Ray before Stephan Gregoire leaped past Ray for second position and began to reel in the leader.

Gregoire, running strong, cut Hornish's lead to 1.223 seconds by Lap 54. But Ray wasn't done for the day. He picked up the pace and steadily marched forward. First he retook second spot from Gregiore. Then Ray took the lead from Hornish on Lap 69 before a round of pit stops shuffled the order of the field, which sent Castroneves, de Ferran, and Scott Sharp briefly to the front. In his first outing in an Indy Racing League car, Castroneves turned in an impressive performance as he stormed up to the front from a 17th place starting position. Ray, however, regained the point on Lap 82 during a caution period caused by a three-car incident in Turn Four involving de Ferran, Jeret Schroeder, and Mark Dismore.

After the cleanup, Ray led Gregoire, Castroneves, Sharp, and Hornish in the restart line. Ray quickly built a three-second lead over Gregoire by the middle of the race while Hornish held fifth. But Gregoire came back to challenge and pass Ray for the lead on Lap 119.

Three laps later, Ray's day ended with a plume of smoke trailing his machine. "The car was running great all day," Ray said. "It was handling well and I could run anywhere on the track I wanted. About 30 laps ago, I

Only 21 years old, Sam Hornish Jr. (4) became the youngest winner in IRL history with his Phoenix victory. His commanding performance was even more impressive because it was his first outing with the Panther Racing team. Hornish dominated the meeting and was passed only once, on Lap 68, by Greg Ray.

Savvy Eliseo Salazar (14) worked his way through traffic and accidents to finish second after starting 13th in the Harrah's A. J. Foyt Dallara-Oldsmobile.

started to lose power. I think the fuel pressure went low and I cracked my block."

Hornish charged ahead and moved up to second place, trailing Gregoire by five seconds. A caution on Lap 125 for oil on the track erased Gregiore's lead. After pit stops, Hornish took the lead under the caution on Lap 128. When the race was restarted, Gregoire spun and hit the Turn Two wall, ending an exceptional run. "The car might not have been good enough to win, but it was good enough to lead," Gregoire said. "It's really a shame. I needed a break. I went on the outside of Robbie Buhl and we touched. It's a shame."

Green-flag racing resumed on Lap 138, and Hornish pulled away in the lead. On Lap 158, Stan Wattles brought out the race's final caution when he hit the inside wall on the backstretch.

After the accident was cleared up and the race restarted, Hornish opened a comfortable lead and cruised to the finish, scoring his first win in just nine IRL starts. Salazar claimed second, trailing by 1.3786 seconds, followed by Lazier, Sharp and Billy Boat.

It certainly made for a flying start for the young driver with a new team. "I knew that I had a little bit better car than (Castroneves) did in traffic, and he wasn't able to put the car on the high side as I was able to," Hornish said. "So I wasn't really worried about it. I knew as long as I was in front of him and I didn't let him get underneath me, that he wasn't going to be able to go around me on the high side.

"The only other time I felt some real competition was (when) Eliseo (Salazar) started catching up to me before the last yellow flag, and he gained some time on me until we got in traffic. I think that's where my car was the best today, was working through traffic, and I was able to put it anywhere where a lot of guys weren't able to go on the high side."

Helio Castroneves makes a pre-Indianapolis 500 start in an unfamiliar paint job. He did not finish.

With his ever increasing oval-track experience and know-how boosting confidence on the tight Phoenix circuit, Airton Daré (88) improved steadily on his 18th-place start and came home in 10th.

Sam Hornish Jr. and Sarah Fisher, two of the Indy Racing League's young guns, finished one-two and made the first appearance of the Indy Racing League at the Homestead track an event to remember. Like the first race of the season at Phoenix, Hornish dominated the proceedings, passing Indy racing veterans Buddy Lazier and Eliseo Salazar as well as Fisher.

The two young guns provide an interesting history, coming up through the ranks of racing. Hornish and Sarah Fisher raced against each other as kids on the go-kart tracks of Ohio, then they went their separate ways in their middle teens. Hornish turned to Formula 2000 cars at 16 after winning the World Karting Association U.S. Grand National Championship in 1995, then stepped up to Formula Atlantic. Fisher won the Grand National title in 1994 and moved over to sprint cars at 15 and then on to midgets.

Their paths finally crossed again while driving at Phoenix International Raceway in the Indy Racing Northern Light Series in March 2000. They came to Indy, passed their rookie tests, and qualified for the Indy 500. When the season was over, Fisher, driving for the well-funded Derrick Walker Racing, was 18th in the final standings and Hornish 21st. However, Hornish's strong impression, both in competition and during tryouts, led to his selection as replacement for veteran Scott Goodyear in the seat of the strong Pennzoil Panther Racing team for 2001.

Hornish won his second consecutive race by a mere 1.8701 seconds over Fisher. Never in the history of major auto racing had two

Although many predicted strong performances from young gun Sam Hornish, few expected him to bag wins in the first two races of the season. A stall in his pit box dropped him from first to fourth, but the determined Ohioan sliced through the field to take the lead and an eventual win.

so young done so well. And never had a woman finished second. It was a race for the record books.

After the epic race, Hornish said, "She gave me a good run."

"I don't know if I could've caught him; I tried," Fisher said.

The race was Hornish's 10th in the Indy Racing League and Fisher's 11th.

The Homestead-Miami Speedway, built beside a cornfield some 30 miles south of Miami, was the first of several new venues for the 2001 IRL season. CART previously had raced once a year on the 1.5-mile circuit.

MBNA Pole qualifying provided a surprise when veteran Jeff Ward, driving for the new Heritage Racing team jointly owned by Jim Rathmann Jr. and John Mecom III, captured the favored front-row inside starting spot in only the team's second race. Ward's speed of 201.551 mph knocked Greg Ray, the Indy Racing League's most prolific pole winner, to the outside of the front row with a speed of 199.893.

NFL Hall-of-Famer Nick Buoniconti gave the command to start the engines to 26 starters. At the drop of the green flag, Ward immediately opened a gap on Ray to lead the first circuit by 1.6377 seconds. Seconds later the yellow caution flag came out as Florida driver Stan Wattles spun into the inside retaining wall at Turn Four and suffered moderate damage. Wattles climbed out unscathed.

On the next lap rookie Jon Herb's day ended when his engine exploded on the front straight, which brought out the yellow flag. The green reappeared for Lap six, but as the leaders rapidly pulled away, Robbie Buhl's Infiniti-powered Dreyer & Reinbold Purex machine lost power and coasted to a halt at the entrance of the pit.

Meanwhile, Ward, leading the race, put some distance between his G Force/Oldsmobile/Firestone and Ray. But Ray was under attack from behind. A hard-charging Hornish made the pass on the Team Menard driver on Lap eight. Six laps later Hornish dove under Ward's car and swept into the lead. Though he soon encountered traffic, Hornish eked out a 1.331-second advantage.

Frenchman Stephan Gregoire made the first official pit stop—an early one—on Lap 22 for tires and fuel. The Dick Simon team reported a tire-pressure problem that was upsetting the handling.

Three laps later, Buddy Lazier got around Ray for second place. After Buhl reentered the race, he lasted two laps before his car stalled again for another yellow. Most of the leaders used this caution to pit. Hornish and Ward were

first out of the pits after service as rookie Felipe Giaffone assumed the lead. However, the Brazilian pitted on the next lap after misunderstanding the radio order to come in with the front-runners.

The track went green on Lap 35. Ward ducked under Hornish in Turn Three on Lap 36 to regain the lead, and Lazier got by Hornish a few moments later for second. By Lap 50, Ward, Lazier, Hornish and Mark Dismore were leading the race. Al Unser Jr. moved methodically through the field, coming from 19th to 8th. But even more impressive was Hornish. He reclaimed second, running side by side and eventually overhauling Ward for the lead. The Defiance, Ohio, driver backed off as he and Ward approached a slower car, but shot by his rival between Turns Three and Four on Lap 63.

On Lap 65, Brazilian Airton Daré, 2000 Indy Racing rookie of the year, brought out the yellow when his TeamXtreme G Force/Oldsmobile engine blew and spun in Turn Two. Then, Unser made a costly mistake. He entered the pits for fuel and tires while the pits were closed and was assessed a stop-and-go penalty.

The race resumed on Lap 71 and Hornish began to pull away at the front. Unser, despite his penalty, clung to fifth. Twelve cars still ran in the lead lap as Hornish led the pack at the halfway mark by five seconds over Ward. Hornish lengthened his lead, but lost the advantage when the yellow came out for debris on the track, with Dismore and Eddie Cheever Jr. holding second and third.

Hornish stormed away from the pack at the restart. By Lap 127 he had built up a 10-second lead over Unser. Hornish widened the gap to 16 seconds as Eliseo Salazar closed to third place. Meanwhile, Unser Jr. ran out of fuel and coasted into the pits without power. Trouble restarting the car took Unser out of contention.

Ray slammed into the Turn Two wall on Lap 166 and the leaders dashed in for their final pit stops. Hornish stalled his car as he started to exit his pitbox and after a quick engine restart, departed in fourth place. Salazar, driving the A. J. Foyt Harrah's Dallara,

snatched the lead. Hornish, who had shown superior speed all day, began to close in for the kill. After Hornish passed Lazier for third, the defending Indy Racing League champion slid high into the wall, ending his day. On the ensuing restart, Hornish blasted by Fisher to take second and set chase after Salazar. He caught him on Lap 183, and with the race on the line, they bitterly contested the position. Hornish found an advantage, inched by Salazar, and then pulled away.

Fisher then slipped by Salazar and charged after Hornish. She slashed the margin to .666 of a second by Lap 192 as the crowd stood and cheered her magnificent drive. But then Hornish slowly added another second to his margin at the checkered flag for his second victory in a row.

"She was always real tough competition," Hornish said about his early days of racing against Sarah. "I was worried that she was going to pull one of those kart moves on me today. Thankfully, everything worked out right."

Despite starting 19th, fan favorite Al Unser Jr. (3) led a lap early in the race. However, a stop-and-go penalty set him back and he could only climb back to sixth.

Former motocross champion Jeff Ward (35) continued to show race-winning form in the IRL by taking the MBNA Pole in the Heritage Motorsports/Menards G Force-Oldsmobile and then finishing fifth.

Pushing the Walker Racing/Kroger Special (15) to the limit, young Sarah Fisher used muscle and finesse to close to within .6 seconds of leader Sam Hornish Jr. and take second.

Greg Ray and Team Menard have been at the top of their game at 1.5-mile Atlanta oval. This year's zMax 500 was no different. Ray didn't give his competition a glimmer of hope and won convincingly. The 1999 Indy Racing League champion's dominating performance looked even more impressive than his 2000 win at this track. In 2000 he won the pole and led 182 of 208 laps, which he backed up this year by capturing the pole and leading 184 of 200 laps. In fact, Ray led 403 laps over a three-year span driving for John Menard.

"It's certainly on my bio as my favorite track," Ray said after bringing his Johns Manville/Menard's Dallara-Oldsmobile/Firestone home 19.857 seconds in front of runner-up Scott Sharp. "To have two fairy-tale race weekends (at the same track) is very rare. Very rarely does a driver and a team have two races so flawless at a track."

Ray averaged 133.647 mph in a race slowed by 55 caution laps. Despite qualifying on the front row in the first two rounds, Ray suffered through two miserable performances (22nd at Phoenix and 21st at Miami). However, when the series traveled to Atlanta, he picked up right where he left off the year before. He easily led both practices with speeds over 217 mph and qualified at 24.7406 seconds for a speed average of 218.265 mph. Jeff Ward came up second-quick but almost two mph slower at 216.144 in his Heritage Motorsports' G Force-Oldsmobile/Firestone car.

At the drop of the green flag, Ward snuck by Ray in Turn 1 and led the first lap by .2571 of a second. However, Ward's run at the front would be short-lived. Ray sliced the margin to .0331 on the second circuit, then snatched the lead away on the back straight of Lap three. Once in front, Ray took firm command of the race.

The yellow waved on Lap four when rookie Brandon Erwin spun and hit the Turn Four wall. He climbed from his cockpit unharmed. It took five laps for Erwin's car to be removed before the field returned to green-flag racing. Ray held off Ward on the restart and began to slip

Call him "The Dominator" at Atlanta. For the second-straight season at Atlanta, Greg Ray (2) sped to the pole in qualifying and ran away from the field to win the zMAX 500. He established a 10-second lead and was able to conserve fuel and cruise to the win while fellow competitors were forced to pit in the late stages of the race.

Despite fighting a balance problem and a deflating tire, Scott Sharp (8) ran well in the Delphi Automotive Systems Dallara-Oldsmobile/Firestone, moving up from a 13th-place start to finish second, but no one could catch race winner Greg Ray.

away as Sam Hornish Jr. closed in on third-place Mark Dismore. Hornish in his Pennzoil Panther Racing Dallara moved past Dismore on Lap 13 and set after Ward. Dismore's brief stint near the front ended as the specter of an engine failure reared its ugly head.

Ray increased his lead over Ward from .9217 seconds on Lap 16 to 1.811 by Lap 25. The Team Menard driver extended his lead to 3.7668 seconds by Lap 34 when Eddie Cheever Jr.'s new 35A Infiniti engine expired. Hornish proved that his pace in the first two races of the season was no fluke as he battled wheel to wheel with Ward for second position. The 21-year-old Ohioan made the pass stick on the back straight of Lap 40, but he trailed Ray by 5.5677 seconds.

A yellow for oil on the track bunched the field up and erased Ray's lead. The leaders took the opportunity to pit for fuel and tires. The Menard team quickly serviced Ray's Dallara, got him back out and retained the lead. On Lap 53, a massive accident eliminated nine cars from the running. As rookie Cory Witherill exited Turn Four, he slowed dramatically. As fellow competitors tried to avoid Witherill's car, it set off a chain-reaction crash that caught Jeret Schroeder, Billy Boat, Robbie Buhl, Robby McGehee, Casey Mears, Davey Hamilton, Al Unser Jr. and Sarah Fisher.

"Somebody hit me from behind, and somebody came over the top of me," said two-time Indy 500 winner Al Unser Jr. "Then it was all smoke and flames, and I hit the wall." Schroeder added, "I was praying we'd get through it, but they started coming up high and took me with them. A couple of cars got airborne and they went over me on fire."

Ray and Hornish took advantage of the yellow to visit the pits. Ward stayed out and assumed the lead on Lap 84, and Kelley Racing's Scott Sharp moved up to claim second position. Sharp hounded Ward on the Lap 87 restart and Ray rejoined the race. Ray charged back up the order, first passing Sharp, and then moving past Ward in the span of three laps.

On Lap 77, rookie Jon Herb stalled in Turn Two, bringing out yet another yellow. This caution prompted Ward and Sharp to pit, but it was disastrous for Ward, who stalled twice and had to have his battery replaced. The mechanical maladies effectively eliminated his chances for victory. After racing resumed on Lap 102, Ray reestablished his lead over Hornish. Hemelgarn Racing's, and defending series champion, Buddy Lazier and Chilean Eliseo Salazar, driving for A. J. Foyt, battled for fourth for 13 consecutive laps. While Salazar and Lazier battled for fourth, Ray dropped the hammer and extended his lead to seven seconds.

Ray made his final stop for fuel and tires on Lap 146. He rejoined the race and set a torrential pace. By Lap 156, Ray held a mammoth lead over Hornish. Salazar and Lazier were the only other cars on the lead lap at that stage of the race.

With 30 laps to go, Team Menard and Ray changed strategy and ran in fuel-conservation mode in order to prevent an additional pit stop. Ray ran in traffic and dropped his pace from 215 to 195 mph. Hornish was in hot pursuit and began to cut huge chunks of time out of Ray's lead. By Lap 188, he had whittled it down to 5.8294 seconds.

It was clear that no one was going to match Ray's pace and mileage. Hornish and Lazier made their final stops on Lap 191. Thus, they were shuffled down the order. Their late-race pit stop moved Sharp into second, although a lap down, and Buzz Calkins was promoted to third. Sharp and Calkins made up enough ground to get back on the lead lap, but neither had the time nor the speed to catch Ray. Hornish came back to pass Salazar and finished fourth while Lazier took sixth.

But on this day, Ray was in a league of his own. He took the checkered flag ahead of Sharp by 19.857 and Calkins by 26.69 seconds. Hornish's fourth-place finish allowed him to maintain his points lead.

Ray's fifth career victory was the ninth win for Team Menard, the most successful team in league history. "For me, I think the big thing is for the guys (crew)," Ray said. "These guys busted their tails. The fun part is for me. I get to get in the car and drive."

Gaining valuable points he needed to move up in the race for the series championship, Buzz Calkins (12) brought the Bradley Food Marts/Sav-O-Mat Dallara-Oldsmobile/Firestone home in third place.

After finishing ninth and 16th in the season's first two races, Buzz Calkins (12) was happy to earn his first podium finish of 2001 with a third place at Atlanta.

SHARP WINS TEXAS SHOOTOUT

The true indicator of an athlete's character is the ability to rebound from adversity. Race driver Scott Sharp sure did that in the Indy Racing Northern Light Series Casino Magic 500 at Texas Motor Speedway. He won a no-holds-barred shootout with Greg Ray in the final stages of the race to take the victory, his sixth in his Indy Racing League career.

Two weeks before, in the Indy 500, Sharp suffered one of the most devastating blows of his racing career. Sitting on the pole position, he crashed in Turn 1 on the opening lap. The 1996 co-Indy Racing League champion took the mishap hard, spending a long time in his Kelley Racing garage before finally meeting the press. "It took me a while to come to the conclusion I'm going to run 4,000 laps this year, and everyone is going to make mistakes," he said. "I picked the worst possible time to make mine."

Days later as Sharp, driver of the Delphi Automotive Systems Dallara-Oldsmobile/Firestone car, prepared to head for the Texas race, he said he still hadn't recovered mentally, and probably wouldn't until he returned to Indy the following May. However, the Indy setback provided extra fuel to his competitive fires as he took a determined approach to the Casino Magic race. It helped to be defending champion of the event. Sharp stated, "I'm moving on and taking out my frustrations on the rest of the season."

He went out and made 23 other drivers feel his furor. In qualifying, he snatched the pole briefly before teammate Mark Dismore wrested it away with a top speed of 215.508 mph. Still, Sharp would start beside him on the front row with a clocking of 215.065. "I might be a little bit more bashful this time," Sharp said about the start. Sharp took a conservative approach to the start of the second night race of the season. Instead of trying to immediately pull away from the field, he made a conservative start and slipped back to fifth as

Texan Greg Ray (2) hoped to claim victory at his home track. He got caught in a late-race accident, though, and ended up 11th.

Scott Sharp (8) ran fast all weekend, qualifying second and going on to win. He earned enough points to move up in the points standings and gain momentum for the middle of the season.

Eddie Cheever Jr., Sam Hornish Jr. and Shigeaki Hattori all drove around him.

Cheever quickly moved up to battle Dismore. On Lap three, he took the lead as he drove around the outside of the Kelley driver. Dismore slipped back to third and then Sharp, now finding his rhythm, edged around his teammate into third on Lap nine and began closing on second-place Hornish. Sharp was not the only driver on the move. Greg Ray and Al Unser Jr., who started 20th and 21st respectively, had each advanced 10 positions.

Sharp took second away from Hornish on Lap 19, and shortly thereafter Hornish succumbed to an attack from Dismore as well. On Lap 27, the yellow flag came out because of debris on the track. The entire field, minus Jaques Lazier and Buzz Calkins, took the opportunity to pit.

When the race restarted on Lap 31, Jaques Lazier, younger brother of Buddy Lazier, ran out front. Team Xtreme's Airton Daré applied pressure to the young Lazier and was able to snatch the lead away after one lap. Daré did not have to contend with a counterattack from Lazier. Instead, Daré had his hands full with Cheever as he moved past Lazier to challenge Daré for the lead. Infiniti-powered driver Robbie Buhl charged up through the field and took second away from Hornish on Lap 44. At Lap 50, the one-quarter mark, Cheever held a 3.9408-second advantage over Buhl. Both demonstrated that the Infiniti powerplant possessed race-winning form. Hornish trailed another 1.5 seconds in third place, and Ray moved up to fourth.

On Lap 73, Jeret Schroeder spun in Turn Two and took Davey Hamilton's car with him into the wall. Sarah Fisher came upon the site of the accident and struck an errant tire. Although able to continue on, she eventually retired on Lap 176. The collision left Hamilton with severe ankle and leg injuries, from which he is expected to recover.

In the close racing typical of exciting IRL races at Texas, Donnie Beechler (11) pulls past Billy Boat (98), while Robbie Buhl (24) is pinned to the outside wall.

Later, Schroeder said, "It felt like I lost an engine. I just decreased my speed, oiled up my tires, and crashed in Turn Two."

The accident initiated a round of pit stops on Lap 75. Ray won the pit scramble followed by Cheever, Giaffone, Hornish and Sharp. When green-flag racing resumed, Ray and Cheever staged an intense battle for the top spot. Shortly thereafter, Jeff Ward joined the fray as he maneuvered his Heritage Motorsports machine into second while Cheever and then Ray pitted. Hornish and Giaffone passed Ward to take over the first and second positions. Once again, Ray was on a charge. He chased down and passed both Hornish and Giaffone for the lead again on Lap 116. Buhl, meanwhile, found himself battling alternator problems, which eventually took him out of contention.

At Lap 150, Sharp climbed back into second and Cheever, rebounding from his unscheduled pit stop, hung on in fifth. A yellow followed on Lap 156, and Sharp forged ahead of Ray to lead the race for the first time on the restart. Evenly matched, the two former champions waged a high-speed chess game in search of the ultimate victory. For the final third of the race, Ray and Sharp were separated by a couple of feet as the two raced wheel to wheel and flat-out. In fact, Ray and Sharp battled for 83 laps of the race. Without a doubt, it provided some of the closest and exciting racing to that point in the 2001 season.

Ward's run ended on Lap 183 when his engine let go, bringing out another yellow. When the green flag waved again, Cheever joined the pack at the front. Ray held an edge of 1.227 seconds over Sharp and .2157 in front of Cheever on Lap 195. Ray and Sharp approached the lapped car of Robby McGehee in Turn Three. Running significantly faster, Ray dived underneath McGehee while Sharp took the high groove. Ray's right-front wheel touched McGehee's left rear and the pair spun across the track. Sharp narrowly missed the pair,

but Cheever, following closely behind, was not so lucky. Cheever plowed into McGehee as he slid in front of him.

The track marshals were not able to clean up the wreckage in time for a green-flag finish. Thus, Sharp took the checkered under yellow-course conditions, followed by Hornish and Buddy Lazier. Giaffone advanced from fourth to second for the Brazilian's best finish. McGehee was airlifted to Parkland Hospital with a concussion and fracture of his lower left leg.

Sharp became the fourth driver in the IRL to finish last in a race and then win the next one. "Everybody's been so supportive after what happened in Turn 1 at Indianapolis," Sharp said. "I just kept my faith in the Man upstairs. I didn't quite know why that happened at Indy, but I kept my trust in Him, and He delivered me today."

The "Most Improved" award could have gone to Jaques Lazier (77), who started a disappointing 19th but worked his way through the field to finish ninth.

LAZIER RULES THE DAY

With his father and his son watching, Buddy Lazier (91) celebrated Father's Day in style by winning the Radisson Indy 200 on what the Colorado resident considers to be his home track.

After a mediocre start to the season, reigning Indy Racing Northern Light Series champion Buddy Lazier was languishing fifth in the points standings, and his chances for defending the title seemed bleak. This year the challenge came not from one of the wily veterans, but instead from young upstart Sam Hornish Jr. In the five prior races, Lazier finished third to Hornish's initial victory at Phoenix; 20th to Hornish's win at Homestead/Miami; sixth to Hornish's fourth at Atlanta; 18th to Hornish's 14th at Indy; and fourth to Hornish's third at Texas.

To mount a successful title defense, Lazier needed to change the tide of current events. And in the past, the Hemelgarn Racing driver delivered the goods when the pressure was on.

In the Radisson Indy 200 at Pikes Peak International Raceway, Lazier put in an inspired drive, taking the win over Hornish in second place. The victory moved Lazier from fifth to fourth in the standings and reduced Hornish's points lead to 62. In addition, as a native of Vail, Colorado, Lazier gave Colorado racing fans an extra reason to be proud. Ron Hemelgarn, owner of Hemelgarn Racing and Lazier's Tae-Bo/Coors Light/Delta Faucet Dallara-Oldsmobile/Firestone, had a hunch, too, that this time it would be Lazier's turn to take the checkered flag. "We're pretty confident," he said. "We've been running pretty good on these short ovals, and Buddy wants to do exceptionally well, this being his home track. I feel we're going to do quite well there."

Lazier recorded his second-best qualifying run of the season to take the fifth starting position, only two spots behind Hornish in third in the Pennzoil Panther Racing Dallara-Oldsmobile/Firestone. Once again, Greg Ray showed blistering speed over a single lap and captured the pole with a speed of 176.585 mph.

At the 2 P.M. race start time, the thermometer read a scorching 95 degrees, with the track temperature reaching 134 degrees. Ray charged away from the field at the drop of the green flag, but it only took Hornish about three laps to overtake and pass him entering Turn Three of Lap four. Robbie Buhl, also on the move, drove his Infiniti-powered Team Purex Dreyer & Reinbold G Force machine by Ray for second on Lap eight.

Lazier showed his cards early by moving past Ray to take third on Lap 11. Meanwhile, Hornish sliced through the field, building a 7.1516-second lead by Lap 22. Three circuits later, he had lapped all cars up to 10th.

Lazier bolted past Buhl in Turn Three on Lap 34 to grab second place. At the front, Hornish pushed hard and extended his lead to 16.10 seconds on Lap 58. But it evaporated when the yellow flag came out for debris on the track. Hornish and Lazier dashed to the pits for service. Hornish took on tires and fuel and retained his lead. Lazier added downforce to his car and returned to the track in second position.

Once again, Hornish quickly pulled away from the field and established an 11.53-second lead over Lazier at the 100-lap, or halfway, mark. But another yellow on Lap 115 killed all the hard work. Buddy pulled up on Hornish's gearbox in second while Jaques resided in third. Pitting did not change the order as Hornish took the green flag on Lap 124 and held his lead. But this

Scott Sharp (8) started on the front row but never led a lap and had to settle for an eighth-place finish that, while disappointing, kept him in the thick of the points race.

Despite leading 152 laps in a row, points leader Sam Hornish Jr. (4) fell victim to an ill-handling car following a late pit stop and finished second behind Buddy Lazier.

Hoping that his strong finish would give him the momentum to finish the season strongly, Billy Boat (98) brought the CURB Records Dallara-Oldsmobile/Firestone home fourth after starting eighth.

time he was not able to build the margin as Buddy Lazier matched Hornish's lap times over the several laps.

Jaques Lazier fell out of the running on Lap 147 with engine problems, following pole sitter Ray, Didier André and Billy Roe to the sidelines. Back at the front, Buddy Lazier set his sights on Hornish. When the track went green on Lap 155, Lazier slipped back. But on the next lap, he reasserted himself and shadowed the Ohioan down the back straight. He slipped by Hornish in Turn Three to assume the lead for the first time. Hornish continued to fall back due to a deteriorating setup. In his efforts to keep the loose car on pace, he grazed the Turn Two wall five laps later and was lucky to be able to continue. Consequently, Hornish shifted his attention to defending second rather than retaking the lead. His misfortunes were Lazier's gains. The defending champ initially opened up a gap of five seconds, which increased to 7.543 seconds with 25 miles left to go. Buhl, meanwhile, closed on his tail and pressured him hard as 15 laps remained.

Lazier increased his lead margin to 10 seconds by Lap 190, while Hornish led Buhl by only a 10th of a second. Billy Boat, driving the CURB Records Dallara-Oldsmobile/Firestone, was the only other driver on the lead lap.

With his first victory since winning the inaugural race at Kentucky Speedway on August 27, 2000 in sight, Lazier paced himself in the closing stages. Still, he took the checkered flag 10.108 seconds in front of Hornish, who was able to hold off Buhl by a car length. Boat finished fourth 19.7498 seconds back. Lazier led 44 laps to Hornish's 152 and averaged 142.987 mph for the 200-mile distance.

"Huge," Lazier exclaimed. "This is huge. I couldn't believe it. I didn't want to believe it until the end. My engineer did a great job. We just kept counting the laps down. We just kept digging and digging. I wanted to win so bad. It's Father's Day. I guess I won it for him (son Flynn, 2)."

Hemelgarn said, "We're just so proud of what Buddy has done.

Our goal is to end up in September and win the championship."

Hornish was pleased to hang onto second after nearly smacking the wall.

"I thought it was over," he said. "I have to thank the guy upstairs for helping me keep it out of the wall. I'm happy the way things are going."

A third-place finish gave Robbie Buhl (24) a welcome dose of points. Buhl could not challenge leader Sam Hornish Jr. or winner Buddy Lazier, but he was pleased with his top-five finish.

LAZIER STAKES TWO IN A ROW

Speed. Savvy. Versatility. Buddy Lazier Jr. possesses these qualities in spades. And when Eddie Cheever and Eliseo Salazar faltered in the SunTrust Indy Challenge, Lazier did not need a second invitation. He won the race by 4.888 seconds over second-place Sam Hornish Jr. Lazier won his second consecutive race, the fifth driver in league history to accomplish the feat, and breathed new life into his championship defense. Whether on a short oval or super speedway, Lazier continues to prove he can rise to the challenge. He won six Indy Racing League races (including the Indy 500) on a variety of tracks. In the League's first trip to Richmond, Lazier quickly adapted to the .75-mile bullring.

Although Lazier took victory by nearly five seconds, the win did not come without drama. On his last pit stop, Lazier's helmet visor fogged and he overshot his pit box. But he took the setback in stride and pitted on the next lap. However, championship rival Sam Hornish Jr. nabbed second, and in turn scored 35 points, keeping a firm grasp on the championship points lead. Beyond the thickening points battle, the Indy Racing League hosted the event in front of 40,000 spectators. Those numbers marked sizable gains in attendance, especially in Richmond, the hotbed of NASCAR racing.

Greg Ray's erratic season suffered another knock in practice. Ray's Dallara-Oldsmobile smacked the outside retaining wall in Turn Four. He climbed out of his car with assistance from the IRL safety crew. On Saturday, Ray met with Dr. Henry Bock, IRL director of medical services. Ray, still complaining about back spasms, was not cleared to race. "I'm a little stiff," Ray said. "That was a straight-on impact. I'd be in the car if it was me. But you can't argue with the doctors."

Jaques Lazier, Buddy's brother, captured his first career pole driving for Sam Schmidt Motorsports, turning a fast lap of 160.417 mph. Buddy started fourth. In her 17th Indy Racing League start, Sarah Fisher qualified in the second position for the first time.

At the drop of the green flag, Fisher sliced past pole sitter Lazier on the inside in Turn 1, to briefly lead. But reigning champion Buddy was the driver on the move. Lazier quickly passed Fisher and dispatched his brother, taking the lead. Hornish, who started sixth, charged into second place on Lap eight and set his sights on the elder Lazier. But Lazier responded to the competition move for move, lap time for lap time.

On Lap 15, Jaques Lazier spun into the Turn Four wall to bring out the first yellow flag. He escaped without injury. After the restart, Buddy seized firm command of the race, staying just out of striking distance from Hornish. From Lap 25 to Lap 50, Lazier's lead over Hornish fluctuated between the high one-second and four-second range. Lazier upped the pace and stretched his lead to 10.72 seconds by Lap 62 when the track went yellow for debris.

Lazier, Hornish and the other leaders peeled into the pits for service. Lazier beat Hornish out, but Salazar stopped in the wrong pit box and had to make another circuit before receiving fuel and tires.

Momentum and valuable driver points were among the benefits Buddy Lazier (91) reaped by winning his second-straight race. He led an IRL record-setting 224 of 250 laps to claim the victory.

SunTrust
INDY Challenge
At Richmond International Raceway

SUNTRUST INDY CHALLENGE
●RICHMOND INTERNATIONAL RACEWAY
June 30, 2001

INDY RACING
Northern Light
Series

Running smooth and steady, Al Unser Jr. (3) earned a podium finish by taking third after starting 11th in the Galles Racing Starz SuperPak car.

A brief light rain brought out the yellow for Laps 92 through 100.

Lazier edged away from Hornish when the track went green again, but 11 laps later Fisher spun into the outside wall in Turn Three, and that bunched the field up again. Shortly thereafter, Jeret Schroeder stalled on the track and subsequently spun out, bringing out the yellow flag. On Lap 150, green-flag racing resumed. Team Xtreme's Airton Daré moved into the lead group. Last year's rookie of the year slid into second with Eddie Cheever Jr., Hornish and Salazar in tow. Daré's run did not last, however. He tangled with rookie standout Felipe Giaffone on the back straight exiting Turn Two in his pursuit of Lazier. Both were sidelined.

The accident and the resulting yellow flag prompted the leaders to make their final pit stops. Like Salazar earlier in the race, Lazier missed his box and made an additional lap in order to get service, but Lazier was not the only driver making mistakes at this critical stage of the race. Hornish stalled his machine, which required considerable time to restart. Hornish, unable to leave his pit box immediately after service, watched an excellent shot at the win stall with his car. When the racing resumed, Salazar led, followed by Cheever, Lazier, Hornish and Al Unser Jr.

But once again luck or fate played into Lazier's hands. Salazar led the way into Turn Three on Lap 214. Cheever made a daring pass attempt on the outside and the two cars touched. An opportunistic Lazier roared through an opening in the spinning wreck and seized the lead, a lead he never gave up. Lazier proved to be the class of the field. He easily dictated the pace, leading 224 of 250 laps, and often pulling out a lead that was a half a lap ahead of the field. Lazier extended his lead over Hornish to 6.6598 seconds with six laps remaining and

took the checkered flag by nearly 5 seconds. Once again Hornish provided Lazier with the stiffest competition, but overrevving his engine on a Lap 185 pit stop proved to be a costly mistake for Hornish. For the rest of the race, he experienced an engine misfire–a misfire that prevented him from hunting down and challenging Lazier. Two-time Indy 500 winner and Galles Racing driver Unser Jr. came home third.

In the physically demanding race, drivers navigated the .75-mile D-shaped oval over 250 laps and averaged about 155 mph. According to telemetry, the drivers experienced a consistent 4–5 gs, which is considerably higher than most IRL tracks. Even though the drivers felt the effects of the stress, they handled it well.

"I'm beat," Lazier said. "This is two weeks in a row. I can't believe it. It's an amazing day."

After this quick pit stop, young Didier André (32) posted his best finish of the season, finishing fourth after starting 14th in the Galles Racing G Force-Oldsmobile/Firestone.

The 43-year-old driver led seven times for a commanding 104 laps, including the last three after making an amazing pass on Sam Hornish Jr. The 35A finally came of age. "We've worked very hard these last three years," Cheever said. "It's been a struggle. I had an advantage here."

Before the green even fell, Greg Ray, who sat out during the previous race due to a crash, turned into the pits on the first pace lap with the engine losing power. Chilean driver Eliseo Salazar made an amazing start. He sped by Cheever and then rocketed around the outside of Sharp in Turn Four to lead the first lap in his Harrah's A. J. Foyt Racing Dallara-Oldsmobile/Firestone. Salazar maintained his edge over Cheever in second as Buhl, in the other Infiniti, slipped by Hornish to regain fourth.

The first caution flag appeared on Lap 15 when liquid was spotted spraying from Billy Roe's Zali Racing car. Roe stopped on the inside of Turns Three and Four.

The Team Menard crew, who had been working feverishly to get Ray's car restarted, finally fired up the engine and sent him out for his

A full house was on hand to see Eddie Cheever Jr. (51) make history. Cheever won the first-ever IRL race at Kansas Speedway with a late-race pass of Sam Hornish Jr.

For 1998 Indy 500 winner Eddie Cheever Jr. the 2001 season looked like a mountain of frustration. He won Infiniti's first race at the Pikes Peak 200 the previous season and set out to build upon that success. In the seven races run in the 2001 IRL season, engine, electrical and throttle problems, in addition to an accident fighting for the lead at Texas, knocked him out of races. To date, he finished 19th, 9th, 24th, 26th, 12th, 6th, and 13th. But Cheever came to Kansas armed with the all-new and all-powerful 35A engine. He used the horsepower to dispatch all challengers and capture the Ameristar Casino Indy 200 at the new 1.5-mile Kansas City track.

Cheever readily admitted the role the engine played in the race. "It wasn't superior driving skill," he said. "It was the Infiniti in the back of my car. My engine ran impeccably. Everything was perfect, one of those days you want to happen more often than they do. . . . I can't thank the Infiniti engineers enough."

Ever since signing on with Infiniti, Cheever pursued an aggressive engine development program. The Infiniti engine, he felt, offered potential but lacked reliability. He won Pikes Peak in 2000, but he knew he could not be truly competitive race after race until the new engine arrived. Cheever needed power and dependability to win. He anticipated unveiling the 35A engine in the next race at Atlanta Motor Speedway, but delays in parts manufacturing prevented it.

It was not until just before the 2001 IRL season opener at Phoenix in March that Cheever and Robbie Buhl, the other Infiniti driver, got the new engine to race. It was still in the developmental stage and not until Pikes Peak, on June 17, did the engine reach its breakthrough. Buhl finished third and Cheever sixth. They slipped back at Richmond, but then no one could beat Cheever at Kansas.

Felipe Giaffone (21) led two laps but was not pressing for the victory at the end. Still, he was happy with his fourth-place finish in the Hollywood G Force-Oldsmobile/Firestone.

first circuit on Lap 17. After checking the entire electrical system, they changed the rev limiter.

During the yellow, several drivers pitted. Racing resumed on Lap 27 and Salazar led the way over Cheever, Sharp, Buhl and Hornish. Cheever took the lead for the first time on Lap 33 when he dived under Salazar in Turn Three. Behind him, Hornish continued to charge. He overtook Buhl and then Sharp to grab second place on Lap 42, and Foyt's other driver, Donnie Beechler, climbed to fourth.

On Lap 47, Hornish's yellow Pennzoil Panther Racing Dallara powered by Cheever at the exit of Turn Two to assume the front spot. Two laps later, Cheever returned the favor by darting past Hornish on the low side of Turn Two for the lead. The terrific duel between the cagey veteran and young lion brought the sellout crowd to its feet. It was just a precursor of what was to transpire at the end.

Hornish charged back to the front on Lap 53. Cheever pitted on Lap 60, followed by Hornish one lap later. During the pit sequence, rookie Felipe Giaffone moved to the top, with Jaques Lazier and two-time Indy 500 champion Al Unser Jr. right behind him.

During this same time, Buhl's day ended when his engine failed as he drove down pit lane. Dismore and Robby McGehee each briefly held the lead before pitting, but the leaders—Hornish, Cheever and Sharp—soon resumed their battle up front. Cheever led on Lap 104 when Jon Herb brought out the yellow. The leaders pitted and Hornish lost precious time when his car stalled. Defending Indy Racing champion Buddy Lazier quietly slipped into the lead.

When the green flag dropped on Lap 111, Cheever quickly assumed the lead. Hornish slid high in Turn Two and opened the door for Sharp to nab second on Lap 127. Ten laps later, his Delphi Automotive Systems Dallara spun into the Turn Four wall.

The pit stops briefly put Buddy Lazier and McGehee out front, but Cheever's much quicker pace thrust him back into the lead. The cars returned to full speed on Lap 158, and again it became a fierce duel between Cheever and Hornish, with Beechler hanging a close third. Hornish snatched the lead away on Lap 191, knifing under Cheever in Turn Three. Cheever faded slightly, but then regained his momentum.

Cheever caught up to Hornish with three laps to go and used all of his quarter-century of racing savvy to get his nose under the youngster's car in Turn Four for the lead. There was no catching Cheever then, and he took the checkered flag by .1976 in front of Hornish, who finished second in his third-straight race.

In his winning effort, Cheever averaged 148.914 mph. Ten cars finished the tight race on the winner's lap and 14 were still running at the end.

In a race that included 20 lead changes, Donnie Beechler (11) led three laps and challenged for the victory before finishing third, a strong improvement over his 11th-place start.

"I had a phenomenal time racing with Hornish," said Cheever. "What I love about racing with Sam is that Sam plays by the rules. He understands if you have a run on him. He will give you a hard time and he will hold his line. And I did that with him. He came up with nine laps to go. It would be easy for me to shut the door on him and start weaving. But he had treated me correctly the whole race and I did the same to him."

Points leader Sam Hornish Jr. (4) led 25 laps, but was passed two laps from the checkered flag by winner Eddie Cheever Jr. and had to settle for second place.

Running strong and steady, Airton Daré (88) moved up to finish sixth in the 1-800-BAR-NONE/Team Xtreme G Force-Oldsmobile/Firestone.

By Jan Shaffer

Hemelgarn Racing is a veteran team, led by owner Ron Hemelgarn and the triumvirate of team manager Lee Kunzman, engineer Ronnie Dawes and crew chief Dennis LaCava. All of their close-working efforts go behind Buddy Lazier when he straps into the seat of one of their machines. The driver is fearless, the race strategy flawless.

Lazier and team are especially competitive at tracks where nobody has gone before. They won the first pole in Indy Racing League history at Walt Disney World. They won the first race held at Charlotte (now Lowe's) Motor Speedway. Now comes the Harrah's 200, a test at the new Nashville Superspeedway, and Lazier already with two victories under his belt before this mid-July whirl. Even with confidence from those two wins, Lazier had to contend with illness and a difficult time developing a setup.

"I had the flu the whole time," Lazier said. "You know, a lot of times when the driver is not feeling too good, the team has to really step it up because you can't give as much feedback. So, they really

A sellout crowd at Nashville Superspeedway saw Buddy Lazier (91) win the Harrah's Indy 200 and edge closer in the points race to leader Sam Hornish Jr.

stepped up their game. They had to kind of help me out and give me a really good car for the race and they did that."

Lazier passed MBNA Pole winner Greg Ray on the back straight for the lead on the seventh lap, kept in touch with the leaders all night, and took off after pit stops with 23 laps to go to post a 10.6293-second victory over Billy Boat for his third win of the campaign.

Lazier's brother, Jaques, was running just in front of him at the end. As Buddy waved his arms in victory, Jaques hit the Turn Two wall while attempting to complete his final lap and was credited with third, the best finish for a pair of brothers in recent Indy-style history.

When the 21-car field rolled off the starting grid, Buddy Lazier was in the sixth spot. Ray took the MBNA Pole with a qualifying run

of 199.922 mph, and Northern Light Series points leader Sam Hornish Jr. was alongside. By the fourth lap, Lazier, Hornish and Boat jockeyed for the second, third and fourth spots behind Ray. After Lazier took the lead three circuits later, Hornish also passed Ray for second. Shortly thereafter, Ray fell off the pace and wasn't heard from at the front again.

On Lap 20, Hornish used lapped traffic as a "pick" and soared under Lazier in Turn Three. Contests took place elsewhere on the track as various drivers got up a head of steam. On a Lap 27 restart after a debris caution, Felipe Giaffone came from ninth to fifth. Forty laps later, he was a lap down. Jaques Lazier started 14th and wheeled to fourth by Lap 42.

Buddy Lazier retook command on Lap 52 from Hornish, who slid high to avoid a car. Two laps later, Hornish beat Lazier out of the pits after a caution caused by debris to lead again.

Just before the halfway point, Sarah Fisher pulled to the pits, joining Jeff Ward and Didier André as early dropouts.

"It doesn't know what it wants to do," she told her crew over the radio. Reason out: handling.

Then it happened. Some in the sport call it The Big Wreck. Cheever was running fifth at the time, Beechler sixth, Unser seventh, Dismore eighth, and Daré ninth when Eddie Cheever Jr. and Ray touched wheels off Turn Two and hit the wall. Donnie Beechler, running right behind the pair, spun and was clipped by Al Unser Jr. Mark Dismore slowed to avoid the melee and was hit in the right rear by Airton Daré, who catapulted over the wheel, nose up into the wall.

Of the group, only Beechler returned to the race. The other five were out. That left the frontrunners to slug it out. Hornish lost the lead to Eliseo Salazar when his crew had trouble with a tire change on a pit stop during the caution, and Hornish came out sixth. He had led 86 of the first 110 laps. Later, he complained the engine was going sour. The culprit was a faulty fuel injector, and essentially Hornish lost the use of that cylinder. He was unable to retake the lead.

Buddy Lazier made short work of Salazar on the restart after the cleanup, then Boat went to the front three laps later for his first lead of the season.

Lazier let him stay there, stalking him until Lap 148, when he got past Boat in traffic. The final pit stops came under the green. Buddy Lazier pitted first, sending Jaques Lazier to the lead. When Jaques pitted, Robby McGehee led for two laps. And when McGehee pitted, Buddy regained the lead en route to victory in the No. 91 Tae-Bo/Coors Light/Delta Faucet Dallara-Oldsmobile/Firestone under the lights before a packed house.

After the race, Lazier put his current run of success in perspective. "Dennis (LaCava) said before the season, 'Buddy, this year we're

Robby McGehee (10) gave up the lead when he made his final pit stop and never made it back to first. He finished fourth in Cahill Racing's Dallara-Oldsmobile/Firestone after starting in 11th.

going to get you the most victories, career victories' and I just don't believe it, but I'll be danged if they haven't gone out and got it done," he said. "It's a huge amount of pride I have for that because I just really love driving Indy cars. I think this is just the series of the future. It's something I'm really proud to be a part of and now to have the best record, it's awesome.

"In racing, a lot of times if you can win 10 or 15 percent of the time, you're wildly successful because there are so many competitors out there, you wind up not winning most of the time. It just feels so good to win and now to have the most victories, it's very special to me."

Although Lazier continued to chip away at Hornish's points lead, the young lion from Ohio retained a 40-point advantage over Lazier at 339 points to Lazier's 299.

Second place was a high-water mark for Boat's season to date. He managed to pass Lazier in the middle stages of the race and hold the lead for 26 laps, but Lazier proved his toughness in the closing stages of the race.

"I think when we were in the lead, Buddy was an awful close match," Boat said. "A lot of traffic won this race . . . won it for Buddy, probably lost it for me. A big track like this, it's awful tough to pass and you've got to kind of have a little bit of luck and time your passes right. I came upon two lapped cars and Buddy got around me. I lost some momentum and he had a little more time to recover and he got by me.

"I think that was really the difference in the race. And once he got by me, it was awful hard for me to catch him. I think he probably would have had a hard time catching us, passing us in a clear track."

For Lazier, it was his 22nd race lead in Indy Racing League competition, a series record. It was his fifth-consecutive top-five finish, also a series record. His third win tied him with Kenny Brack and Greg Ray for most victories in a season.

Billy Boat (98) put CURB Records' Dallara-Oldsmobile/Firestone in the lead for 26 laps before settling for a runner-up finish at Nashville, giving him a valuable boost in the driver standings.

For the first four races of the season, Buddy Lazier and Hemelgarn Racing were far from spectacular, but their mid-season run was nothing short of stunning. Lazier prevailed over Scott Sharp by 1.5822 seconds in the Beleterra Casino Indy 300 at Kentucky Speedway and became a back-to-back winner in the series at the track.

In his quest to become the first two-time Indy Racing Northern Light Series champion, Lazier set a series record by winning more races than any other driver. But if Lazier was going to realize his goal, the Indy Racing championship, he needed Sam Hornish Jr. to suffer some misfortune. Hornish's consistent podium finishes in the four previous races, including his third at Kentucky, allowed Lazier to put a serious dent in his points lead, but not erase it. In fact, Lazier had trimmed a 70-point lead to 26 as he stood on 349 points to Hornish's 375.

The Kentucky win was Lazier's eighth in the series, a league record as well. "What a great second half of the season we're having," Lazier said. "We're coming hard. I think it's going to be real tight for the points battle. It's going to be close there at the end of the season."

To keep himself in the thick of the race for the championship, Buddy Lazier (91) won the Belterra Casino Indy 300 while averaging nearly 175 mph. *Jim Haines*

Sharp qualified his Delta Automotive Systems Dallara-Oldsmobile/Firestone machine 1 mile per hour faster than his competitors at 214.507 miles per hour. Mark Dismore ran the closest at 213.646 miles per hour, which put the two Kelley Racing teammates on the front row. Lining up behind them were the two Infiniti-powered cars of Eddie Cheever Jr. and Robbie Buhl. Ricky Treadway, son of Fred Treadway, co-owner of Treadway/Hubbard Racing, qualified for his first IRL race in 15th place.

Sharp pulled away from the field at the start, and only teammate Dismore kept pace in the early going. Sharp averaged 208.836 after 10 circuits. Dismore shadowed his teammate by only .191 of a

second and recorded the quickest lap in the early stage of the race at 212.693. On Lap 11, Dismore tried to slip under Sharp in Turn 1, but Sharp held his line and thwarted the move.

Jeff Ward, driving for Heritage Motorsports, began to slow on Lap 16 when he reported his car was loose. Sharp and Dismore continued their heated battle in front of the pack. On Lap 29, Dismore's tire deflated, sending him spinning and eventually tapping the Turn Two wall. Dismore rolled into the pits for a tire change, and rejoined the race several laps down. But Dismore eventually returned to the pits and parked it.

When the incident brought out the yellow, Sharp and most of the leaders pitted. The Kelley team serviced Sharp's car fast enough to retain the lead. Hornish moved up and challenged Sharp, but Sharp fended off the attack and held on to the lead. Then Robbie Buhl, piloting the Dreyer & Reinbold Dallara-Infiniti, sliced past Hornish to take second on Lap 56. Once again, the usual suspects (Hornish and Lazier) were forging their way to the front of the field as defending series champion Buddy Lazier charged into second on Lap 63. Lazier momentarily slipped back as Hornish moved up to take second behind the leader, Sharp. In a brave move on the front straight, Hornish dove between Buhl and the slower Billy Roe to take over second again.

At the midstage of the race, Sharp led with Buddy Lazier in second by .328 of a second and Cheever in third by .653.

Airton Daré brushed the wall between Turns Three and Four and the leaders used the yellow period to pit. Hornish won the pit contest and assumed the front spot behind the Pace Car for the race's first change of leaders.

As in previous races, Lazier asserted his presence at the front of the field as the race wound down. Running side by side on Lap 111, Lazier muscled his way past Hornish on the back straight to retake the lead. But Lazier and Hornish circulated in close proximity and were eventually joined by Boat. The trio threaded their way through traffic together. In a heart-pounding moment, Lazier narrowly swept past the lapped car of Buzz Calkins as Hornish and Boat snapped at his heels.

Eliseo Salazar brought out the final yellow by spinning and stalling in the pits. Subsequently, the crew pushed his car nearly the entire length of the pit lane to the A. J. Foyt Racing team pit box. During the last round of pit stops, Buhl's team manager John O'Gara made a costly error. He waved Buhl out of his pit while the fuel hose was still connected to the car. The methanol tank fell over and some fuel spilled on the ground, but it was quickly cleaned up.

Buhl's mishap didn't distract him from the task at hand. He valiantly charged from sixth to second in the span of 17 laps and demonstrated that the competitive form of the new 35A Infiniti powerplant was for real. On Laps 186 and 187, locked in a wheel-to-wheel battle, neither Lazier nor Buhl held a decisive advantage. But Buhl managed to get a strong enough line out of Turn Two on Lap 189

to take the lead from Lazier. However, Lazier is tough when the race is on the line, and the previous pit episode prevented valuable fuel from getting into Buhl's fuel cell. Entering Turn Three on Lap 196, Buhl's car abruptly slowed, out of fuel. Sharp picked up second from a slowing Buhl, but could not challenge for the lead. Lazier was out of reach. The Hemelgarn driver roared to the checkered flag by 1.582 seconds in front of the Kelley Racing driver.

Buhl expressed his profound disappointment. "Leaving the pits early on that last pit stop while the fuel hose was still hooked up hurt us. Johnny (O'Gara, who doubles as the right-front tire changer on pit stops) anticipated the drop of the car and the fuel coming out. He waved me out and Bubba (Martin), our fuel guy, was just trying to release the hose and it hung up. It's a game where tenths of a second make a difference and we were just trying to make everything work perfectly."

Lazier, who led 84 of the final 89 laps, summed up his battle with Buhl. "I'm watching in the mirror and he's reeling me in," he said. "I'm going as fast as I can go. I'm wide open, got the car trimmed out to the point where the rear end is wiggling. I can't go anywhere. At some point, you realize, boy, this can go any way. I've got to make the right decision here."

But in the end, Lazier, once again, came up with the goods.

Billy Boat (98) generated some much-needed momentum for his team with a sixth-place finish at Kentucky in his Dallara-Oldsmobile/Firestone. *Steve Snoddy*

Scott Sharp (8) leads Sam Hornish Jr. (4) and eventual winner Buddy Lazier (91). Five drivers led before Lazier won by 1.56 seconds over Sharp. Steve Snoddy

UNSER'S FUEL GAMBLE PAYS OFF

By Joe Crowley

With two major championships and two Indy 500 victories under his belt, Al Unser Jr. will go down in history as one of the best drivers of his era. Unser added another impressive achievement to his resume by winning the Gateway Indy 250 through stunning driving and a gutsy strategy. In the process, the 39-year-old ended a 16-race winless streak and erased any questions about his competitiveness.

Off-track developments made nearly as much news as Unser's latest win. Team Menard replaced Greg Ray, the 1999 Indy Racing League champion, with Jaques Lazier, brother of defending Indy Racing champion Buddy Lazier. Ray, who had been with Team Menard since 1999, scored only four top-10 finishes, including two wins since his championship season.

It was the League's first trip to the peculiar 1.25-mile oval. Gateway adds a unique twist with tight Turns 1 and Two and long, sweeping Turns Three and Four, linked by two long straightaways.

Scott Sharp led the divided practice session with a lap of 168.262 miles per hour in his No. 8T Delphi Automotive Systems Dallara-Oldsmobile/Firestone. But that lap would prove moot for qualifying when the MBNA Pole Qualifying session was washed out the next day. Sam Hornish Jr. was placed in the top starting spot with Buddy Lazier on the outside of the front row as the qualifying lineup was determined by accumulated entrant points in accordance with Indy Racing League rules.

Hornish led the points ever since the opening race in Phoenix. But with four victories in the last five Indy Racing events, Lazier trimmed Hornish's once commanding lead to just 25 points. Now the two drivers would line up side by side to battle for victory with the championship on the line. Lazier provided some perspective: "It's just a matter of real-izing, being mature about things, and knowing that the race is won 200 laps into the race as opposed to the first or second lap."

Though qualifying was canceled, two practice sessions were scheduled for the remainder of the day in order to give teams time to adapt to a new venue. Sharp again posted the fastest lap of the divided first practice session, turning a lap of 169.562 miles per hour. The lap would end up being the fastest of the day as yet more rain fell in the St. Louis area, causing the final 30-minute practice session to be postponed to race morning.

Race morning dawned clear and sunny, and Hornish led the final practice session with a lap of 166.230 miles per hour. During the morning warm-up, Lazier's engine was running too hot, so the team decided to change it after the session. The hard work of the Hemelgarn Racing crew never paid off. Almost immediately after the cars rolled off the grid, Lazier experienced fuel-pressure problems. On the start he fell back to third in the first turn as Hornish grabbed the lead. By Lap four, Lazier dropped to 12th place, well off the pace. His chances of winning back-to-back Indy Racing championships were slipping away. And Lazier wasn't alone. Rookie Felipe Giaffone began slowing on Lap eight with a wheel-bearing problem. He would ultimately fall out of the race on Lap 84, his first DNF for 2001.

After a yellow on Lap 40 for debris, most of the field headed toward the pits for service. Hornish stayed in the lead, exiting the pits while Al Unser Jr., who came in seventh, received fast service from his Galles Racing crew and came out behind Hornish in second. During the flurry of pit stops, Buzz Calkins made contact with Alex Barron on pit road, taking both cars out of the race.

Hornish led the restart on Lap 49, followed by Unser, Sharp, Eliseo Salazar and Robbie Buhl, but a Turn Two crash by Chris Menninga brought the yellow flag out a few laps later. On the Lap 58 restart, Unser swept by Hornish on the front straight and took the lead entering Turn 1. Unser, a wily veteran with a good car underneath him, obviously got up to speed on the new track.

By the halfway point, it was still Unser and Hornish running one-two with Jaques Lazier—in his first race with Team Menard—running third, followed by Buhl and Sharp. Most teams made pit stops just past the 100-lap halfway mark, but the frontrunners stayed out and Unser extended his lead over Hornish. A caution period started on Lap 129 when Eliseo Salazar slowed on the deceleration lane. That caution brought a large part of the field into the pits for what some thought would be the final service of the day. Unser, Dismore, Sharp and Cheever all pitted, but Buhl and Hornish both remained on the track. Both had pitted on Lap 107.

After lengthy pit stops, Jaques Lazier's first drive with Team Menard ended with engine problems after 139 laps. On Lap 169, Buhl headed to the pits for his

Without much breathing room, Al Unser Jr. (3) eked out a gritty win by 1.1 seconds over Mark Dismore in the Gateway Indy 250.
Roger Bedwell

A fast pit stop helped Mark Dismore (28) get in and out of the pits quickly. He came in second to Al Unser Jr., the winner in his Starz G Force-Oldsmobile/Firestone. *Jerry Lawrence*

final stop of the day, relinquishing the lead to Hornish, who was running a comfortable 10-second lead over Unser.

Then Donnie Beechler hit the wall in Turn Two on Lap 188, changing the complexion of the race. Unser spent the entire race running full lean, and the strategy paid off. Unser was able to stay out, assume the lead, and cruise to the checkered. After running hard trying to get back into the lead, Hornish was forced to head in when the pits opened on Lap 190. He spent 4.4 seconds getting a splash of fuel and rejoined the race in third position. However, he had four lapped cars in between him and Dismore. Hornish was unable to make up the time to the leader with 12 laps remaining.

Dismore in second couldn't match Unser's pace in the final stint. Unser earned his second Indy Racing League victory crossing the line 1.1834 seconds ahead of Dismore and Hornish. "I thought we were going all the way to the end without another yellow," said Unser. "So maybe I should have run a little richer to keep up with Sam. And then on that yellow, Sam Hornish pulled in the pits. Rick (Galles) made the right decision, and that's why he's the strategist, and I'm the driver."

Dismore scored his best finish since placing second, ironically to Unser, in April 2000 at Las Vegas. Hornish, who also finished third behind Unser at that Las Vegas event, stretched his overall points lead. He stood at 411 to Lazier's 366.

"It's a very disappointing day," said Lazier, who came home 13th. "All day long, the fuel alarm was going off in the car; probably a couple of hundred times the fuel alarm went off. It's miserable."

A season's worth of highs and lows finally leveled ouyt for Eddie Cheever, Jr. (51) as he challenged for the win and came home fourth in St. Louis." *Roger Bedwell*

Jaques Lazier and championship leader Sam Hornish Jr. made history in the Delphi Indy 300 at Chicagoland Speedway. Lazier won his first Indy Racing League race after his second start with the Menard team, and Sam Hornish Jr., who showed speed, consistency, and maturity beyond his years, clinched the Indy Racing Northern Light Series championship with a second-place finish.

From the start of the season, Hornish demonstrated he was a force to be reckoned with by dominating the first two races. When it looked as though Hornish would run away with the season, the competition caught up, but Hornish didn't overdrive. He simply drove his best and kept it off the walls, racking up two wins, four seconds and three thirds. It was that cool, calm, confident attitude displayed by Hornish, age 22, that erased any doubts the Pennzoil Panther team may have had when it took a chance on second-year driver Hornish rather than a veteran with much more experience in Indy Racing.

Despite the youthful Hornish taking the prerace spotlight, veterans led the first practice day on the new 1.5-mile oval at Joliet, Illinois. Three drivers topped 220 miles per hour, with Robbie Buhl leading at 221.002 in his No. 24 Team Purex Dryer and Reinbold Racing G Force-Infiniti/Firestone. Scott Sharp posted a lap of 220.424 in his No. 8 Delphi Automotive Systems Dallara-Oldsmobile/Firestone, while Eddie Cheever Jr. was third fastest in the only other Infiniti-powered car in the field, posting a speed of 220.380 in his #51 Cheever Indy Racing Dallara-Infiniti/Firestone.

Jaques Lazier, quiet all weekend, threw down the gauntlet as the fifth car out to qualify by turning a lap of 221.740 in his No. 2 Johns Manville/Menards Dallara-Oldsmobile/Firestone. Buhl and Sharp both failed to break into the 221-mile-per-hour range, leaving only Cheever to knock off Lazier. Cheever topped 221 miles per hour, but his lap of 221.105 was not enough to secure the pole. Jaques Lazier earned his second MBNA Pole of the year but his first with Team Menard. His other pole, at Richmond, Virginia, came with Sam Schmidt Motorsports. "I thought I had a good shot," said Lazier. "I was still a little hesitant when Eddie was going out there, but the time really surprised me. A 221.7 was more than I ever expected."

On race day, clear skies and warm temperatures greeted competitors prior to the final 30-minute practice session. Buhl led the session with a lap of 221.634, but the news was bittersweet for the Infiniti brigade as Cheever suffered an engine failure in the session, forcing a change prior to the race. The crew changed the engine without a prob-

lem and fired the new engine alongside 24 other Indy Racing machines in front of a sold-out crowd of 75,000 Windy City race fans getting their first glimpse at Indy Racing in the Chicagoland area.

On the start, Lazier jumped to the lead and held Hornish at bay until Lap 30, when Scott Sharp brought out the first yellow flag as he hit the wall in Turn Two. When the field pitted under the caution on Lap 32, Hornish came out first, followed by Buhl, Felipe Giaffone, Mark Dismore, and Cheever. Lazier was delayed in the pits by a slow left-rear tire change and fell out of the top five.

Giaffone took one lap to get by Buhl for second and then set off after Hornish. Giaffone then battled back and forth with Hornish, finally taking the lead on Lap 47 after going three-wide with Hornish and Buhl into Turn 1 on Lap 46.

With Giaffone leading, the top six cars were separated by less than a second. Buhl showed that the Infiniti had more than competi-

After taking over the No. 2 car for team owner John Menard in midseason, Jaques Lazier (2) made the switch pay off with a victory in the Delphi Indy 300 at Chicago. Walt Kuhn

tive horsepower. On the back straight, he made an outside pass around Giaffone on Lap 59 and kept the lead until Lap 87, when he came into the pits for service. Giaffone took the lead until pitting on Lap 90, giving the lead to Dismore, who stayed in front for five laps until he pitted and gave back the lead to Buhl. Unfortunately for Buhl, his season-long bad luck continued on Lap 99. He slowed while leading in Turn Four and eventually fell out of the race on Lap 113 due to a vibration. "Something in the motor broke," said Buhl. "I don't know what I need to do to buy a win."

Jaques Lazier regained the lead from Buhl and led when the yellow flag came out on Lap 124 for debris in Turn Two. Giaffone got out of the pits first and regained the lead. When the race restarted on Lap 130, Giaffone led Jaques Lazier, Hornish, Eliseo Salazar and Donnie Beechler. Giaffone was able to keep Lazier at bay for three laps. But Lazier had a race-winning car and was determined to get

through Giaffone. He made the pass for the lead stick on Lap 133. Behind them, Hornish and Beechler were staging an intense battle. Beechler eventually got around Hornish, but Salazar passed them both, climbing to third by Lap 150. Then the roles were reversed. Giaffone shadowed Lazier, looking for a mistake or the opportunity to pass. On Lap 163, when Salazar veered across the back straight, he hit Dismore before hitting the outside retaining wall. Neither driver was hurt.

"That wasn't bad luck out there, it was bad judgment," said a disgusted Dismore. "I was on the high side for two or three laps, and we were coming up on a slower car. I moved up, and Eliseo needed to go either to the guy's left or check up a little bit, but he chose to drive right across the front of my car."

Said Salazar: "I came up to a back marker and went to move around him, and Dismore didn't give me any room. He tried to snooker me and force me to brake. You have to find room because if you lift, you lose. As it turned out, we both lost."

When the pits opened under caution on Lap 165, Jaques Lazier, Giaffone, Hornish, Beechler, Jeff Ward and Cheever all pitted. Giaffone was out first, followed by Lazier and Hornish, and the order stayed the same as the green flag flew on Lap 173. Two laps later, Lazier and Giaffone were side by side, both racing for their first Indy Racing victory. Meanwhile, Hornish, running third, could lock up the Northern Light Cup if he stayed put. As the trio exited Turn Four on Lap 175, Lazier took the lead for the rest of the way, holding off Giaffone and Hornish.

Giaffone's brilliant run ended on Lap 198 when his engine expired. Lazier took the checkered flag and scored his inaugural Indy Racing League win. He and Buddy Lazier also became the first brothers to win events in Indy Racing competition. "It was a collaborative effort today," said Jaques Lazier. "We have jelled quicker than I ever thought possible. Felipe (Giaffone) did a tremendous job. He definitely made it hard. I tried to break away a couple times, and tried to separate the draft, and he just kept fighting up and up and stayed right with me."

For Giaffone, a strong run ended with a plume of smoke. "I'm just so disappointed and happy at the same time," said Giaffone, who ended up 10th. "I had a car to win this race. We ran up front all day, and I was just pulling out to pass Jaques when the motor let go."

Cheever brought his Infiniti-powered car home in third place, Ward came away with a season-best fourth, and Beechler drove his A. J. Foyt–owned

machine to fifth. But the big winner on the day was Hornish. He finished second and clinched the Northern Light Cup, becoming the youngest driver in North American racing history to win a major-league open-wheel series championship. "It's been a great run this year," said Hornish. "The Pennzoil Panther guys put me in an awesome car all year long." On his way to clinching the championship, with one race still remaining at Texas Motor Speedway, Hornish finished out of the top 10 only once, at Indianapolis. He had only finished off the podium two other times, a fourth at Atlanta, and a sixth at Nashville, Tennessee.

"We may not have always been the fastest, but we always finished up toward the front," Hornish said.

A second-place finish at Chicago strengthened the bid by Sam Hornish Jr. (4), to win the season points race. Here Hornish leads Robbie Buhl (24) through a turn. Jim Haines

Felipe Giaffone (21) pushes the Hollywood G Force-Oldsmobile/Firestone hard on the Chicago oval. Giaffone finished two laps off the pace in 10th place. Jim Haines

HORNISH CAPS TITLE SEASON

By Joe Crowley

With the weight of the battle for championship off his shoulders, Sam Hornish Jr. could focus on just one thing—winning the race. After muscling his way past Robbie Buhl and Scott Sharp on the final lap, Hornish found himself the victor of the most intense three-way dogfight of the season. A crowd estimated at 60,000 watched Hornish edge out Sharp by a mere 0.018 seconds to take the Chevy 500 at Texas Motor Speedway while Buhl came in third.

The season-ending race at Texas Motor Speedway, originally scheduled for September 16, was postponed until October 6th due the terrorist events of September 11th. Many of the teams and racers memorialized the tragedy by carrying special patriotic paint schemes on their cars. Eddie Cheever Jr. #51 Cheever Indy Racing Dallara-Infiniti/Firestone entry sported a special red, white and blue "Stars and Stripes" paint scheme with American Red Cross decals.

The race weekend was shortened from its scheduled three days of competition to two, with qualifying on Friday, October 5th, and the race Saturday, October 6th. MBNA Pole Qualifying was rained out. Thus, starting position was determined by entrant point standings. Sam Hornish Jr., who had clinched the Northern Light Cup on September 2 at Chicagoland Speedway and 2000 series champion Buddy Lazier were placed on the front row. Drivers had only two practice sessions before the race was run.

Before the race, motorcycle daredevil Kaptain Robbie Knievel successfully jumped 20 Indy Racing cars on the main straightaway to kick off the patriotic prerace ceremonies. After driver introductions, the 25 drivers led the crowd in "The Pledge of Allegiance." Miss Texas Stacey James sang "America the Beautiful" and the national anthem.

It did not take long for the first yellow to appear. On the opening lap Sarah Fisher, running in the middle of the pack, spun out in Turn Three and made contact with the wall. In Turn Four, Billy Boat spun into the infield grass. Fisher was done for the day, but Boat pitted for repairs and continued.

The field resumed green flag racing on Lap eight. Lazier took over the point from Hornish on Lap nine, but Hornish regained the lead on Lap 10. The new Menard recruit, Jaques Lazier, had sliced through the field to challenge Hornish for the lead. The two drivers swapped the lead back and forth for about 40 laps, trading the lead nine times in 32 laps.

Most of the field pitted for service on Lap 53. For Jaques Lazier, a mistake in wheel changing cost him a shot at victory. A wheel spun off his Dallara-Olds exiting pits requiring him to drive the three-wheeled machine around the entire 1.5-mile oval and back into the pits. The errant wheel brought out the yellow flag.

Felipe Giaffone assumed the lead at the front of the field after the round of pit stops were completed. Giaffone, who had already clinched the Chevy Rookie of the Year Award, led until Lap 67, when smoke began to pour out of his No. 21 Hollywood G Force-Oldsmobile/Firestone. The rookie's season came to an end on Lap 69 when his engine expired.

With Giaffone falling out of the race, Hornish regained the lead and held it for 30 laps, the longest anyone would hold it all day. By Lap 91, a battle ensued at the front. Hornish led Al Unser Jr. and Scott Sharp. Sharp and Buhl dispatched Unser and set their sites on Hornish. Just before the halfway point of the 200-lap event, Sharp grabbed the lead from Hornish with Buhl close behind. Sharp led for two laps before Hornish regained the lead on Lap 101. The top five were separated by a scant .3610 of a second.

Rick Treadway (23) posted an impressive top-five finish in the Big Tex G Force-Oldsmobile/Firestone at Texas, where the racing is always breathtakingly fast and close. *Roger McQueeney*

Sam Hornish Jr. (4) edged Scott Sharp (8) and Robbie Buhl (24) to win the Chevy 500 by just .0188 seconds over Sharp. It was the third win of the season for points champion Hornish. *Roger Bedwell*

Sharp momentarily fell off the lead pace giving Buhl the opportunity to challenge Hornish for the lead. Buhl trimmed Hornish's lead from .7132 of a second to .2841, then to .1029, and eventually battled hammer and tong with Hornish. Coming out of Turn Four on Lap 117, Buhl sqeezed by Hornish for the lead. The duo took turns in the lead, but Buhl took command on Lap 122 and held on until Lap 135, when he came into the pits for service. Hornish and Sharp briefly assumed the lead until pitting a handful of laps later.

After the round of pit stops, Hornish led Buhl by .0641 of a second with Sharp in third. Buhl roared past Hornish for the lead on Lap 148. The yellow came out nine laps later when rookie Anthony Lazzaro's car had engine trouble. The leaders came in for their final round of pit stops. Hornish got out first, followed by Sharp and Buhl.

Hornish led the field back to the green flag, but the race was slowed when rookie Laurent Redon's engine blew on Lap 167. As the green flag flew again on Lap 172, Hornish and Sharp diced for the lead once again. Sharp regained the lead on Lap 173 while Eliseo Salazar edged past Buhl for third. As they came across the line on Lap 175, Sharp led Hornish by the almost undetectable .0008 of a second.

By Lap 178, Sharp's hair-thin lead somehow was cut in half. The gap was .0004 between the top two, with the top four cars running together, two-by-two and side-by-side. Hornish regained the lead from Sharp on Lap 183 as their game of 215-mph tug-of-war continued. Meanwhile, Buhl had passed Salazar for third.

With 10 laps remaining, Hornish led Sharp and Buhl by less than two-tenths of a second.

Sharp then made what he thought was his decisive move on Lap 193 on the backstretch and took the lead from Hornish. Hornish and Buhl both tried desperately to catch Sharp, who was going for a sweep of both Texas races in 2001. As the white flag came out on Lap 199, Sharp led Hornish by .0764 of a second. As they came through Turn Three on the final lap, Hornish went to the outside of Sharp. As they came off the final turn, Buhl made it three wide.

Hornish got a better drive off the last corner and pulled ahead of Sharp. He took the victory by just .0188 of a second ahead of Sharp and only .0468 ahead of Buhl. The finish was the closest in Indy Racing history as well as the closest three-car finish in Indy Racing history.

Hornish capped his Northern Light Cup championship season with a win in one of the most exciting races in history. The race logged 32 official lead changes, an Indy Racing record. "Unbelievable," said Hornish. "I didn't think I had enough. I just went down another gear and thought I might have enough rpm to get by him. I did, and we won."

Although disappointed with second, Sharp could not downplay the race.

"It's awesome," said Sharp. "I tell you, this place is just magical with our cars, the Indy Racing League cars, with the level of downforce we have, this track, it is just some unbelievable racing."

Perhaps it was Buhl who summed up an amazing afternoon best:

"You know, that's what the Indy Racing League is all about. That's what this series has been building to. What a way to end the year and then going into next year with everything that's going on for the Indy Racing League."

Eliseo Salazar (14) took on tires and fuel in the A. J. Foyt Racing pit. Salazar ran with the lead pack and finished an impressive fourth in the season finale. *Ron McQueeney*

INDY RACING NORTHERN LIGHT SERIES
Phoenix International Raceway, Sunday, March 18, 2001

FP	SP	Car		Driver	Car Name	C/E/T	Laps Comp.	Running/ Reason Out	IRL Pts.	Total Pts.	IRL Standings	IRL Awards	Designated Awards	Total Awards
1	2	4		Sam Hornish Jr.	Pennzoil Panther Racing	D/O/F	200	Running	52	52	1	$93,300	$31,000	$124,300
2	13	14		Eliseo Salazar	Harrah's A.J. Foyt Racing	D/O/F	200	Running	40	40	2	77,900	11,750	89,650
3	6	91		Buddy Lazier	Tae-Bo/Coors Light/Delta Faucet/Hemelgarn Racing	D/O/F	200	Running	35	35	3	66,300	1,350	67,650
4	10	8		Scott Sharp	Delphi Automotive Systems	D/O/F	200	Running	32	32	4	54,700	900	55,600
5	7	98		Billy Boat	CURB Records/Ash Kicker Racing	D/O/F	200	Running	30	30	5	50,400	750	51,150
6	9	21	R	Felipe Giaffone	Hollywood	G/O/F	199	Running	28	28	6	45,200	750	45,950
7	3	35		Jeff Ward	Heritage Motorsports/Firestone/Menards	G/O/F	199	Running	26	26	7	44,100	250	44,350
8	16	10		Robby McGehee	Olympus/Opalescence/Cahill Racing	D/O/F	198	Running	24	24	8	43,100	250	43,350
9	11	12		Buzz Calkins	Bradley Food Marts/Sav-O-Mat	D/O/T	197	Running	22	22	9	43,100	0	43,100
10	18	88		Airton Daré	1-800-BAR-NONE TeamXtreme	G/O/F	197	Running	20	20	10	42,100	0	42,100
11	8	24		Robbie Buhl	Dreyer & Reinbold Racing Team Purex	G/I/F	196	Running	19	19	11	41,000	5,000	46,000
12	20	99		Davey Hamilton	Sam Schmidt Motorsports Racing Special	D/O/F	192	Running	18	18	12	39,900	0	39,900
13	24	55		Shigeaki Hattori	EPSON	G/O/F	192	Running	17	17	13	16,900	0	16,900
14	26	30	R	Brandon Erwin	WorldBestBuy.com/McCormack Motorsports	G/O/F	185	Running	16	16	14	15,800	0	15,800
15	19	6		Tyce Carlson	Tri Star Motorsports Inc.	D/O/F	162	Mechanical	15	15	15	36,800	0	36,800
16	14	92		Stan Wattles	Hemelgarn Racing	D/O/F	157	Accident	14	14	16	35,800	0	35,800
17	21	15		Sarah Fisher	Walker Racing/Kroger Special	D/O/F	145	Engine	13	13	17	12,600	0	12,600
18	17	68		Helio Castroneves	Penske Auto Center Special	D/O/F	142	Engine	12	12	18	34,600	0	34,600
19	12	51		Eddie Cheever Jr.	#51 Excite@Home Indy Race Car	D/I/F	133	Throttle	11	11	19	33,600	0	33,600
20	25	31	R	Casey Mears	Galles Racing SportsLine.com	G/O/F	133	Electrical	10	10	20	10,600	0	10,600
21	4	7		Stephan Gregoire	Tokheim/Jack K. Elrod Co./Nada Guides	D/O/F	131	Accident	9	9	21	32,600	2,000	34,600
22	1	2		Greg Ray	Johns Manville/Menards	D/O/F	121	Engine	8	8	22	32,600	22,500	55,100
23	23	3		Al Unser Jr.	Galles Racing Starz SuperPak	G/O/F	104	Engine	7	7	23	10,600	0	10,600
24	5	66		Gil de Ferran	Penske Auto Center Special	D/O/F	76	Accident	6	6	24	32,600	0	32,600
25	15	28		Mark Dismore	Delphi Automotive Systems/Bryant Heating & Cooling	D/O/F	75	Accident	5	5	25	32,600	0	32,600
26	22	9		Jeret Schroeder	Summit Packaging	D/O/F	74	Accident	4	4	26	10,600	0	10,600
27	27	32	R	Didier André	Galles Racing	G/O/F	53	Handling	3	3	27	10,600	0	10,600
				Speedway Engines									600	600
				Ilmor Engineering									400	400
											TOTAL -	**$1,000,000**	**$77,500**	**$1,077,500**

Time of Race: 1:36:56.7051 **Average Speed:** 125.072 mph **Margin of Victory:** 1.3786 sec.
Fastest Lap: #98 Billy Boat (Race lap 93, 168.769, 21.3309 sec.) / **Fastest Leading Lap:** #4 Sam Hornish Jr. (Race lap 153, 166.483 mph, 21.6238 sec.)
MBNA Pole Winner: #1 Greg Ray (177.663 mph, 20.2631 sec.) **"The Net Race Live Award" Lap Leader:** #4 Sam Hornish Jr.
Firestone "Leader at Halfway" Award: #2 Greg Ray **Coors Light "Pit Performance" Award:** #14 Eliseo Salazar
Legend: R= Indy Racing Northern Light Series Rookie **Chassis Legend:** D=Dallara (18); G=G Force (9)
Engine Legend: O=Oldsmobile (25); I=Infiniti (2) **Tire Legend:** F=Firestone (27)

Lap Leaders:

Laps	Car#	Driver
1-67	#4	Sam Hornish Jr.
68-73	#2	Greg Ray
74-76	#66	Gil de Ferran
77-80	#68	Helio Castroneves
81	#8	Scott Sharp
82-118	#2	Greg Ray
119-127	#7	Stephan Gregoire
128-200	#4	Sam Hornish Jr.

Total: 7 Lead changes among 6 drivers

Lap Leader Summary:

Driver	Times	Total
Sam Hornish Jr.	2	140
Greg Ray	2	43
Stephan Gregoire	1	9
Helio Castroneves	1	4
Gil de Ferran	1	3
Scott Sharp	1	1

Caution Flags:

Laps	Reason/Incident
20-23	#30 Erwin, spin
77-89	#9 Schroeder, #66 de Ferran, #28 Dismore, accident T4
125-130	debris
132-137	#7 Gregoire, accident T2
159-166	#92 Wattles, accident T2

Total: 5 caution flags, 37 laps

INDY RACING NORTHERN LIGHT SERIES
Homestead-Miami Speedway, Sunday, April 8, 2001

FP	SP	Car		Driver	Car Name	C/E/T	Laps Comp.	Running/ Reason Out	IRL Pts.	Total IRL Pts.	IRL Standings	IRL Awards	Designated Awards	Total Awards
1	5	4		Sam Hornish Jr.	Pennzoil Panther Racing	D/O/F	200	Running	52	104	1	$96,650	$41,000	$137,650
2	7	15		Sarah Fisher	Walker Racing/Kroger Special	D/O/F	200	Running	40	53	6	80,200	1,850	82,050
3	6	14		Eliseo Salazar	Harrah's A.J. Foyt Racing	D/O/F	200	Running	35	75	2	68,000	750	68,750
4	4	21	R	Felipe Giaffone	Hollywood	G/O/F	199	Running	32	60	3	55,700	250	55,950
5	1	35		Jeff Ward	Heritage Motorsports/Firestone/Menards	G/O/F	199	Running	30	56	4	51,200	15,150	66,350
6	19	3		Al Unser Jr.	Galles Racing Starz SuperPak	G/O/F	199	Running	28	35	11	26,850	250	27,100
7	9	28		Mark Dismore	Delphi Automotive Systems/Bryant Heating & Cooling	D/O/F	199	Running	26	31	14	25,750	250	26,000
8	8	8		Scott Sharp	Delphi Automotive Systems	D/O/F	198	Running	24	56	4	43,500	0	43,500
9	16	51		Eddie Cheever Jr.	#51 Excite@Home Indy Race Car	D/I/F	198	Running	22	33	12	43,500	5,000	48,500
10	26	32	R	Didier André	Galles Racing	G/O/F	196	Running	20	23	20	23,550	0	23,550
11	24	31	R	Casey Mears	Galles Racing SportsLine.com	G/O/F	196	Running	19	29	15	41,200	0	41,200
12	22	10		Robby McGehee	Cahill Racing	D/O/F	196	Running	18	42	9	40,200	0	40,200
13	12	98		Billy Boat	CURB Records	D/O/F	196	Running	17	47	7	39,100	0	39,100
14	14	9		Jeret Schroeder	Purity Products	D/O/F	195	Running	16	20	21	19,050	0	19,050
15	21	55		Shigeaki Hattori	EPSON	G/O/F	193	Running	15	32	13	36,800	0	36,800
16	15	12		Buzz Calkins	Bradley Food Marts/Sav-O-Mat	D/O/F	193	Running	14	36	10	35,800	10,000	45,800
17	25	30	R	Brandon Erwin	WorldBestBuy.com/McCormack Motorsports	G/O/F	190	Running	13	29	15	34,600	0	34,600
18	18	27		John Hollansworth Jr.	Blueprint Racing Special	G/O/F	189	Running	12	12	26	15,750	0	15,750
19	13	99		Davey Hamilton	Sam Schmidt Motorsports Racing Special	D/O/F	185	Running	11	29	15	33,500	0	33,500
20	3	91		Buddy Lazier	Tae-Bo/Coors Light/Delta Faucet	D/O/F	175	Accident	10	45	8	32,400	0	32,400
21	2	2		Greg Ray	Johns Manville/Menards	D/O/F	161	Accident	9	17	23	13,550	0	13,550
22	11	7		Stephan Gregoire	Tokheim/Jack K. Elrod Co./NADA Guides	D/O/F	69	Mechanical	8	17	23	13,550	0	13,550
23	20	88		Airton Daré	1-800-BAR-NONE	G/O/F	62	Engine	7	27	18	32,400	0	32,400
24	23	24		Robbie Buhl	Team Purex Dreyer & Reinbold Racing	G/I/F	9	Electrical	6	25	19	32,400	0	32,400
25	17	6	R	Jon Herb	Immke/Tri Star Motorsports Inc.	D/O/F	3	Fire	5	5	29	32,400	0	32,400
26	10	92		Stan Wattles	Hemelgarn Racing	D/O/F	0	Accident	4	18	22	32,400	0	32,400
				Comptech Engines									600	600
				Menard Engines									400	400
											TOTAL -	$1,000,000	$75,500	$1,075,500

Time of Race: 2:01:12.3363   **Average Speed:** 148.508 mph   **Margin of Victory:** 1.8701 sec.

Fastest Lap: #4 Sam Hornish (Race lap 175, 195.949 mph, 27.5582 sec.) / **Fastest Leading Lap:** #4 Sam Hornish Jr. (Race lap 185, 194.753 mph, 27.7274 sec.)

MBNA Pole Winner: #35 Jeff Ward (201.551 mph, 26.7922 sec.)   **"The Net Race Live Award" Lap Leader:** #4 Sam Hornish Jr.

Firestone "Leader at Halfway" Award: #4 Sam Hornish   **Coors Light "Pit Performance" Award:** #12 Buzz Calkins

Legend: R= Indy Racing Northern Light Series Rookie   **Chassis Legend:** D=Dallara (16); G=G Force (10)

Engine Legend: O=Oldsmobile (24); I=Infiniti (2)   **Tire Legend:** F=Firestone (26)

Lap Leaders:

Laps	Car#	Driver	Laps	Car#	Driver
1-13	#35	Jeff Ward	63-67	#4	Sam Hornish Jr.
14-31	#4	Sam Hornish Jr.	68	#3	Al Unser Jr.
32	#21	Felipe Giaffone	69-168	#4	Sam Hornish Jr.
33-35	#4	Sam Hornish Jr.	169-184	#14	Eliseo Salazar
36-62	#35	Jeff Ward	185-200	#4	Sam Hornish Jr.

Total: 9 Lead changes among 5 drivers

Lap Leader Summary:

Driver	Times	Total
Sam Hornish Jr.	5	142
Jeff Ward	2	40
Eliseo Salazar	1	16
Felipe Giaffone	1	1
Al Unser Jr.	1	1

Caution Flags:

Laps	Reason/Incident
2-5	#92 Wattles, accident frontstretch
29-34	#24 Buhl, car stalled T1
65-70	#88 Daré, engine
111-116	debris T4
166-171	#2 Ray, accident T2
177-180	#91 Lazier, accident T4

Total: 6 caution flags, 32 laps

INDY RACING NORTHERN LIGHT SERIES
Atlanta Motor Speedway, Sunday, April 28, 2001

FP	SP	Car		Driver	Car Name	C/E/T	Laps Comp.	Running/ Reason Out	IRL Pts.	Total IRL Pts.	IRL Standings	IRL Awards	Designated Awards	Total Awards
1	1	2		Greg Ray	Johns Manville/Menards	D/O/F	200	Running	52	69	9	$73,500	$50,600	$124,100
2	13	8		Scott Sharp	Delphi Automotive Systems	D/O/F	200	Running	40	96	3	79,200	16,400	95,600
3	8	12		Buzz Calkins	Bradley Food Marts/Sav-O-Mat	D/O/F	200	Running	35	71	8	67,100	1,500	68,600
4	6	4		Sam Hornish Jr.	Pennzoil Panther Dallara	D/O/F	199	Running	32	136	1	55,100	250	55,350
5	7	14		Eliseo Salazar	Harrah's A.J. Foyt Racing	D/O/F	199	Running	30	105	2	50,700	0	50,700
6	9	91		Buddy Lazier	Tae-Bo/Coors Light/Delta Faucet	D/O/F	199	Running	28	73	6	45,300	250	45,550
7	2	35		Jeff Ward	Heritage Motorsports/Firestone/Menards	G/O/F	199	Running	26	82	4	44,200	2,250	46,450
8	5	55		Shigeaki Hattori	EPSON	D/O/F	198	Running	24	56	11	43,100	250	43,350
9	11	88		Airton Daré	1-800-BAR-NONE	G/E/T	197	Running	22	49	13	43,100	0	43,100
10	15	21	R	Felipe Giaffone	Hollywood	G/O/F	182	Running	20	80	5	42,000	0	42,000
11	18	15		Sarah Fisher	Walker Racing/Kroger Special	D/O/F	178	Running	19	72	7	40,900	0	40,900
12	16	92		Stan Wattles	Hemelgarn Racing	D/O/F	147	Running	18	36	18	17,800	0	17,800
13	20	32	R	Didier André	Galles Racing	G/O/F	139	Clutch	17	40	16	38,800	0	38,800
14	17	98		Billy Boat	CURB Records	D/O/F	109	Running	16	63	10	37,600	0	37,600
15	21	7		Stephan Gregoire	Tokheim/Jack K. Elrod Co./NADA Guides	D/O/F	95	Mechanical	15	32	22	14,600	0	14,600
16	25	6	R	Jon Herb	Tri Star Motorsports Inc.	D/O/F	77	Engine	14	19	25	13,500	0	13,500
17	14	3		Al Unser Jr.	Galles Racing Starz SuperPak	G/O/F	52	Accident	13	48	14	34,300	0	34,300
18	12	99		Davey Hamilton	Sam Schmidt Motorsports Racing Special	D/O/F	52	Accident	2	41	15	34,300	0	34,300
19	22	9		Jeret Schroeder	Purity Products Summit Packaging	D/O/F	52	Accident	11	31	24	11,300	0	11,300
20	19	24		Robbie Buhl	Team Purex Dreyer & Reinbold Racing	G/I/F	52	Accident	10	35	20	32,200	5,000	37,200
21	10	10		Robby McGehee	Cahill Racing	D/O/F	52	Accident	9	51	12	32,200	0	32,200
22	24	16	R	Cory Witherill	WSA/MOTORS/ Indy Regency Racing	G/O/F	51	Accident	8	8	29	10,200	0	10,200
23	27	31	R	Casey Mears	Galles Racing SportsLine.com	G/O/F	51	Accident	7	36	18	32,200	0	32,200
24	3	51		Eddie Cheever Jr.	#51 Excite@Home Indy Race Car	D/I/F	34	Engine	6	39	17	32,200	0	32,200
25	23	11		Jack Miller	Olympus/Opalescence/Cahill Racing	D/O/F	28	Accident	5	5	31	10,200	0	10,200
26	4	28		Mark Dismore	Delphi Automotive Systems/Bryant Heating & Cooling	D/O/F	15	Engine	4	35	20	32,200	0	32,200
27	26	30	R	Brandon Erwin	WorldBestBuy.com/McCormack Motorsports	G/O/F	3	Accident	3	32	22	32,200	0	32,200
					Menard Engines								600	600
					Ilmor Engineering								400	400
										TOTAL -		$1,000,000	$77,500	$1,077,500

Time of Race: 2:14:40.9890   **Average Speed:** 133.647 mph   **Margin of Victory:** 19.8570 sec.

Fastest Lap / Fastest Leading Lap: #2 Greg Ray (Race lap 155, 215.714 mph, 25.0331 sec.)

MBNA Pole Winner: #2 Greg Ray (218.265 mph, 24.7406 sec.)   **"The Net Race Live Award" Lap Leader:** #2 Greg Ray

Firestone "Leader at Halfway" Award: #2 Greg Ray   **Coors Light "Pit Performance" Award:** #2 Greg Ray

Legend: R= Indy Racing Northern Light Series Rookie   **Chassis Legend:** D=Dallara (18); G=G Force (9)

Engine Legend: O=Oldsmobile (25); I=Infiniti (2)   **Tire Legend:** F=Firestone (27)

Lap Leaders:

Laps	Car#	Driver	Laps	Car#	Driver
1-2	#35	Jeff Ward	83-90	#35	Jeff Ward
3-47	#2	Greg Ray	91-146	#2	Greg Ray
48	#4	Sam Hornish Jr.	147-151	#8	Scott Sharp
49-82	#2	Greg Ray	152-200	#2	Greg Ray

Total: 7 Lead changes among 4 drivers

Lap Leader Summary:

Driver	Times	Total
Greg Ray	4	184
Jeff Ward	2	10
Scott Sharp	1	5
Sam Hornish Jr.	1	1

Caution Flags:

Laps	Reason/Incident
5-8	#30 Erwin, accident T3
46-50	debris
54-88	#3, 6, 9, 10, 11, 15, 16, 24, 31, 98, 99, accident T4
91-101	#6 Herb, car stopped on track

Total: 4 caution flags, 55 laps

OFFICIAL Box Score
ROUND 4: 85TH INDIANAPOLIS 500-MILE RACE

INDY RACING NORTHERN LIGHT SERIES
Indianapolis Motor Speedway, Sunday, May 27, 2001

FP	SP	Car		Driver	Car Name	C/E/T	Laps Comp.	Running/ Reason Out	IRL Pts.	Total IRL Pts.	IRL Standings	IRL Awards	Designated Awards	Total Awards
1	11	68	R	Helio Castroneves	Marlboro Team Penske	D/O/F	200	Running	52	64	13	$954,000	$316,475	$1,270,475
2	5	66		Gil de Ferran	Marlboro Team Penske	D/O/F	200	Running	40	46	19	452,000	30,775	482,775
3	21	39		Michael Andretti	Motorola/Archipelago	D/O/F	200	Running	35	35	25	324,000	22,225	346,225
4	12	44		Jimmy Vasser	Target Chip Ganassi Racing	G/O/F	200	Running	32	32	27	222,000	11,325	233,325
5	20	50	R	Bruno Junqueira	Target Chip Ganassi Racing	G/O/F	200	Running	30	30	29	235,000	20,825	255,825
6	7	33		Tony Stewart	Target Chip Ganassi Racing	G/O/F	200	Running	28	28	30	201,000	17,850	218,850
7	28	14		Eliseo Salazar	Harrah's A.J. Foyt Racing	D/O/F	199	Running	26	131	2	303,000	53,300	356,300
8	30	88		Airton Daré	1-800-BAR NONE TeamXtreme	G/O/F	199	Running	24	73	10	285,000	35,325	320,325
9	32	98		Billy Boat	CURB Records	D/O/F	199	Running	22	85	7	278,000	59,325	337,325
10	33	21	R	Felipe Giaffone*	Hollywood	G/O/F	199	Running	20	100	3	174,000	37,575	211,575
11	14	10		Robby McGehee	Cahill Racing Cure Autism Now	D/O/F	199	Running	19	70	12	271,000	19,825	290,825
12	24	12		Buzz Calkins	Bradley Food Marts/Sav-O-Mat	D/O/F	198	Running	18	89	5	267,000	19,025	286,025
13	6	5	W	Arie Luyendyk	Meijer	G/O/F	198	Running	17	17	33	164,000	18,275	182,275
14	13	4		Sam Hornish Jr.	Pennzoil Panther Dallara	D/O/F	196	Running	16	152	1	261,000	47,825	308,825
15	9	24		Robbie Buhl	Team Purex Dreyer & Reinbold Racing	G/I/F	196	Running	15	50	15	258,000	42,325	300,325
16	4	28		Mark Dismore	Delphi Automotive Systems/Bryant Heating & Cooling	D/O/F	195	Running	14	49	16	255,000	32,375	287,375
17	2	2		Greg Ray	Johns Manville/Menards	D/O/F	192	Running	13	82	9	252,000	83,325	335,325
18	10	91	W	Buddy Lazier	Tae-Bo/Coors Light/Life Fitness/Delta Faucet	D/O/F	192	Running	12	85	7	250,000	12,325	262,325
19	31	16	R	Cory Witherill	Radio Shack	G/O/F	187	Running	11	19	32	148,000	11,575	159,575
20	23	9		Jeret Schroeder	Purity Products	D/O/F	187	Running	10	41	21	246,000	10,325	256,325
21	3	41		Robby Gordon	Team Conseco/Foyt Racing/RCR Childress Racing	D/O/F	184	Running	9	9	36	143,000	30,225	173,225
22	17	77		Jaques Lazier	Classmates.com/Jonathan Byrd's Cafeteria	G/O/F	183	Running	8	8	37	141,000	20,325	161,325
23	26	99		Davey Hamilton	Sam Schmidt Motorsports Racing Special	D/O/F	182	Engine	7	48	18	240,000	40,325	280,325
24	8	35		Jeff Ward	Aerosmith/Heritage Motorsports/Firestone/Menards	G/O/F	168	Running	6	88	6	238,000	10,325	248,325
25	27	84		Donnie Beechler	Harrah's A.J. Foyt Racing	D/O/F	160	Oil Leak	5	5	38	162,000	10,325	172,325
26	25	51	W	Eddie Cheever Jr.	#51 Excite@Home Indy Race Car	D/I/F	108	Electrical	4	43	20	236,000	11,325	247,325
27	18	6	R	Jon Herb	Tri Star Motorsports Inc.	D/O/F	104	Accident	3	22	31	235,000	10,575	245,575
28	29	36		Stephan Gregoire	Heritage Motorsports/Delco Remy/Firestone/Menards	G/O/F	86	Oil Leak	2	34	26	139,000	15,325	154,325
29	22	49	R	Nicolas Minassian	Target Chip Ganassi Racing	G/O/F	74	Gearbox	1	1	40	138,000	11,575	149,575
30	19	3	W	Al Unser Jr.	Galles Racing Starz SuperPak Budweiser	G/O/F	16	Accident	1	49	16	232,000	23,825	255,825
31	15	15		Sarah Fisher	Walker Racing Kroger Special	D/O/F	7	Accident	1	73	10	232,000	15,325	247,325
32	16	52		Scott Goodyear	#52 Thermos® Grill2Go™ Cheever Indy Racing Infiniti	D/I/F	7	Accident	1	1	40	132,000	11,325	143,325
33	1	8		Scott Sharp	Delphi Automotive Systems	D/O/F	0	Accident	1	97	4	232,000	195,325	427,325
				RPM Engines								1,000		1,000
				Speedway Engines								500		500
				Comptech Engines								500		500
											TOTAL -	$8,300,000	$1,310,325	$9,610,325
														(Event Record)

* Qualified by Raul Boesel

Time of Race: 3:31:54.1800 **Average Speed:** 141.574 mph **Margin of Victory:** 1.7373 sec.
Fastest Lap: #4 Sam Hornish Jr. (Race Lap 130, 219.830 mph, 40.9407 sec.) **Fastest Leading Lap:** #66 Gil de Ferran (Race Lap 132, 219.774 mph, 40.9512 sec.)
MBNA Pole Winner: #8 Scott Sharp (226.037 mph, 2:39.2658) **"The Net Race Live Award"** Lap Leader: #68 Helio Castroneves
Firestone "Leader at Halfway" Award: #2 Greg Ray **WorldCom Long Distance Award:** #98 Billy Boat
Coors Light Pit Stop Contest: #8 Scott Sharp (Kelley Racing)
Legend: R=Indianapolis 500-Mile Race Rookie, W=Former Indianapolis 500-Mile Race Winner
Chassis Legend: D=Dallara (20); G=G Force (13) **Engine Legend:** O=Oldsmobile (30); I=Infiniti (3) **Tire Legend:** F=Firestone (33)

Lap Leaders:

Laps	Car#	Driver	Laps	Car#	Driver
1-22	#41	Robby Gordon	81-84	#39	Michael Andretti
23-45	#2	Greg Ray	85-91	#28	Mark Dismore
46	#33	Tony Stewart	92-102	#2	Greg Ray
47	#5	Arie Luyendyk	103-109	#39	Michael Andretti
48-52	#39	Michael Andretti	110-136	#66	Gil de Ferran
53-74	#28	Mark Dismore	137-148	#33	Tony Stewart
75-80	#2	Greg Ray	149-200	#68	Helio Castroneves

Total: 13 Lead changes among 8 drivers

Lap Leader Summary:

Driver	Times	Total
Helio Castroneves	1	52
Greg Ray	3	40
Mark Dismore	2	29
Gil de Ferran	1	27
Robby Gordon	1	22
Michael Andretti	3	16
Tony Stewart	2	13
Arie Luyendyk	1	1

Caution Flags:

Laps	Reason/Incident
1-5	#8 Sharp, accident T1
8-16	#15 Fisher, #52 Goodyear, accident T2
18-21	#3 Unser, accident T4
90-95	Track Inspection: Oil on Track
107-118	Rain
134-138	#16 Witherill, accident T4
148-157	Track Inspection: Oil on Track/Rain, (Red Flag, Lap 155)
166-170	#24 Buhl, accident T2

Total: 8 caution flags, 56 laps

INDY RACING NORTHERN LIGHT SERIES
Texas Motor Speedway, Saturday, June 9, 2001

FP	SP	Car	Driver	Car Name	C/E/T	Laps Comp.	Running/ Reason Out	IRL Pts.	Total IRL Pts.	IRL Standings	IRL Awards	Designated Awards	Total Awards
1	2	8	Scott Sharp	Delphi Automotive Systems	D/O/F	200	Running	50	147	3	$99,500	$26,100	$125,600
2	14	21 R	Felipe Giaffone	Hollywood	G/O/F	200	Running	40	140	4	82,500	1,250	83,750
3	4	4	Sam Hornish Jr.	Pennzoil Panther Dallara	D/O/F	200	Running	35	187	1	69,800	250	70,050
4	13	91	Buddy Lazier	Tae-Bo/Coors Light/Delta Faucet	D/O/F	200	Running	32	117	5	57,000	650	57,650
5	10	98	Billy Boat	CURB Records	D/O/F	200	Running	30	115	6	52,300	250	52,550
6	6	11	Donnie Beechler	Harrah's A.J. Foyt Racing	D/O/F	200	Running	28	33	28	39,400	250	39,650
7	9	14	Eliseo Salazar	Harrah's A.J. Foyt Racing	D/O/F	200	Running	26	157	2	45,400	250	45,650
8	11	3	Al Unser Jr.	Galles Racing Starz SuperPak	G/O/F	200	Running	24	73	14	44,300	0	44,300
9	19	77	Jaques Lazier	Classmates.com/Jonathan Byrd's Cafeteria	G/O/T	199	Running	22	30	30	29,650	10,000	39,650
10	5	55	Shigeaki Hattori	EPSON	D/O/F	198	Running	20	76	13	43,200	0	43,200
11	20	2	Greg Ray	Johns Manville/Menards	D/O/F	195	Accident	21	103	8	42,000	15,000	57,000
12	3	51	Eddie Cheever Jr.	#51 Cheever Indy Racing Infiniti	D/I/F	195	Accident	18	61	16	40,900	5,000	45,900
13	24	81	Billy Roe	Zali Racing	G/O/F	195	Running	17	17	35	17,700	0	17,700
14	17	10	Robby McGehee	Cahill Racing	D/O/F	188	Accident	16	86	10	38,500	0	38,500
15	16	12	Buzz Calkins	Bradley Food Marts/Sav-O-Mat	D/O/F	188	Running	15	104	7	37,400	0	37,400
16	7	35	Jeff Ward	Heritage Motorsports/Firestone/Menards	G/O/F	184	Half shaft	14	102	9	36,300	0	36,300
17	21	32 R	Didier André	Galles Racing	G/O/F	184	Running	13	53	20	20,450	0	20,450
18	18	15	Sarah Fisher	Walker Racing Kroger Special	D/O/F	176	Running	12	85	11	35,100	0	35,100
19	12	88	Airton Daré	1-800-BAR-NONE	G/O/F	145	Running	11	84	12	33,900	0	33,900
20	1	28	Mark Dismore	Delphi Automotive Systems/Bryant Heating & Cooling	D/O/F	132	Engine	10	59	17	32,800	12,500	45,300
21	8	24	Robbie Buhl	Team Purex Dreyer & Reinbold Racing	G/I/F	116	Electrical	9	59	17	32,800	2,000	34,800
22	23	30 R	Brandon Erwin	McCormack Motorsports/Team Calcium	G/O/F	72	Handling	8	40	23	18,150	0	18,150
23	15	6	Jeret Schroeder	Tri Star Motorsports Inc.	D/O/F	71	Accident	7	48	21	18,150	0	18,150
24	22	99	Davey Hamilton	Sam Schmidt Motorsports Racing Special	D/O/F	71	Accident	6	54	19	32,800	0	32,800
				Ilmor Engineering								600	600
				Speedway Engines								400	400
										TOTAL -	$1,000,000	$74,500	$1,074,500

Time of Race: 1:55:43.5775   **Average Speed:** 150.873 mph   **Margin of Victory:** .7133 of a second (under caution)

Fastest Lap: #51 Eddie Cheever Jr. (Race lap 177, 218.697 mph, 23.9510 sec.)   **Fastest Leading Lap:** #8 Scott Sharp (Race lap 183, 217.538 mph, 24.0785 sec.)

MBNA Pole Winner: #28 Mark Dismore (215.508 mph, 24.3054 sec.)

"The Net Race Live Award" Lap Leader: #2 Greg Ray   **Firestone "Leader at Halfway" Award:** #2 Greg Ray

Legend: R= Indy Racing Northern Light Series Rookie   **Chassis Legend:** D=Dallara(15); G=G Force (9)

Engine Legend: O=Oldsmobile (22); I=Infiniti(2)   **Tire Legend:** F=Firestone (24)

Lap Leaders:

Laps	Car#	Driver	Laps	Car#	Driver
1-2	#28	Mark Dismore	117-158	#2	Greg Ray
3-27	#51	Eddie Cheever Jr.	159-162	#8	Scott Sharp
28-31	#77	Jaques Lazier	163-164	#2	Greg Ray
32-36	#88	Airton Daré	165-169	#8	Scott Sharp
37-75	#51	Eddie Cheever Jr.	170	#2	Greg Ray
76-110	#2	Greg Ray	171-189	#8	Scott Sharp
111-115	#51	Sam Hornish Jr.	190-195	#2	Greg Ray
##	#21	Felipe Giaffone	196-200	#8	Scott Sharp

Total: 15 Lead changes among 8 drivers

Lap Leader Summary:

Driver	Times	Total
Greg Ray	5	86
Eddie Cheever Jr.	2	64
Scott Sharp	4	33
Sam Hornish Jr.	1	5
Airton Daré	1	5
Jaques Lazier	1	4
Mark Dismore	1	2
Felipe Giaffone	1	1

Caution Flags:

Laps	Reason/Incident
25-30	debris
73-87	#6 Schroeder, #99 Hamilton, #15 Fisher, accident T2
107-114	#88 Dare, stalled T1
157-160	debris
184-187	debris
196-200	#2 Ray, #10 McGehee, #51 Cheever, accident backstretch

Total: 6 caution flags, 42 laps

INDY RACING NORTHERN LIGHT SERIES
Pikes Peak International Raceway, Sunday, June 17, 2001

FP	SP	Car		Driver	Car Name	C/E/T	Laps Comp.	Running/ Reason Out	IRL Pts.	Total IRL Pts.	IRL Standings	IRL Awards	Designated Awards	Total Awards
1	5	91		Buddy Lazier	Tae-Bo/Coors Light/Delta Faucet	D/O/F	200	Running	50	167	4	$102,200	$29,100	$131,300
2	3	4		Sam Hornish Jr.	Pennzoil Panther Dallara	D/O/F	200	Running	42	229	1	85,100	25,750	110,850
3	4	24		Robbie Buhl	Team Purex Dreyer & Reinbold Racing	G/I/F	200	Running	35	94	12	72,000	6,150	78,150
4	8	98		Billy Boat	CURB Records	D/O/F	200	Running	32	147	6	58,900	1,250	60,150
5	13	88		Airton Daré	1-800-BAR-NONE	G/O/F	198	Running	30	114	10	54,100	750	54,850
6	10	51		Eddie Cheever Jr.	#51 Cheever Indy Racing Infiniti	D/I/F	198	Running	28	89	14	48,200	750	48,950
7	9	21	R	Felipe Giaffone	Hollywood	G/O/F	198	Running	26	166	5	46,900	250	47,150
8	2	8		Scott Sharp	Delphi Automotive Systems	D/O/F	197	Running	24	171	3	45,800	0	45,800
9	15	99		Richie Hearn	Sam Schmidt Motorsports Racing Special	D/O/F	197	Running	22	22	34	45,800	0	45,800
10	14	15		Sarah Fisher	Walker Racing Kroger Special	D/O/F	197	Running	20	105	11	44,600	0	44,600
11	17	3		Al Unser Jr.	Galles Racing Starz SuperPak	G/O/F	196	Running	19	92	13	43,400	0	43,400
12	18	35		Jeff Ward	Heritage Motorsports/Firestone/Menards	G/O/F	196	Running	18	120	7	42,200	0	42,200
13	6	28		Mark Dismore	Delphi Automotive Systems/Bryant Heating & Cooling	D/O/F	196	Running	17	76	17	41,100	0	41,100
14	11	14		Eliseo Salazar	Harrah's A.J. Foyt Racing	D/O/F	194	Running	16	173	2	39,800	0	39,800
15	7	12		Buzz Calkins	Bradley Food Marts/Sav-O-Mat	D/O/F	193	Running	15	119	8	38,700	0	38,700
16	16	11		Donnie Beechler	Harrah's A.J. Foyt Racing	D/O/F	192	Running	14	47	22	37,500	0	37,500
17	12	77		Jaques Lazier	Classmates.com/Jonathan Byrd's Cafeteria	G/O/F	145	Engine	13	43	24	25,300	0	25,300
18	1	2		Greg Ray	Johns Manville/Menards	D/O/F	132	Handling	12	115	9	36,300	12,500	48,800
19	19	32	R	Didier André	Galles Racing	G/O/F	104	Mechanical	11	64	18	35,100	0	35,100
20	20	81		Billy Roe	Zali Racing	G/O/F	34	Oil Pressure	10	27	33	23,000	0	23,000
21	21	55		Shigeaki Hattori	EPSON	D/O/F	0	Did not start	9	85	16	34,000	0	34,000
				Speedway Engines									600	600
				TWR Engines									400	400
											TOTAL -	$1,000,000	$77,500	$1,077,500

Time of Race: 1:23:55.4261   **Average Speed:** 142.987 mph   **Margin of Victory:** 10.1080 sec.
Fastest Lap: #98 Billy Boat (Race lap 169, 167.546 mph, 21.4866 sec.)   **Fastest Leading Lap:** #4 Sam Hornish Jr. (Race lap 72, 167.060 mph, 21.5491 sec.)
MBNA Pole Winner: #2 Greg Ray (176.585 mph, 20.3868 sec.)   **"The Net Race Live Award" Lap Leader:** #4 Sam Hornish Jr.
Firestone "Leader at Halfway" Award: #4 Sam Hornish Jr.   **Coors Light "Pit Performance" Award:** #4 Sam Hornish Jr.
Legend: R= Indy Racing Northern Light Series Rookie   **Chassis Legend:** D=Dallara (13); G=G Force (8)
Engine Legend: O=Oldsmobile (19); I=Infiniti (2)   **Tire Legend:** F=Firestone (21)

Lap Leaders:

Laps	Car#	Driver
1-4	#2	Greg Ray
5-156	#4	Sam Hornish Jr.
157-200	#91	Buddy Lazier

Total: 2 Lead changes among 3 drivers

Lap Leader Summary:

Driver	Times	Total
Sam Hornish Jr.	1	152
Buddy Lazier	1	44
Greg Ray	1	4

Caution Flags:

Laps	Reason/Incident
58-64	debris
115-122	debris
146-153	#77 J. Lazier, stalled

Total: 3 caution flags, 23 laps

INDY RACING NORTHERN LIGHT SERIES
Richmond International Raceway, Saturday, June 30, 2001

FP	SP	Car	Driver	Car Name	C/E/T	Laps Comp.	Running/ Reason Out	IRL Pts.	Total IRL Pts.	IRL Standings	IRL Awards	Designated Awards	Total Awards
1	4	91	Buddy Lazier	Tae-Bo/Coors Light/Delta Faucet	D/O/F	250	Running	52	219	2	$102,200	$54,100	$156,300
2	6	4	Sam Hornish Jr.	Pennzoil Panther Dallara	D/O/F	250	Running	40	269	1	85,100	1,250	86,350
3	11	3	Al Unser Jr.	Galles Racing Starz SuperPak	G/O/F	250	Running	35	127	10	72,000	900	72,900
4	14	32 R	Didier André	Galles Racing	G/O/F	250	Running	32	96	17	58,900	10,250	69,150
5	10	8	Scott Sharp	Delphi Automotive Systems	D/O/F	249	Running	30	201	3	54,100	250	54,350
6	13	28	Mark Dismore	Delphi Automotive Systems/Bryant Heating & Cooling	D/O/F	249	Running	28	104	15	48,200	250	48,450
7	15	11	Donnie Beechler	A.J. Foyt Racing	D/O/F	247	Running	26	73	19	46,900	0	46,900
8	19	35	Jeff Ward	Heritage Motorsports/Firestone/Menards	G/O/F	247	Running	24	144	7	45,800	0	45,800
9	9	24	Robbie Buhl	Team Purex Dreyer & Reinbold Racing	G/I/F	247	Running	22	116	13	45,800	5,000	50,800
10	16	12	Buzz Calkins	Bradley Food Marts/Sav-O-Mat	D/O/F	239	Running	20	139	8	44,600	0	44,600
11	8	21 R	Felipe Giaffone	Hollywood	G/O/F	215	Running	19	185	5	43,400	0	43,400
12	7	14	Eliseo Salazar	Harrah's A.J. Foyt Racing	D/O/F	213	Accident	18	191	4	42,200	0	42,200
13	3	51	Eddie Cheever Jr.	#51 Cheever Indy Racing Infiniti	D/I/F	213	Accident	17	106	14	41,100	0	41,100
14	18	55	Shigeaki Hattori	EPSON	D/O/F	199	Accident	16	101	16	39,800	0	39,800
15	5	88	Airton Daré	1-800-BAR-NONE	G/O/F	182	Accident	15	129	9	38,700	0	38,700
16	12	6	Jeret Schroeder	Tri Star Motorsports Inc.	D/O/F	126	Accident	14	62	21	37,500	0	37,500
17	2	15	Sarah Fisher	Walker Racing Kroger Special	D/O/F	107	Accident	13	118	12	36,300	0	36,300
18	20	98	Billy Boat	CURB Records	D/O/F	31	Oil pressure	12	159	6	36,300	0	36,300
19	1	99	Jaques Lazier	Sam Schmidt Motorsports Racing Special	D/O/F	13	Accident	11	54	22	35,100	12,500	47,600
20	17	81	Billy Roe	Zali Racing	G/O/F	9	Handling	10	37	26	12,000	0	12,000
21	21	2	Greg Ray	Johns Manville/Menards	D/O/F	0	Did not start	9	124	11	34,000	0	34,000
			Speedway Engines									600	600
			VDS Engines									400	400
										TOTAL -	**$1,000,000**	**$85,500**	**$1,085,500**

Time of Race: 1:55:27.7300 **Average Speed:** 97.435 mph **Margin of Victory:** 4.8828 sec.

Fastest Lap / Fastest Leading Lap: #91 Buddy Lazier (Race lap 232, 154.896 mph, 17.4311 sec.) **Sony Disc 10,000 Indy Racing Lap Award:** #91 Buddy Lazier (Lap 75)

MBNA Pole Winner: #99 Jaques Lazier (160.417 mph, 16.8311 sec.) **"The Net Race Live Award" Lap Leader:** #91 Buddy Lazier

Firestone "Leader at Halfway" Award: #91 Buddy Lazier **Coors Light "Pit Performance" Award:** #32 Didier André

Legend: R= Indy Racing Northern Light Series Rookie **Chassis Legend:** D=Dallara (14); G=G Force (7)

Engine Legend: O=Oldsmobile (19); I=Infiniti (2) **Tire Legend:** F=Firestone (21)

Lap Leaders:

Laps	Car#	Driver
1-187	#91	Buddy Lazier
188-213	#14	Eliseo Salazar
214-250	#91	Buddy Lazier

Total: 2 Lead changes among 2 drivers

Lap Leader Summary:

Driver	Times	Total
Buddy Lazier	2	224
Eliseo Salazar	1	26

Caution Flags:

Laps	Reason/Incident
15-21	#77 J. Lazier, accident T4
65-72	debris
92-99	moisture
111-125	#15 Fisher, accident T4
128-132	#6 Schroeder, stalled frontstretch
139-149	#6 Schroeder, accident exiting pits T2
183-196	#88 Daré, #21 Giaffone, accident T2
206-212	#55 Hattori, accident T3
214-227	#14 Salazar, #51 Cheever, accident T3

Total: 9 caution flags, 89 laps

INDY RACING NORTHERN LIGHT SERIES
Kansas Speedway, Sunday, July 8, 2001

FP	SP	Car		Driver	Car Name	C/E/T	Laps Comp.	Running/ Reason Out	IRL Pts.	Total IRL Pts.	IRL Standings	IRL Awards	Designated Awards	Total Awards
1	2	51		Eddie Cheever Jr.	#51 Cheever Indy Racing Infiniti	D/I/F	200	Running	52	158	7	$102,200	$37,100	$139,300
2	5	4		Sam Hornish Jr.	Pennzoil Panther Dallara	D/O/F	200	Running	40	309	1	84,900	20,750	105,650
3	11	11		Donnie Beechler	A.J. Foyt Racing	D/O/F	200	Running	35	108	18	71,700	750	72,450
4	6	21	R	Felipe Giaffone	Hollywood	G/O/F	200	Running	32	217	3	58,500	250	58,750
5	12	91		Buddy Lazier	Tae-Bo/Coors Light/Delta Faucet	D/O/F	200	Running	30	249	2	53,600	650	54,250
6	22	88		Airton Daré	1-800-BAR-NONE/TeamXtreme	G/O/F	200	Running	28	157	8	47,700	250	47,950
7	3	14		Eliseo Salazar	Harrah's A.J. Foyt Racing	D/O/F	200	Running	26	217	3	46,400	2,250	48,650
8	9	55		Shigeaki Hattori	EPSON	D/O/F	200	Running	24	125	14	45,200	0	45,200
9	8	98		Billy Boat	CURB Records	D/O/F	200	Running	22	181	6	45,200	0	45,200
10	14	10		Robby McGehee	Cahill Racing	D/O/F	200	Running	20	106	19	44,100	0	44,100
11	7	28		Mark Dismore	Delphi Automotive Systems/Bryant Heating & Cooling	D/O/F	199	Running	19	123	16	42,800	0	42,800
12	17	15		Sarah Fisher	Walker Racing Kroger Special	D/O/F	197	Running	18	136	13	41,600	0	41,600
13	18	12		Buzz Calkins	Bradley Food Marts/Sav-O-Mat	D/O/F	191	Running	17	156	9	40,500	0	40,500
14	10	2		Greg Ray	Johns Manville/Menards	D/O/F	180	Running	16	140	11	39,200	0	39,200
15	20	9		Jeret Schroeder	High Plains Corp. AMVETS PDM Racing	D/O/F	147	Accident	15	77	20	27,000	0	27,000
16	16	32	R	Didier André	Galles Racing	G/O/F	138	Mechanical	14	110	17	36,900	0	36,900
17	1	8		Scott Sharp	Delphi Automotive Systems	D/O/F	136	Accident	13	214	5	35,600	12,500	48,100
18	13	99		Jaques Lazier	Sam Schmidt Motorsports Racing Special	D/O/F	123	Engine	12	66	21	35,600	0	35,600
19	19	6	R	Jon Herb	Tri Star Motorsports Inc.	D/O/F	101	Engine	11	33	31	23,400	0	23,400
20	15	3		Al Unser Jr.	Galles Racing Starz SuperPak	G/O/F	82	Electrical	10	137	12	33,300	0	33,300
21	4	24		Robbie Buhl	Team Purex Dreyer & Reinbold Racing	G/I/F	54	Engine	9	125	14	33,300	0	33,300
22	21	81		Billy Roe	Zali Racing	G/O/F	14	Engine	8	45	25	11,300	0	11,300
				TWR Engines									600	600
				Speedway Engines									400	400
											TOTAL -	$1,000,000	$75,500	$1,075,500

Time of Race: 2:02:29.2032 **Average Speed:** 148.914 mph **Margin of Victory:** 0.1976 of a second
Fastest Lap: #28 Mark Dismore (Race lap 125, 217.347 mph, 25.1763 sec.) **Fastest Leading Lap:** #51 Eddie Cheever Jr. (Race lap 200, 216.241 mph, 25.3051 sec.)
MBNA Pole Winner: #8 Scott Sharp (216.175 mph, 25.3128 sec.) **"The Net Race Live Award" Lap Leader:** #51 Eddie Cheever Jr.
Firestone "Leader at Halfway" Award: #51 Eddie Cheever Jr. **Coors Light "Pit Performance" Award:** #51 Eddie Cheever Jr.
Legend: R= Indy Racing Northern Light Series Rookie **Chassis Legend:** D=Dallara (16); G=G Force (6)
Engine Legend: O=Oldsmobile (20); I=Infiniti (2) **Tire Legend:** F=Firestone (22)

Lap Leaders:

Laps	Car#	Driver	Laps	Car#	Driver
1-32	#14	Eliseo Salazar	94-96	#4	Donnie Beechler
33-46	#51	Eddie Cheever Jr.	97-105	#51	Eddie Cheever Jr.
47-49	#4	Sam Hornish Jr.	106	#4	Sam Hornish Jr.
50-52	#51	Eddie Cheever Jr.	107-118	#91	Buddy Lazier
53-59	#4	Sam Hornish Jr.	119-139	#51	Eddie Cheever Jr.
60-61	#21	Felipe Giaffone	140	#91	Buddy Lazier
62-71	#28	Mark Dismore	141-145	#10	Robby McGehee
72-77	#10	Robby McGehee	146-190	#51	Eddie Cheever Jr.
78-81	#4	Sam Hornish Jr.	191-197	#4	Sam Hornish Jr.
82-90	#51	Eddie Cheever Jr.	198-200	#51	Eddie Cheever Jr.
91-93	#4	Sam Hornish Jr.			

Total: 20 Lead changes among 8 drivers

Lap Leader Summary:

Driver	Times	Total
Eddie Cheever Jr.	7	104
Eliseo Salazar	1	32
Sam Hornish Jr.	6	25
Buddy Lazier	2	13
Robby McGehee	2	11
Mark Dismore	1	10
Donnie Beechler	1	3
Felipe Giaffone	1	2

Caution Flags:

Laps	Reason/Incident
16-26	#81 Roe, engine T2
75-79	debris
87-89	debris
104-109	#6 Herb, engine T4
137-147	#8 Sharp, accident T4
149-156	#9 Schroeder, accident T2

Total: 6 caution flags, 44 laps

INDY RACING NORTHERN LIGHT SERIES
Nashville Superspeedway, Saturday, July 21, 2001

FP	SP	Car		Driver	Car Name	C/E/T	Laps Comp.	Running/ Reason Out	IRL Pts.	Total IRL Pts.	IRL Standings	IRL Awards	Designated Awards	Total Awards
1	6	91		Buddy Lazier	Tae-Bo/Coors Light/Delta Faucet	D/O/F	200	Running	50	299	2	$104,200	$39,100	$143,300
2	4	98		Billy Boat	CURB Records	D/O/F	200	Running	40	221	6	86,200	2,650	88,850
3	14	99		Jaques Lazier	Sam Schmidt Motorsports Racing Special	D/O/F	199	Accident	35	101	20	72,700	1,000	73,700
4	11	10		Robby McGehee	Cahill Racing	D/O/F	199	Running	32	138	16	59,200	250	59,450
5	13	8		Scott Sharp	Delphi Automotive Systems	D/O/F	199	Running	30	244	3	54,200	750	54,950
6	2	4		Sam Hornish Jr.	Pennzoil Panther Dallara	D/O/F	198	Running	30	339	1	48,200	15,000	63,200
7	16	55		Shigeaki Hattori	EPSON	D/O/F	197	Running	26	151	13	46,900	250	47,150
8	9	21	R	Felipe Giaffone	Hollywood	G/O/F	195	Running	24	241	4	45,700	0	45,700
9	15	12		Buzz Calkins	Bradley Food Marts/Sav-O-Mat	D/O/F	193	Running	22	178	7	45,700	0	45,700
10	10	11		Donnie Beechler	A.J. Foyt Racing	D/O/F	190	Running	20	128	18	44,500	0	44,500
11	12	14		Eliseo Salazar	Harrah's A.J. Foyt Racing	D/O/F	148	Engine	19	236	5	43,200	0	43,200
12	21	81		Billy Roe	Zali Racing Belterra Casino Resort	G/O/F	146	Radiator	18	63	23	20,000	0	20,000
13	7	24		Robbie Buhl	Team Purex Dreyer & Reinbold Racing	G/I/F	145	Radiator	17	142	15	40,800	5,000	45,800
14	19	3		Al Unser Jr.	Galles Racing Starz SuperPak	G/O/F	103	Accident	16	153	11	39,500	0	39,500
15	5	51		Eddie Cheever Jr.	#51 Cheever Indy Racing Infiniti	D/I/F	102	Accident	15	173	8	38,300	0	38,300
16	3	28		Mark Dismore	Delphi Automotive Systems/Bryant Heating & Cooling	D/O/F	102	Accident	14	137	17	37,200	0	37,200
17	18	88		Airton Daré	1-800-BAR-NONE/TeamXtreme	G/O/F	102	Accident	13	170	9	35,900	0	35,900
18	1	2		Greg Ray	Johns Manville/Menards	D/O/F	98	Accident	12	152	12	35,900	12,500	48,400
19	17	15		Sarah Fisher	Walker Racing Kroger Special	D/O/F	82	Handling	11	147	14	34,700	0	34,700
20	8	35		Jeff Ward	Heritage Motorsports Firestone Menards	G/O/F	81	Engine	10	154	10	33,500	0	33,500
21	20	32	R	Didier André	Galles Racing	G/O/F	17	Suspension	9	119	19	33,500	0	33,500
				Speedway Engines									1,000	1,000
											TOTAL -	$1,000,000	$77,500	$1,077,500

Time of Race: 1:47:43.6823   **Average Speed:** 144.809 mph   **Margin of Victory:** 10.6293 sec.
Fastest Lap: #91 Buddy Lazier (Race lap 102, 199.160 mph, 23.4987 sec.)   **Fastest Leading Lap:** #91 Buddy Lazier (Race lap 165, 199.115 mph, 23.5040 sec.)
MBNA Pole Winner: #2 Greg Ray (199.922 mph, 23.4091 sec.)
"The Net Race Live Award" Lap Leader: #4 Sam Hornish Jr.   **Firestone "Leader at Halfway" Award:** #4 Sam Hornish Jr.   **Coors Light "Pit Performance" Award:** #91 Buddy Lazier
Legend: R= Indy Racing Northern Light Series Rookie   **Chassis Legend:** D=Dallara (14); G=G Force (7)
Engine Legend: O=Oldsmobile (19); I=Infiniti (2)   **Tire Legend:** F=Firestone (21)

Lap Leaders:

Laps	Car#	Driver	Laps	Car#	Driver
1-6	#2	Greg Ray	119-121	#91	Buddy Lazier
7-19	#91	Buddy Lazier	122-147	#98	Billy Boat
20-51	#4	Sam Hornish Jr.	148-173	#91	Buddy Lazier
52-56	#91	Buddy Lazier	174	#99	Jaques Lazier
57-110	#4	Sam Hornish Jr.	175-176	#10	Robby McGehee
111-118	#14	Eliseo Salazar	177-200	#91	Buddy Lazier
Total: 11 Lead changes among 7 drivers					Jaques Lazier

Lap Leader Summary:

Driver	Times	Total
Sam Hornish Jr.	2	86
Buddy Lazier	5	71
Billy Boat	1	26
Eliseo Salazar	1	8
Greg Ray	1	6
Robby McGehee	1	2
	1	1

Caution Flags:

Laps	Reason/Incident
22-26	debris
54-60	debris
83-88	#35 Ward, engine
103-119	#2 Ray, #3 Unser Jr., #11 Beechler,
	#28 Dismore, #51 Cheever, #88 Daré,
	accident T2
Total: 4 caution flags, 35 laps	

INDY RACING NORTHERN LIGHT SERIES
Kentucky Speedway, Sunday, August 12, 2001

FP	SP	Car		Driver	Car Name	C/E/T	Laps Comp.	Running/ Reason Out	IRL Pts.	Total IRL Pts.	IRL Standings	IRL Awards	Designated Awards	Total Awards
1	11	91		Buddy Lazier	Tae-Bo/Coors Light/Delta Faucet	D/O/F	200	Running	50	349	2	$102,200	$27,100	$129,300
2	1	8		Scott Sharp	Delphi Automotive Systems	D/O/F	200	Running	42	286	3	84,900	28,400	113,300
3	8	4		Sam Hornish Jr.	Pennzoil Panther Dallara	D/O/F	200	Running	35	374	1	71,700	10,500	82,200
4	9	3		Al Unser Jr.	Galles Racing Starz SuperPak	G/O/F	200	Running	32	185	8	58,500	250	58,750
5	22	11		Donnie Beechler	A.J. Foyt Racing	D/O/F	200	Running	30	158	15	53,600	250	53,850
6	6	98		Billy Boat	CURB Records	D/O/F	200	Running	28	249	6	47,700	250	47,950
7	18	55		Shigeaki Hattori	EPSON	D/O/F	200	Running	26	177	11	46,400	0	46,400
8	12	21	R	Felipe Giaffone	Hollywood	G/O/F	200	Running	24	265	4	45,200	0	45,200
9	4	24		Robbie Buhl	Team Purex Dreyer & Reinbold Racing	G/I/F	199	Running	22	164	14	45,200	7,000	52,200
10	7	35		Jeff Ward	Heritage Motorsports Firestone Menards	G/O/F	198	Running	20	174	12	44,100	0	44,100
11	17	32	R	Didier André	Galles Racing	G/O/F	198	Running	19	138	19	42,800	0	42,800
12	13	99		Jaques Lazier	Sam Schmidt Motorsports Racing Special	D/O/F	198	Running	18	119	20	41,600	0	41,600
13	5	2		Greg Ray	Johns Manville/Menards	D/O/F	197	Running	17	169	13	40,500	0	40,500
14	21	81		Billy Roe	Zali Racing Belterra Casino Resort	G/O/F	196	Running	16	79	21	17,200	0	17,200
15	14	14		Eliseo Salazar	Harrah's A.J. Foyt Racing	D/O/F	196	Running	15	251	5	38,000	0	38,000
16	19	12		Buzz Calkins	Bradley Food Marts/Sav-O-Mat	D/O/F	195	Running	14	192	7	36,900	0	36,900
17	15	5	R	Rick Treadway	Meijer	G/O/F	190	Running	13	13	39	13,600	0	13,600
18	10	10		Robby McGehee	Cahill Racing	D/O/F	157	Running	12	150	17	35,600	0	35,600
19	20	15		Sarah Fisher	Walker Racing Kroger Special	D/O/F	154	Gearbox	11	158	15	34,400	0	34,400
20	16	88		Airton Daré	1-800-BAR-NONE/TeamXtreme	G/O/F	133	Oil pressure	10	180	10	33,300	0	33,300
21	3	51		Eddie Cheever Jr.	#51 Cheever Indy Racing Infiniti	D/I/F	105	CV joint	9	182	9	33,300	0	33,300
22	2	28		Mark Dismore	Delphi Automotive Systems/Bryant Heating & Cooling	D/O/F	31	Accident	8	145	18	33,300	0	33,300
				Speedway Engines									600	600
				Ilmor Engineering									400	400
											TOTAL -	$1,000,000	$74,750	$1,074,750

Time of Race: 1:42:54.5930   **Average Speed:** 174.910 mph   **Margin of Victory:** 1.5822 sec.
Fastest Lap: #28 Mark Dismore (Race lap 20, 214.132 mph, 25.2181 sec.)   **Fastest Leading Lap:** #8 Scott Sharp (Race lap 21, 213.948 mph, 25.2398 sec.)
MBNA Pole Winner: #8 Scott Sharp (214.598 mph, 25.1633 sec.)
"The Net Race Live Award" Lap Leader: #8 Scott Sharp   **Firestone "Leader at Halfway" Award:** #8 Scott Sharp   **Coors Light "Pit Performance" Award:** #4 Sam Hornish Jr.
Legend: R= Indy Racing Northern Light Series Rookie   **Chassis Legend:** D=Dallara (14); G=G Force (8)
Engine Legend: O=Oldsmobile (20); I=Infiniti (2)   **Tire Legend:** F=Firestone (22)

Lap Leaders:

Laps	Car#	Driver
1-105	#8	Scott Sharp
106	#11	Donnie Beechler
107-111	#4	Sam Hornish Jr.
112-188	#91	Buddy Lazier
189-192	#24	Robbie Buhl
193	#91	Lazier
194	#24	Buhl
195-200	#99	Lazier

Total: 7 Lead changes among 5 drivers

Lap Leader Summary:

Driver	Times	Total
Scott Sharp	1	105
Buddy Lazier	3	84
Robbie Buhl	2	5
Sam Hornish Jr.	1	5
Donnie Beechler	1	1

Caution Flags:

Laps	Reason/Incident
30-34	#28 Dismore, accident T2
74-78	debris
103-108	debris
156-164	#14 Salazar, spin in pits

Total: 4 caution flags, 25 laps

INDY RACING NORTHERN LIGHT SERIES
Gateway International Raceway, Sunday, August 26, 2001

FP	SP	Car		Driver	Car Name	C/E/T	Laps Comp.	Running/ Reason Out	IRL Pts.	Total IRL Pts.	IRL Standings	IRL Awards	Designated Awards	Total Awards
1	8	3		Al Unser Jr.	Galles Racing Starz SuperPak	G/O/F	200	Running	50	235	7	$101,100	$33,100	$134,200
2	19	28		Mark Dismore	Delphi Automotive Systems/Bryant Heating & Cooling	D/O/F	200	Running	40	185	14	83,700	15,900	99,600
3	1	4		Sam Hornish Jr.	Pennzoil Panther Dallara	D/O/F	200	Running	37	411	1	70,700	5,250	75,950
4	9	51		Eddie Cheever Jr.	#51 Cheever Indy Racing Infiniti	D/I/F	200	Running	32	214	8	57,700	5,750	63,450
5	14	24		Robbie Buhl	Team Purex Dreyer & Reinbold Racing	G/I/F	199	Running	30	194	12	53,000	2,250	55,250
6	5	98		Billy Boat	CURB Records	D/O/F	199	Running	28	277	4	47,100	750	47,850
7	12	35		Jeff Ward	Heritage Motorsports Firestone Menards	G/O/F	199	Running	26	200	10	45,900	250	46,150
8	3	8		Scott Sharp	Delphi Automotive Systems	D/O/F	199	Running	24	310	3	44,800	0	44,800
9	10	88		Airton Daré	1-800-BAR-NONE/TeamXtreme	G/O/F	199	Running	22	202	9	44,800	0	44,800
10	18	10		Robby McGehee	Cahill Racing	D/O/F	197	Running	20	170	17	43,600	0	43,600
11	15	15		Sarah Fisher	Walker Racing Kroger Special	D/O/F	195	Running	19	177	15	42,400	0	42,400
12	20	32	R	Didier André	Galles Racing	G/O/F	193	Running	18	156	19	41,200	0	41,200
13	2	91		Buddy Lazier	Tae-Bo/Coors Light/Delta Faucet	D/O/F	190	Running	17	366	2	40,100	0	40,100
14	16	11		Donnie Beechler	A.J. Foyt Racing	D/O/F	186	Accident	16	174	16	38,800	0	38,800
15	11	55		Shigeaki Hattori	EPSON	D/O/F	185	Running	15	192	13	37,700	0	37,700
16	13	2		Jaques Lazier	Johns Manville/Menards	D/O/F	139	Engine	14	133	20	36,600	0	36,600
17	4	14		Eliseo Salazar	Harrah's A.J. Foyt Racing	D/O/F	127	Engine	13	264	6	35,300	0	35,300
18	23	44	R	Anthony Lazzaro	Parsons' Project	G/O/F	77	Engine	12	12	40	13,300	0	13,300
19	22	92	R	Chris Menninga	Hemelgarn/Metro Racing	D/O/F	50	Accident	11	11	42	12,200	0	12,200
20	6	21	R	Felipe Giaffone	Hollywood	G/O/F	44	Mechanical	10	275	5	33,000	0	33,000
21	17	99		Alex Barron	Sam Schmidt Motorsports Racing Special	D/O/F	41	Accident	9	9	43	33,000	0	33,000
22	7	12		Buzz Calkins	Bradley Food Marts/Sav-O-Mat	D/O/F	40	Suspension	8	200	10	33,000	0	33,000
23	21	81		Billy Roe	Juno Online Services/Blair.com/Zali Racing	G/O/F	32	Handling	7	86	21	11,000	0	11,000
				Speedway Engines									600	600
				Ilmor Engineering									400	400
											TOTAL -	$1,000,000	$64,250	$1,064,250

Time of Race: 1:49:59.2682   **Average Speed:** 136.379 mph   **Margin of Victory:** 1.1834 sec.

Fastest Lap / Fastest Leading Lap: #24 Robbie Buhl (Race lap 168, 166.487 mph, 27.0291 sec.)

The Net Race Live Award" Lap Leader: #4 Sam Hornish Jr.

Firestone "Leader at Halfway" Award: #3 Al Unser Jr.   **Coors Light "Pit Performance" Award:** #3 Al Unser Jr.

Legend: R= Indy Racing Northern Light Series Rookie   **Chassis Legend:** D=Dallara (15); G=G Force (8)

Engine Legend: O=Oldsmobile (21); I=Infiniti (2)   **Tire Legend:** F=Firestone (23)

Lap Leaders:

Laps	Car#	Driver
1-58	#4	Sam Hornish Jr.
59-107	#3	Al Unser Jr.
108	#88	Airton Daré
109-116	#28	Mark Dismore
117-132	#3	Al Unser Jr.
133	#4	Sam Hornish Jr.
134-168	#24	Robbie Buhl
169-190	#4	Sam Hornish Jr.
191-200	#3	Al Unser Jr.

Total: 8 Lead changes among 5 drivers

Lap Leader Summary:

Driver	Times	Total
Sam Hornish Jr.	3	81
Al Unser Jr.	3	75
Robbie Buhl	1	35
Mark Dismore	1	8
Airton Daré	1	1

Caution Flags:

Laps	Reason/Incident
40-48	debris
52-57	#92 Menninga, accident T2
129-136	#14 Salazar, tow-in
188-193	#11 Beechler, accident T2

Total: 4 caution flags, 29 laps

INDY RACING NORTHERN LIGHT SERIES
Chicagoland Speedway, Sunday, September 2, 2001

FP	SP	Car		Driver	Car Name	C/E/T	Laps Comp.	Running/ Reason Out	IRL Pts.	Total IRL Pts.	IRL Standings	IRL Awards	Designated Awards	Total Awards
1	1	2		Jaques Lazier	Johns Manville/Menards	D/O/F	200	Running	52	185	16	$98,100	$39,600	$137,700
2	8	4		Sam Hornish Jr.	Pennzoil Panther Dallara	D/O/F	200	Running	40	451	1	81,300	26,250	107,550
3	2	51		Eddie Cheever Jr.	#51 Cheever Indy Racing Infiniti	D/I/F	200	Running	35	249	8	68,900	5,650	74,550
4	10	35		Jeff Ward	Heritage Motorsports Firestone Menards	G/O/F	200	Running	32	232	9	56,400	250	56,650
5	17	11		Donnie Beechler	A.J. Foyt Racing	D/O/F	200	Running	30	204	12	51,800	250	52,050
6	20	99		Richie Hearn	Sam Schmidt Motorsports Racing Special	D/O/F	199	Running	28	50	25	46,200	250	46,450
7	13	34	R	Laurent Redon	Mi-Jack	D/O/F	199	Running	26	26	37	23,000	0	23,000
8	12	3		Al Unser Jr.	Galles Racing Starz SuperPak	G/O/F	199	Running	24	259	7	43,900	250	44,150
9	18	12		Buzz Calkins	Bradley Food Marts/Sav-O-Mat	D/O/F	199	Running	22	222	10	43,900	0	43,900
10	6	21	R	Felipe Giaffone	Hollywood	G/O/F	198	Engine	20	295	4	42,800	2,000	44,800
11	9	91		Buddy Lazier	Tae-Bo/Coors Light/Delta Faucet	D/O/F	198	Running	19	385	2	41,600	0	41,600
12	11	98		Billy Boat	CURB Records	D/O/F	198	Running	18	295	4	40,500	0	40,500
13	21	32	R	Didier André	Galles Racing	G/O/F	198	Running	17	173	19	39,400	0	39,400
14	15	5	R	Rick Treadway	Meijer	G/O/F	198	Running	16	29	35	16,200	0	16,200
15	24	18	R	Jon Herb	Star Registry	G/O/F	192	Running	15	48	26	15,100	0	15,100
16	23	92	R	Chris Menninga	Hemelgarn/Metro Racing	D/O/F	191	Running	14	25	38	14,000	0	14,000
17	5	28		Mark Dismore	Delphi Automotive Systems/Bryant Heating & Cooling	D/O/F	164	Accident	13	198	15	34,800	0	34,800
18	7	14		Eliseo Salazar	Harrah's A.J. Foyt Racing	D/O/F	162	Accident	12	276	6	34,800	0	34,800
19	19	88		Airton Daré	1-800-BAR-NONE/TeamXtreme	G/O/F	147	Bell Housing	11	213	11	33,700	0	33,700
20	16	10		Robby McGehee	Cahill Racing	D/O/F	108	Suspension	10	180	18	32,600	0	32,600
21	14	55		Shigeaki Hattori	EPSON	D/O/F	104	Gearbox	9	201	14	32,600	0	32,600
22	4	24		Robbie Buhl	Team Purex Dreyer & Reinbold Racing	G/I/F	102	Gearbox	8	202	13	32,600	0	32,600
23	25	81		Billy Roe	Juno Online Services/Blair.com/Zali Racing	G/O/F	89	Gearbox	7	93	21	10,600	0	10,600
24	22	15		Sarah Fisher	Walker Racing Kroger Special	D/O/F	37	Electrical	6	183	17	32,600	0	32,600
25	3	8		Scott Sharp	Delphi Automotive Systems	D/O/F	29	Accident	5	315	3	32,600	0	32,600
				Menard Engines									600	600
				TWR Engines									400	400
											TOTAL -	$1,000,000	$75,500	$1,075,500

Time of Race: 1:45:57.4030   **Average Speed:** 172.146 mph   **Margin of Victory:** 1.4609 sec.

Fastest Lap / Fastest Leading Lap: #24 Robbie Buhl (Race lap 73, 222.137 mph, 24.6334 sec. - Track Record)

MBNA Pole Winner: #2 Jaques Lazier (221.740 mph, 24.6776 sec.)   **"The Net Race Live Award"** Lap Leader: #2 Jaques Lazier

Firestone "Leader at Halfway" Award: #2 Jaques Lazier   **Coors Light "Pit Performance" Award:** #4 Sam Hornish Jr.

Legend: R= Indy Racing Northern Light Series Rookie   **Chassis Legend:** D=Dallara (16); G=G Force (9)

Engine Legend: O=Oldsmobile (23); I=Infiniti (2)   **Tire Legend:** F=Firestone (25)

Lap Leaders:

Laps	Car#	Driver	Laps	Car#	Driver
1-32	#2	Jaques Lazier	100-114	#2	Jaques Lazier
33-45	#4	Sam Hornish Jr.	115-116	#21	Felipe Giaffone
46-58	#21	Felipe Giaffone	117-126	#2	Jaques Lazier
59-86	#24	Robbie Buhl	127-132	#21	Felipe Giaffone
87-90	#21	Felipe Giaffone	133-165	#2	Jaques Lazier
91-95	#28	Mark Dismore	166-174	#21	Felipe Giaffone
96-99	#24	Robbie Buhl	175-200	#2	Jaques Lazier

Total: 13 Lead changes among 5 drivers

Lap Leader Summary:

Driver	Times	Total
Jaques Lazier	5	116
Felipe Giaffone	5	34
Robbie Buhl	2	32
Sam Hornish Jr.	1	13
Mark Dismore	1	5

Caution Flags:

Laps	Reason/Incident
30-38	#8 Sharp, accident T2
124-129	debris
163-172	#14 Salazar, #28 Dismore, accident backstretch

Total: 3 caution flags, 25 laps

INDY RACING NORTHERN LIGHT SERIES
Texas Motor Speedway, Saturday, October 6, 2001

FP	SP	Car		Driver	Car Name	C/E/T	Laps Comp.	Running/ Reason Out	IRL Pts.	Total IRL Pts.	IRL Standings	IRL Awards	Designated Awards	Total Awards
1	1	4		Sam Hornish Jr.	Pennzoil Panther Dallara	D/O/F	200	Running	52	503	1	$98,100	$41,000	$139,100
2	3	8		Scott Sharp	Delphi Automotive Systems	D/O/F	200	Running	40	355	3	81,300	11,600	92,900
3	14	24		Robbie Buhl	Team Purex Dreyer & Reinbold Racing	G/I/F	200	Running	35	237	12	68,900	5,650	74,550
4	5	14		Eliseo Salazar	Harrah's A.J. Foyt Racing	D/O/F	200	Running	32	308	5	56,400	500	56,900
5	23	5	R	Rick Treadway	Big Tex Trailers	G/O/F	200	Running	30	59	25	29,800	500	30,300
6	7	3		Al Unser Jr.	Galles Racing Starz SuperPak	G/O/F	200	Running	28	287	7	46,200	0	46,200
7	12	88		Airton Daré	1-800-BAR-NONE	G/O/F	199	Running	26	239	10	45,000	0	45,000
8	13	11		Greg Ray	A.J. Foyt Racing	D/I/F	197	Running	24	193	18	43,900	0	43,900
9	25	18	R	Jon Herb	Star Registry	G/O/F	191	Running	22	70	23	21,900	0	21,900
10	11	12		Buzz Calkins	Bradley Food Marts/Sav-O-Mat	D/O/F	176	Engine	20	242	9	42,800	0	42,800
11	24	34	R	Laurent Redon	Mi-Jack	D/O/F	168	Engine	19	45	29	19,600	0	19,600
12	4	98		Billy Boat	CURB Records	D/O/F	159	Running	18	313	4	40,500	0	40,500
13	17	99	R	Anthony Lazzaro	Sam Schmidt Motorsports Racing Special	D/O/F	155	Engine	17	29	38	39,400	0	39,400
14	19	10		Robby McGehee	Cahill Racing	D/O/F	151	Engine	16	196	16	38,200	0	38,200
15	20	32	R	Didier André	Galles Racing	G/O/F	140	Accident	15	188	20	37,100	0	37,100
16	15	55		Shigeaki Hattori	EPSON	D/O/F	113	Handling	14	215	13	36,000	0	36,000
17	2	91		Buddy Lazier	Tae-Bo/Coors Light/Delta Faucet	D/O/F	102	Engine	13	398	2	34,800	0	34,800
18	8	51		Eddie Cheever Jr.	#51 Cheever Indy Racing Infiniti	D/I/F	91	Electrical	12	261	8	34,800	0	34,800
19	22	92	R	Chris Menninga	Hemelgarn/Metro Racing/Planet Hollywood	D/O/F	85	Suspension	11	36	33	11,700	0	11,700
20	9	2		Jaques Lazier	Johns Manville/Menards	D/O/F	70	Suspension	10	195	17	32,600	2,000	34,600
21	6	21	R	Felipe Giaffone	Hollywood	G/O/F	69	Engine	9	304	6	32,600	0	32,600
22	21	81		Billy Roe	Juno Online Services/Blair.com/Zali Racing	G/O/F	44	Fuel Pressure	8	101	21	10,600	0	10,600
23	16	28		Mark Dismore	Delphi Automotive Systems/Bryant Heating & Cooling	D/O/F	41	Fuel Pressure	7	205	14	32,600	0	32,600
24	10	35		Jeff Ward	Heritage Motorsports Firestone Menards	G/I/F	19	Suspension	6	238	11	32,600	0	32,600
25	18	15		Sarah Fisher	Walker Racing Kroger Special	D/O/F	0	Accident	5	188	19	32,600	0	32,600
				Ilmor Engineering									600	600
				TWR Engines									400	400
											TOTAL -	$1,000,000	$62,250	$1,062,250

Time of Race: 1:43:36.3757　**Average Speed:** 168.523 mph　**Margin of Victory:** .0188 of a second

Fastest Lap: #21 Felipe Giaffone (Race lap 52, 221.540 mph, 23.6436 sec.)　**Fastest Leading Lap:** #4 Sam Hornish Jr. (Race lap 45, 221.348 mph, 23.6641 sec.)

The Net Race Live Award" Lap Leader: #4 Sam Hornish Jr.

Firestone "Leader at Halfway" Award: #8 Scott Sharp　**Coors Light "Pit Performance" Award:** #4 Sam Hornish Jr.

Legend: R= Indy Racing Northern Light Series Rookie　**Chassis Legend:** D=Dallara (16); G=G Force (9)

Engine Legend: O=Oldsmobile (21); I=Infiniti (4)　**Tire Legend:** F=Firestone (25)

Lap Leaders:

Laps	Car#	Driver	Laps	Car#	Driver
1-8	#4	Sam Hornish Jr.	99-100	#8	Scott Sharp
9	#91	Buddy Lazier	101-116	#4	Sam Hornish Jr.
10-18	#4	Sam Hornish Jr.	117-121	#24	Robbie Buhl
19	#2	Jaques Lazier	122	#4	Sam Hornish Jr.
20-21	#4	Sam Hornish Jr.	123-135	#24	Robbie Buhl
22	#2	Jaques Lazier	136-140	#4	Sam Hornish Jr.
23-29	#4	Sam Hornish Jr.	141-144	#8	Scott Sharp
30-31	#2	Jaques Lazier	145-147	#4	Sam Hornish Jr.
32-34	#4	Sam Hornish Jr.	148-160	#24	Robbie Buhl
35	#2	Jaques Lazier	161-172	#4	Sam Hornish Jr.
36-37	#4	Sam Hornish Jr.	173-178	#8	Scott Sharp
38-44	#2	Jaques Lazier	179	#4	Sam Hornish Jr.
45-46	#4	Sam Hornish Jr.	180-182	#8	Scott Sharp
47-52	#2	Jaques Lazier	183-192	#4	Sam Hornish Jr.
53-54	#4	Sam Hornish Jr.	193-199	#8	Scott Sharp
55-67	#21	Felipe Giaffone	200	#4	Sam Hornish Jr.
68-98	#4	Sam Hornish Jr.	**Total: 32 Lead changes among 6 drivers**		

Lap Leader Summary:

Driver	Times	Total
Sam Hornish Jr.	17	115
Robbie Buhl	3	31
Scott Sharp	5	22
Jaques Lazier	6	18
Felipe Giaffone	1	13
Buddy Lazier	1	1

Caution Flags:

Laps	Reason/Incident
1-7	#15 Fisher, accident T4
	#98 Boat, spin frontstretch
55-62	#2 J. Lazier, Lost wheel leaving pits
85-90	#92 Menninga, suspension
157-163	#99 Lazzaro, fire
168-171	#34 Redon, engine

Total: 5 caution flags, 32 laps

Track	Date	Winner (start)	Time of Race	Average Speed (mph)	Margin of Victory	Second	Third	Fourth	Fifth
PIR	3/18	Sam Hornish Jr. (2)	1:35:56.7051	125.072	1.3786 sec.	Salazar	B. Lazier	Sharp	Boat
HMS	4/8	Sam Hornish Jr. (5)	2:01:12.3363	148.508	1.8701 sec.	Fisher	Salazar	Giaffone	Ward
AMS	4/28	Greg Ray (1)	2:14:40.9890	133.647	19.8570 sec.	Sharp	Calkins	Hornish	Salazar
IMS	5/27	Helio Castroneves (11)	3:31:54.1800	141.574	1.7373 sec.	de Ferran	Andretti	Vasser	Junqueira
TMS	6/9	Scott Sharp (2)	1:55:43.5775	150.873	Under Caution	Giaffone	Hornish	B. Lazier	Boat
PPIR	6/17	Buddy Lazier (5)	1:23:55.4261	142.987	10.1080 sec.	Hornish	Buhl	Boat	Daré
RIR	6/30	Buddy Lazier (4)	1:55:27.7300	97.435	4.8828 sec.	Hornish	Unser	André	Sharp
KaS	7/8	Eddie Cheever Jr. (2)	2:02:29.2032	148.914	0.1976 sec.	Hornish	Beechler	Giaffone	B. Lazier
NS	7/21	Buddy Lazier (6)	1:47:43.6823	144.809	10.6293 sec.	Boat	J. Lazier	McGehee	Sharp
KyS	8/12	Buddy Lazier (11)	1:42:54.5930	174.910	1.5822 sec.	Sharp	Hornish	Unser	Beechler
GIR	8/26	Al Unser Jr. (8)	1:49:59.2682	136.379	1.1834 sec.	Dismore	Hornish	Cheever	Buhl
CS	9/2	Jaques Lazier (1)	1:45:57.4030	172.146	1.4609 sec.	Hornish	Cheever	Ward	Beechler
TMS 2	10/6	Sam Hornish Jr. (1)	1:43:36.3757	168.523	0.0188 sec.	Sharp	Buhl	Salazar	Treadway

Track	Pole (finish)	Average Qualifying Speed	Starters	Running at Finish	Cars On Lead Lap	Race Leaders	Lead Changes	Caution Flags	Laps Under Caution
PIR	Greg Ray (22)	177.663	27	14	5	6	7	5	37
HMS	Jeff Ward (5)	201.551	26	19	3	5	9	6	32
AMS	Greg Ray (1)	218.265	27	13	3	4	7	4	55
IMS	Scott Sharp (33)	226.037	33	22	6	8	13	8	56
TMS	Mark Dismore (20)	215.508	24	15	8	8	15	6	42
PPIR	Greg Ray (18)	176.585	20	16	4	3	2	3	23
RIR	Jaques Lazier (19)	160.417	20	11	4	2	2	9	89
KaS	Scott Sharp (17)	216.175	22	14	10	8	20	6	44
NS	Greg Ray (18)	199.922	21	9	2	7	11	4	36
KyS	Scott Sharp (2)	214.598	22	18	8	5	7	4	25
GIR	Sam Hornish Jr.(3)	Points*	23	14	4	5	8	4	29
CS	Jaques Lazier (1)	221.740	25	15	5	5	13	3	25
TMS 2	Sam Hornish Jr.(1)	Points*	25	10	6	6	32	5	32

* = Starting Line-up based on entrant points as qualifications were rained out.

Key: PIR-Phoenix International Raceway; HMS-Homestead-Miami Speedway; AMS-Atlanta Motor Speedway; IMS-Indianapolis Motor Speedway; TMS-Texas Motor Speedway; PPIR-Pikes Peak International Raceway; RIR-Richmond International Raceway; KaS-Kansas Speedway; NS-Nashville Speedway; KyS-Kentucky Speedway; GIR-Gateway International Raceway; CS-Chicagoland Speedway.

2 0 0 1   I N D I A N A P O L I S   5 0 0   E N T R Y   L I S T

Car	Driver	Car Name	C/E	Entrant
2	Greg Ray	Johns Manville/Menards	D/O/F	Team Menard
2T	Greg Ray	Johns Manville/Menards	D/O/F	Team Menard
3	Al Unser Jr. (W)	Galles Racing Starz SuperPak	G/O/F	Galles Racing
3T	Al Unser Jr. (W)	Galles Racing Starz SuperPak	G/O/F	Galles Racing
4	Sam Hornish Jr.	Pennzoil Panther Dallara	D/O/F	Panther Racing
4T	Sam Hornish Jr.	Pennzoil Panther Dallara	D/O/F	Panther Racing
5	Arie Luyendyk (W)	Meijer	G/O/F	Treadway/Hubbard Racing
5T	Arie Luyendyk (W)	Meijer	G/O/F	Treadway/Hubbard Racing
6	Jon Herb (R)	Tri Star Motorsports Inc.	D/O/F	Tri Star Motorsports
6T	Jon Herb (R)	Tri Star Motorsports Inc.	D/O/F	Tri Star Motorsports
7	Stephan Gregoire	Jack K. Elrod Co./Tokheim/NADA Guides	D/O/F	Dick Simon Racing
7T	Stephan Gregoire	Jack K. Elrod Co./Tokheim/NADA Guides	G/O/F	Dick Simon Racing
8	Scott Sharp	Delphi Automotive Systems	D/O/F	Kelley Racing
8T	Scott Sharp	Delphi Automotive Systems	D/O/F	Kelley Racing
9	Jeret Schroeder	Purity Products	D/O/F	PDM Racing
9T	Jeret Schroeder	Purity Products	TBA	PDM Racing
10	Robby McGehee	Cahill Racing	D/O/F	Cahill Racing
10T	Robby McGehee	Cahill Racing	D/O/F	Cahill Racing
11	Jack Miller	Olympus/Opalescence/Cahill Racing	D/O/F	Cahill Racing
11T	Jack Miller	Olympus/Opalescence/Cahill Racing	D/O/F	Cahill Racing
12	Buzz Calkins	Bradley Food Marts/Sav-O-Mat	D/O/F	Bradley Motorsports
12T	Buzz Calkins	Bradley Food Marts/Sav-O-Mat	D/O/F	Bradley Motorsports
14	Eliseo Salazar	Harrah's A.J. Foyt Racing	D/O/F	A.J. Foyt Enterprises
14T	Eliseo Salazar	Harrah's A.J. Foyt Racing	D/O/F	A.J. Foyt Enterprises
15	Sarah Fisher	Walker Racing/Kroger Special	D/O/F	Walker Racing
15T	Sarah Fisher	Walker Racing/Kroger Special	D/O/F	Walker Racing
16	Cory Witherill (R)	WSA/MOTORS/Indy Regency Racing	G/O/F	Indy Regency Racing
17	TBA	Dick Simon Racing	TBA	Dick Simon Racing
17T	TBA	Dick Simon Racing	TBA	Dick Simon Racing
18	Johnny Unser	Truscelli Team Racing		Truscelli Team Racing
19	TBA	Della Penna Motorsports	D/O/F	Della Penna Motorsports
20	TBA	TBA	D/O/F	Kelley Racing
20T	TBA	TBA	D/O/F	Kelley Racing
21	Felipe Giaffone (R)	Hollywood	G/O/F	Treadway/Hubbard Racing
21T	Felipe Giaffone (R)	Hollywood	G/O/F	Treadway/Hubbard Racing
22	TBA	Johns Manville/Menards	D/O/F	Team Menard
22T	TBA	Johns Manville/Menards	D/O/F	Team Menard
23	TBA	Dreyer & Reinbold Racing	G/I/F	Dreyer & Reinbold Racing
23T	TBA	Dreyer & Reinbold Racing	G/I/F	Dreyer & Reinbold Racing
24	Robbie Buhl	Team Purex Dreyer & Reinbold Racing	G/I/F	Dreyer & Reinbold Racing
24T	Robbie Buhl	Team Purex Dreyer & Reinbold Racing	G/I/F	Dreyer & Reinbold Racing
25	TBA	Walker Racing TBA Special	TBA	Walker Racing
25T	TBA	Walker Racing TBA Special	TBA	Walker Racing
27	TBA	Blueprint Racing Special	G/O/F	Blueprint Racing Enterprises
27T	TBA	Blueprint Racing Special	G/O/F	Blueprint Racing Enterprises
28	Mark Dismore	Delphi Automotive Systems Bryant Heating & Cooling	D/O/F	Kelley Racing
28T	Mark Dismore	Delphi Automotive Systems Bryant Heating & Cooling	D/O/F	Kelley Racing
30	Brandon Erwin (R)	WorldBestBuy.com/McCormack Motorsports	G/O/F	McCormack Motorsports

2 0 0 1   I N D I A N A P O L I S   5 0 0   E N T R Y   L I S T

Car	Driver	Car Name	C/E	Entrant
30T	Brandon Erwin (R)	WorldBestBuy.com/McCormack Motorsports	G/O/F	McCormack Motorsports
31	Casey Mears (R)	Galles Racing SportsLine.com	G/O/F	Galles Racing
31T	Casey Mears (R)	Galles Racing SportsLine.com	G/O/F	Galles Racing
32	Didier André (R)	Galles Racing	G/O/F	Galles Racing
33	Nicolas Minassian (R)	Target Chip Ganassi Racing	G/O/F	Chip Ganassi Racing Teams
33T	Nicolas Minassian (R)	Target Chip Ganassi Racing	G/O/F	Chip Ganassi Racing Teams
35	Jeff Ward	Heritage Motorsports/Firestone/Menards	G/O/F	Heritage Motorsports
35T	Jeff Ward	Heritage Motorsports/Firestone/Menards	G/O/F	Heritage Motorsports
37	TBA	Brayton Racing		
38				Neinhouse Motorsports
38T				Neinhouse Motorsports
39	Michael Andretti	Motorola/Archipelago	D/O/F	Team Green
39T	Michael Andretti	Motorola/Archipelago	D/O/F	Team Green
41	Robby Gordon	A.J. Foyt Racing	D/O/F	A.J. Foyt Enterprises
41T	Robby Gordon	A.J. Foyt Racing	D/O/F	A.J. Foyt Enterprises
44	Bruno Junqueira (R)	Target Chip Ganassi Racing	G/O/F	Chip Ganassi Racing Teams
44T	Bruno Junqueira (R)	Target Chip Ganassi Racing	G/O/F	Chip Ganassi Racing Teams
51	Eddie Cheever Jr. (W)	#51 Excite@Home Indy Race Car	D/I/F	Cheever Indy Racing
51T	Eddie Cheever Jr. (W)	#51 Excite@Home Indy Race Car	D/I/F	Cheever Indy Racing
52	Scott Goodyear	Cheever Indy Racing	D/I/F	Cheever Indy Racing
52T	Scott Goodyear	Cheever Indy Racing	D/I/F	Cheever Indy Racing
55	Shigeaki Hattori (R)	EPSON	G/O/F	Vertex/Cunningham Racing
55T	Shigeaki Hattori (R)	EPSON	G/O/F	Vertex/Cunningham Racing
60	TBA	Tri Star Motorsports Inc.	D/O/F	Tri Star Motorsports
60T	TBA	Tri Star Motorsports Inc.	D/O/F	Tri Star Motorsports
66	Gil de Ferran	Marlboro Team Penske	D/O/F	Penske Racing
66T	Gil de Ferran	Marlboro Team Penske	D/O/F	Penske Racing
68	Helio Castroneves (R)	Marlboro Team Penske	D/O/F	Penske Racing
68T	Helio Castroneves (R)	Marlboro Team Penske	D/O/F	Penske Racing
77	Jaques Lazier	Jonathan Byrd's Cafeteria TeamXtreme	G/O/F	Jonathan Byrd TeamXtreme Racing
77T	Jaques Lazier	Jonathan Byrd's Cafeteria TeamXtreme	G/O/F	Jonathan Byrd TeamXtreme Racing
81	John Paul			Team Pelfrey
88	Airton Daré	1-800-BAR NONE TeamXtreme	G/O/F	TeamXtreme Racing
88T	Airton Daré	1-800-BAR NONE TeamXtreme	G/O/F	TeamXtreme Racing
91	Buddy Lazier (W)	Tae-Bo/Coors Light/LifeFitness/Delta Faucet	D/O/F	Hemelgarn Racing
91T	Buddy Lazier (W)	Tae-Bo/Coors Light/LifeFitness/Delta Faucet	D/O/F	Hemelgarn Racing
92	Stan Wattles	Hemelgarn/Firestone/Dallara/Oldsmobile	D/O/F	Hemelgarn Racing
92T	Stan Wattles	Hemelgarn/Firestone/Dallara/Oldsmobile	D/O/F	Hemelgarn Racing
93	TBA	Metro Management/Super Fitness/Firestone	D/O/F	Hemelgarn Racing
93T	TBA	Metro Management/Super Fitness/Firestone	D/O/F	Hemelgarn Racing
94	TBA	Hemelgarn Racing	D/O/F	Hemelgarn Racing
94T	TBA	Hemelgarn Racing	D/O/F	Hemelgarn Racing
98	Billy Boat	Curb Records	D/O/F	Curb-Agajanian/Beck Motorsports
98T	Billy Boat	Curb Records	D/O/F	Curb-Agajanian/Beck Motorsports
99	Davey Hamilton	Sam Schmidt Motorsports Racing Special	D/O/F	Sam Schmidt Motorsports
99T	Davey Hamilton	Sam Schmidt Motorsports Racing Special	D/O/F	Sam Schmidt Motorsports

Legend: C/E/T=Chassis/Engine/Tire Chassis: D=Dallara, G=G Force
Engine: O=Oldsmobile, I=Infiniti Tire: F=Firestone
W=Indy 500 Winner R=Indy 500 Rookie
Entry List as of April 11, 2001

The 2001 Indianapolis 500 purse exceeded $9 million for the third time in Speedway history. While the Indianapolis Motor Speedway contributes over $6 million to the purse, over 50 participating sponsors posted more than $1 million in cash and prizes.

Helio Castroneves took home $130,000 from Borg-Warner Inc. for winning the 85th Indianapolis 500 and $25,000 for being the Bank One Rookie of the Year. He also was awarded a 2002 Oldsmobile Bravada. Scott Sharp and the Kelley Racing team won the Coors Indy Pit Stop Challenge on Coors Carb Day taking home $42,500 of the $80,000 purse posted by Coors Brewing Company. Kelley Racing presented $5,000 of their winning sum to the American Red Cross. The Firestone "Leader at Halfway Award" of $20,000 went to Greg Ray, while the WorldCom "Long Distance Award" of $20,000 went to Billy Boat.

$100,000

MBNA Pole Award
$100,000

OLDSMOBILE POLE AWARD
2001 Oldsmobile Aurora
(pole winner)

$30,000

Verizon "Front Runner" Award - $30,000
$10,000 awarded to each front row driver
VERIZON

$11,000

Monarch Beverage "Inside Track" Award - $11,000
$1,000 to starters on the inside of each row
MONARCH BEVERAGE

$5,000

Bruno Junqueira
American Dairy Association
"Fastest Qualifying Rookie"
Award - $5,000
AMERICAN DAIRY ASSOCIATION

Sarah Fisher
Ameritech "Youngest Starting Driver"
Award - $5,000
awarded to the youngest driver to qualify
AMERITECH

Stephan Gregoire
Buckeye Machine/Race Spec
"Final Measure"
Award - $5,000
awarded to last team to pass inspection
and qualify for the race
BUCKEYE MACHINE/RACE SPEC

Billy Boat
Ferguson Steel
"Most Consistent Qualifier"
Award - $5,000
awarded to the driver who records the
four most consistent qualifying laps
FERGUSON STEEL COMPANY, INC.

Bruno Junqueira
Gregory & Appel, Inc.
"Fastest Rookie Qualifier"
Award - $5,000
GREGORY & APPEL, INC.

Filipe Giaffone
Buildings To Go
"Most Consistent Rookie Qualifier"
Award - $5,000
awarded to the rookie who records
the four most consistent qualifying laps
BUILDINGS TO GO

Scott Sharp
Mi-Jack "Top Performance"
Award - $5,000
awarded to the driver recording
the fastest single qualifying lap
MI-JACK PRODUCTS

John O'Gara
Snap-On/CAM "Top Wrench"
Award - $5,000
recognizes mechanical excellence
by a chief mechanic during practice
and qualifying
SNAP-ON TOOLS/CAM

Helio Castroneves
T.P. Donovan
"Top Starting Rookie"
Award - $5,000
T.P. DONOVAN INVESTMENTS

The Indianapolis Motor Speedway and it's presenting sponsors I the 85th Indianapolis 500 were pleased to offer the following qualifying incentives. For the first time, MBNA Motorsports presented the "MNBA Pole Award" worth $100,000 to the pole position winner. In addition to the $100,000, pole winner Scott Sharp was presented a 2001 Oldsmobile Aurora. Sharp, Greg Ray and Robby Gordon each took home $10,000 from Verizon for qualifying in the front row, and Monarch Beverage awarded $1,000 to the starters on the inside of each row.

$125,000

PENNZOIL
$125,000

$30,000

INFINITI

INFINITI MOTORSPORTS
$30,000

Oldsmobile

OLDSMOBILE
$30,000

$50,000

Digital Audio Disc Corporation

Sony Disc Manufacturing

DIGITAL AUDIO DISC CORPORATION/ SONY DISC MANUFACTURING
$50,000

$10,000

TEAM SIMPSON RACING
$10,000

$6,000

BELL RACING
$6,000

KLOTZ SPECIAL FORMULA PRODUCTS
$6,000

$35,000

BOSCH

ROBERT BOSCH CORPORATION
$35,000

$5,000

BG PRODUCTS
$5,000

CREATIVE COMMUNICATIONS
$5,000

EARL'S INDY
$5,000

EMCO GEARS
$5,000

HYPERCO
$5,000

IDEAL DIVISION/ STANT CORPORATION
$5,000

KECO COATINGS
$5,000

Motorsport Spares
$5,000

The 2001 Indianapolis 500 purse exceeded 9 million dollars for the third time in Speedway history. While the Indianapolis Motor Speedway contributes over 6 million dollars to this purse, over 50 participating sponsors have posted more than $1,000,000 in cash and prizes.

Borg-Warner Inc. leads the postings for race day awards with $130,000 in cash for the winner and a $120,000 bonus if a back-to-back win is recorded. Coors Brewing Company has posted $80,000 for the Carburetion Day "Coors Indy Pit Stop Challenge." Bank One awards $25,000 to the "Rookie of the Year," Firestone awards $20,000 for the "Leader at Halfway Award" and WorldCom posts $20,000 for the "Long Distance Award."

The 2001 race winner will also receive a 2002 Oldsmobile Bravada.

$130,000

BORG-WARNER INC. TROPHY AWARD

$130,000 plus trophy replica
$120,000 bonus if the 2000 winner repeats his victory
($20,000 added to the bonus each year until a back-to-back win is recorded)

Borg-Warner, Inc.
(race winner)
Helio Castroneves

OLDSMOBILE OFFICIAL PACE VEHICLE AWARD

2002 Oldsmobile Bravada
(race winner) **Helio Castroneves**

$80,000

$80,000 - Coors Brewing Company
(contest held May 24, 2001)
Scott Sharp

$25,000

BANK ONE "ROOKIE OF THE YEAR" AWARD

$25,000 - Bank One, Indianapolis
Helio Castroneves

SCOTT BRAYTON DRIVERS TROPHY
$25,000
(awarded to the driver who most exemplifies the attitude, spirit and competitive drive of the late Scott Brayton)
Davey Hamilton

$20,000

FIRESTONE "LEADER AT HALFWAY" AWARD

$20,000 - Bridgestone/Firestone Inc.
(awarded to the race leader at lap 100 using Firestone tires)
Greg Ray

UNION PLANTERS BANK "LEADERS' CIRCLE" AWARD

$20,000 - Union Planters Bank
Helio Castroneves

WorldCom "LONG DISTANCE" AWARD

$20,000 - WorldCom
(awarded to the driver who most improves their position during the race)
Billy Boat

$15,000

DELCO REMY "QUICK START" AWARD

$15,000 - Delco Remy
(awarded to the driver who records the fastest lap during the first 50 laps)
Helio Castroneves

$10,000

C&R RACING "TRUE GRIT" AWARD

$10,000 - C&R Racing co-sponsored by Visteon Climate Control
(awarded to the mechanic that exemplifies outstanding achievement and excellence in preparation and management)
John O'Gara

MAURICE LACROIX SWISS WATCHES "TOMORROW'S CLASSICS" AWARD

$10,000 Value - Maurice Lacroix USA
(Limited edition 18-karat rose-gold Masterpiece Indy 500 Flyback Annuaire awarded to the race winner)
Helio Castroneves

NATIONAL CITY BANK "CHECKERED FLAG" AWARD

$10,000 - National City Bank, Indiana
(race winner)
Helio Castroneves

INDY NET RACE LIVE/ANIVISION

$10,000 - Net Race Live/AniVision
(awarded to the eligable driver who leads the most laps during the race)
Greg Ray

TRUE VALUE "MECHANICS OF THE INDY 500" AWARD

$10,000 - True Value
(awarded to the winning team's mechanic)
Rick Rinaman

$8,500

CLARIAN HEALTH PARTNERS
"FASTEST LAP" AWARD
$8,500 - Clarian Health Partners
(awarded to the driver with the fastest lap)
Sam Hornish Jr.

$7,000

SUMMIT CONSTRUCTION
"PAGODA" AWARD
$7,000 - Summit
(awarded to the race leader at lap 99)
Greg Ray

$5,500

AMERICAN DAIRY AWARDS
$5,500 - American Dairy Association
($5,000 to the race winner,
$500 to winning chief mechanic)
Helio Castroneves, Rick Rinaman

OFFICIAL SPONSORS OF THE 2001 INDIANAPOLIS 500

Anivision	Official Online Entertainment
Barrington Jewels	Official Fine Jeweler
Clarian Health Partners	Official Healthcare Provider
Coors Brewing Company	Official Beer
Digital Audio Disc Corporation/ Sony Disc Manufacturers	Official Media Duplication Partner
Emergency One	Official Fire Truck
Featherlite Trailers	Official Motorhome & Trailer
Holmatro Rescue Tools	Official Safety Equipment Supplier
Keystone Grill	Official Restaurant
Maurice Lacroix USA	Official Watch
MBNA	Official Sponsor, Pole Award
Miller Industries	Official Race Recovery
Nokia	Official Wireless Communications Device
Northern Light	Official Search Engine
Oldsmobile	Official Pace Vehicle
Pennzoil	Official Motor Oil
Pepsi	Official Soft Drink
Perkin Elmer	Official Fuel Analysis Instrumental Supplier & Fuel Certification
Safety-Kleen	Official Supplier of Environmental Services
St. Clair Apparel	Official Clothier
Tokheim Corporation	Official Fuel Dispenser
Whistler Corporation	Official Radar Detector/Power Inverter
WorldCom	Official Communications Company

$5,000

CLINT BRAWNER
"MECHANICAL EXCELLENCE" AWARD
$5,000 - Clint Brawner Mechanical Excellence Foundation
Tom Bose

DANA BRAKE & CHASSIS/RAYBESTOS
"SAFETY IN SPEED" AWARD
$5,000 - Dana Brake & Chassis/Raybestos
(awarded to the car owner of the race winner)
Roger Penske

LINCOLN ELECTRIC
"HARD CHARGER" AWARD
$5,000 - Lincoln Electric
Racing's #1 Choice in Welding
(awarded to the lowest qualifier to lead the race)
Michael Andretti

ROCHE DIAGNOSTICS FASTEST TWO RACE LAPS AWARD
$5,000
(awarded to the driver who records the fastest two lap average
during the race)
Sam Hornish Jr.

WHISTLER RADAR DETECTOR
"FASTEST LAP" AWARD
$5,000 - Whistler Corporation
(awarded to the driver who records the fastest lap time
during the race, driver and crew chief also receive a
limited edition IMS model radar detector)
Sam Hornish Jr.

INDY RACING LEAGUE PROMOTIONAL PARTNERS

Rank	Driver	Total Points	Starts	Best Start	Best Finish	Laps Comp. (2,650)	Running At Finish	Races Led	Total Laps Led	Season Earnings
1	Sam Hornish Jr.	503	13	1st	1st	2,643	13	11	765	$2,477,025
2	Buddy Lazier	398	13	2nd	1st	2,506	11	6	437	1,196,525
3	Scott Sharp	355	13	1st	1st	2,207	10	5	166	1,234,425
4	Billy Boat	313	13	4th	2nd	2,291	12	1	26	925,025
5	Eliseo Salazar	308	13	3rd	2nd	2,438	9	4	82	949,900
6	Felipe Giaffone (R)	304	13	4th	2nd	2,298	10	5	51	839,825
7	Al Unser Jr.	287	13	7th	1st	2,020	8	2	76	844,525
8	Eddie Cheever Jr.	261	13	2nd	1st	1,977	5	2	168	881,275
9	Buzz Calkins	242	13	7th	3rd	2,402	11	0	0	807,025
10	Airton Daré	239	13	5th	5th	2,160	8	2	6	806,025
11	Jeff Ward	238	12	1st	4th	2,089	9	2	50	742,775
12	Robbie Buhl	237	13	4th	3rd	1,915	7	4	103	873,375
13	Shigeaki Hattori	215	11	5th	7th	1,979	8	0	0	459,100
14	Mark Dismore	205	13	1st	2nd	1,798	6	5	54	793,325
15	Donnie Beechler	204	9	6th	3rd	1,775	7	2	4	558,025
16	Robby McGehee	196	11	10th	4th	1,845	7	2	13	698,625
17	Jaques Lazier	195	10	1st	1st	1,469	4	4	139	633,675
18	Greg Ray	193	10	1st	1st	1,673	5	6	363	859,875
19	Sarah Fisher	188	13	2nd	2nd	1,675	6	0	0	717,175
20	Didier André (R)	188	12	14th	4th	1,810	6	0	0	428,550
21	Billy Roe	101	9	20th	12th	759	2	0	0	133,400
22	Jeret Schroeder	77	7	12th	14th	852	2	0	0	379,925
23	Jon Herb (R)	70	6	17th	9th	649	2	0	0	351,875
24	Helio Castroneves	64	2	11th	1st	342	1	2	56	1,305,075
25	Rick Treadway (R)	59	3	15th	5th	588	3	0	0	60,100
26	Davey Hamilton	54	5	12th	12th	682	2	0	0	420,825
27	Richie Hearn	50	2	15th	6th	396	2	0	0	92,250
28	Gil de Ferran	46	2	5th	2nd	276	1	2	30	515,375
29	Laurent Redon (R)	45	2	13th	7th	367	1	0	0	42,600
30	Brandon Erwin (R)	40	4	23rd	14th	450	2	0	0	100,750
31	Casey Mears (R)	36	3	24th	11th	380	1	0	0	84,000
32	Stan Wattles	36	3	10th	12th	304	1	0	0	86,000
33	Chris Menninga (R)	36	3	22nd	16th	326	1	0	0	37,900
34	Michael Andretti	35	1	21st	3rd	200	1	1	16	346,225
35	Stephan Gregoire	34	4	4th	15th	381	0	1	9	217,075
36	Jimmy Vasser	32	1	12th	4th	200	1	0	0	233,325
37	Bruno Junqueira	30	1	20th	5th	200	1	0	0	255,825
38	Anthony Lazzaro (R)	29	2	17th	3rd	232	0	0	0	52,700
39	Tony Stewart	28	1	7th	6th	200	1	1	13	218,850
40	Cory Witherill (R)	19	2	24th	19th	238	1	0	0	169,775
41	Arie Luyendyk	17	1	6th	13th	198	1	1	1	182,275
42	John Hollansworth Jr.	12	1	18th	18th	189	1	0	0	15,750
42	Tyce Carlson	15	1	19th	15th	162	0	0	0	36,800
44	Alex Barron	9	1	17th	21st	41	0	0	0	33,000
45	Robby Gordon	9	1	3rd	21st	184	1	1	22	173,225
46	Jack Miller	5	1	23rd	25th	28	0	0	0	10,200
47	Nicolas Minassian	1	1	22nd	29th	74	0	0	0	149,575
48	Scott Goodyear	1	1	16th	32nd	7	0	0	0	143,325

Total: $23,574,075

Key: (R) - Indy Racing Northern Light Series Rookie   Note: Total Season Earnings include season-ending contingency awards.

Number of Races

1	Billy Boat	13
	Robbie Buhl	13
	Buzz Calkins	13
	Eddie Cheever Jr.	13
	Airton Daré	13
	Mark Dismore	13
	Sarah Fisher	13
	Felipe Giaffone (R)	13
	Sam Hornish Jr.	13
	Buddy Lazier	13
	Eliseo Salazar	13
	Scott Sharp	13
	Al Unser Jr.	13
14	Didier André (R)	12
	Jeff Ward	12
16	Shigeaki Hattori	11
	Robby McGehee	11
18	Greg Ray	10
	Jaques Lazier	10
20	Donnie Beechler	9
	Billy Roe	9

Laps Completed (2,650 poss.)

1	Sam Hornish Jr.	2,643
2	Buddy Lazier	2,506
3	Eliseo Salazar	2,438
4	Buzz Calkins	2,402
5	Felipe Giaffone (R)	2,298
6	Billy Boat	2,291
7	Scott Sharp	2,207
8	Airton Daré	2,160
9	Jeff Ward	2,089
10	Al Unser Jr.	2,020
11	Shigeaki Hattori	1,979
12	Eddie Cheever Jr.	1,977
13	Robbie Buhl	1,915
14	Robby McGehee	1,845
15	Didier André (R)	1,810
16	Mark Dismore	1,798
17	Donnie Beechler	1,775
18	Sarah Fisher	1,675
19	Greg Ray	1,673
20	Jaques Lazier	1,469

Race Wins

1	Buddy Lazier	4
2	Sam Hornish Jr.	3
3	Helio Castroneves	1
	Eddie Cheever Jr.	1
	Jaques Lazier	1
	Greg Ray	1
	Scott Sharp	1
	Al Unser Jr.	1

Poles

1	Greg Ray	4
2	Scott Sharp	3
3	Jaques Lazier	2
4	Mark Dismore	1
	Jeff Ward	1

Races Led

1	Sam Hornish Jr.	11
2	Buddy Lazier	6
	Greg Ray	6
4	Mark Dismore	5
	Felipe Giaffone	5
	Scott Sharp	5
7	Robbie Buhl	4
	Jaques Lazier	4
	Eliseo Salazar	4

Total Season Earnings

1	Sam Hornish Jr.	$2,477,025
2	Helio Castroneves	1,305,075
3	Scott Sharp	1,234,425
4	Buddy Lazier	1,196,525
5	Eliseo Salazar	949,900
6	Billy Boat	925,025
7	Eddie Cheever Jr.	881,275
8	Robbie Buhl	873,375
9	Greg Ray	859,875
10	Al Unser Jr.	844,525
11	Felipe Giaffone (R)	839,825
12	Buzz Calkins	807,025
13	Airton Daré	806,025
14	Mark Dismore	793,325
15	Jeff Ward	742,775
16	Sarah Fisher	717,175
17	Robby McGehee	698,625
18	Jaques Lazier	633,675
19	Donnie Beechler	558,025
20	Gil de Ferran	515,375

Laps Led

1	Sam Hornish Jr.	765
2	Buddy Lazier	437
3	Greg Ray	363
4	Eddie Cheever Jr.	168
5	Scott Sharp	166
6	Jaques Lazier	139
7	Robbie Buhl	103
8	Eliseo Salazar	82
9	Al Unser Jr.	76
10	Helio Castroneves	56

Running at Finish

1	Sam Hornish Jr.	13
2	Billy Boat	12
3	Buzz Calkins	11
	Buddy Lazier	11
5	Felipe Giaffone (R)	10
	Scott Sharp	10
7	Jeff Ward	9
	Eliseo Salazar	9
9	Shigeaki Hattori	8
	Airton Daré	8
	Al Unser Jr.	8
12	Donnie Beechler	7
	Robbie Buhl	7
	Robby McGehee	7

Indianapolis 500 Winners

Year	St. Pos.	Car #	Driver	Car Name & Sponsor Chassis/Engine	Qualify Speed	Race Time	Race Speed
1911	28	32	Ray Harroun	Nordyke & Marmon Marmon / Marmon		6:42:08.000	74.602
1912	7	8	Joe Dawson	National Motor Vehicle National / National	86.130	6:21:06.000	78.719
1913	7	16	Jules Goux	Peugeot Peugeot / Peugeot	86.030	6:35:05.000	75.933
1914	15	16	Rene Thomas	L. Delage Delage / Delage	94.540	6:03:45.000	82.474
1915	2	2	Ralph DePalma	Mercedes/E.C. Patterson Mercedes / Mercedes	98.580	5:33:55.510	89.840
1916	4	17	Dario Resta	Peugeot Auto Racing Peugeot / Peugeot	94.400	3:34:17.000	84.001 a
1919	2	3	Howdy Wilcox	Peugeot/Indpls Spdway Team Peugeot / Peugeot	100.010	5:40:42.870	88.050
1920	6	4	Gaston Chevrolet	Monroe/William Small Frontenac / Frontenac	91.550	5:38:32.000	88.618
1921	20	2	Tommy Milton	Frontenac/Louis Chevrolet Frontenac / Frontenac	93.050	5:34:44.650	89.621
1922	1	35	Jimmy Murphy	Jimmy Murphy Duesenberg / Miller	100.500	5:17:30.790	94.484
1923	1	1	Tommy Milton	H.C.S. Motor Miller / Miller	108.170	5:29:50.170	90.954
1924	21	15	L.L. Corum-J. Boyer	Duesenberg Duesenberg / Duesenberg	93.330	5:05:23.510	98.234
1925	2	12	Peter DePaolo	Duesenberg Duesenberg / Duesenberg	113.080	4:56:39.460	101.127
1926	20	15	Frank Lockhart	Miller/Peter Kreis Miller / Miller	95.780	4:10:14.950	95.904 b
1927	22	32	George Souders	Duesenberg/William White Duesenberg / Duesenberg	111.550	5:07:33.080	97.545
1928	13	14	Louie Meyer	Miller/Alden Sampson, II Miller / Miller	111.350	5:01:33.750	99.482
1929	6	2	Ray Keech	Simplex Piston Ring/Nagle Miller / Miller	114.900	5:07:25.420	97.585
1930	1	4	Billy Arnold	Miller-Hartz Summers / Miller	113.260	4:58:39.720	100.448
1931	13	23	Louis Schneider	Bowes Seal Fast/Schneider Stevens / Miller	107.210	5:10:27.930	96.629
1932	27	34	Fred Frame	Miller-Harry Hartz Wetteroth / Miller	113.850	4:48:03.790	104.144
1933	6	36	Louie Meyer	Tydol/Louie Meyer Miller / Miller	116.970	4:48:00.750	104.162
1934	10	7	Bill Cummings	Boyle Products/Henning Miller / Miller	116.110	4:46:05.200	104.863
1935	22	5	Kelly Petillo	Gilmore Speedway/Petillo Wetteroth / Offy	115.090	4:42:22.710	106.240
1936	28	8	Louie Meyer	Ring Free/Lou Meyer Stevens / Miller	114.170	4:35:03.390	109.069
1937	2	6	Wilbur Shaw	Shaw-Gilmore Shaw / Offy	122.790	4:24:07.800	113.580
1938	1	23	Floyd Roberts	Burd Piston Ring/Lou Moore 125.680 Wetteroth / Miller		4:15:58.400	117.200
1939	3	2	Wilbur Shaw	Boyle Racing Headquarters Maserati / Maserati	128.970	4:20:47.390	115.035
1940	2	1	Wilbur Shaw	Boyle Racing Headquarters Maserati / Maserati	127.060	4:22:31.170	114.277
1941	17	16	F. Davis-M. Rose	Noc-Out Hose Clamp/Moore Wetteroth / Offy	121.100	4:20:36.240	115.117
1946	15	16	George Robson	Thorne Engineering Adams / Sparks	125.540	4:21:16.700	114.820
1947	3	27	Mauri Rose	Blue Crown Spark Plug/Moore Deidt / Offy	120.040	4:17:52.170	116.338
1948	3	3	Mauri Rose	Blue Crown Spark Plug/Moore Deidt / Offy	129.120	4:10:23.330	119.814
1949	4	7	Bill Holland	Blue Crown Spark Plug/Moore Deidt / Offy	128.670	4:07:15.970	121.327
1950	5	1	Johnnie Parsons	Wynn's Friction/Kurtis-Kraft Kurtis / Offy	132.040	2:46:55.970	124.002 c
1951	2	99	Lee Wallard	Murrell Belanger Kurtis / Offy	135.030	3:57:38.050	126.244
1952	7	98	Troy Ruttman	J.C. Agajanian Kuzma / Offy	135.360	3:52:41.880	128.922
1953	1	14	Bill Vukovich	Fuel Injection/Howard Keck KK500A / Offy	138.390	3:53:01.690	128.740
1954	19	14	Bill Vukovich	Fuel Injection/Howard Keck KK500A / Offy	138.470	3:49:17.270	130.840
1955	14	6	Bob Sweikert	John Zink KK500C / Offy	139.990	3:53:59.130	128.213

Indianapolis 500 Winners

Year	St. Pos.	Car #	Driver	Car Name & Sponsor Chassis/Engine	Qualify Speed	Race Time	Race Speed
1956	1	8	Pat Flaherty	John Zink / Watson / Offy	145.590	3:53:28.840	128.490
1957	13	9	Sam Hanks	Belond Exhaust/George Salih / Salih / Offy	142.810	3:41:14.250	135.601
1958	7	1	Jimmy Bryan	Belond AP/George Salih / Salih / Offy	144.180	3:44:13.800	133.791
1959	6	5	Rodger Ward	Leader Card 500 Roadster / Watson / Offy	144.030	3:40:49.200	135.857
1960	2	4	Jim Rathmann	Ken-Paul / Watson / Offy	146.370	3:36:11.360	138.767
1961	7	1	A.J. Foyt, Jr.	Bowes Seal Fast/Bignotti / Trevis / Offy	145.900	3:35:37.490	139.130
1962	2	3	Rodger Ward	Leader Card 500 Roadster / Watson / Offy	149.370	3:33:50.330	140.293
1963	1	98	Parnelli Jones	J.C. Agajanian/Willard Battery / Watson / Offy	151.150	3:29:35.400	143.137
1964	5	1	A.J. Foyt, Jr.	Sheraton-Thompson/Ansted / Watson / Offy	154.670	3:23:35.830	147.350
1965	2	82	Jim Clark	Lotus powered by Ford / Lotus / Ford	160.720	3:19:05.340	150.686
1966	15	24	Graham Hill	American Red Ball/Mecom / Lola / Ford	159.240	3:27:52.530	144.317
1967	4	14	A.J. Foyt, Jr.	Sheraton-Thompson/Ansted / Coyote / Ford	166.280	3:18:24.220	151.207
1968	3	3	Bobby Unser	Rislone/Leader Cards / Eagle / Offy	169.500	3:16:13.760	152.882
1969	2	2	Mario Andretti	STP Oil Treatment / Hawk / Ford	169.850	3:11:14.710	156.867
1970	1	2	Al Unser	Johnny Lightning/Parnelli Jones / P.J. Colt / Ford	170.220	3:12:37.040	155.749
1971	5	1	Al Unser	Johnny Lightning/Parnelli Jones / P.J. Colt / Ford	174.520	3:10:11.560	157.735
1972	3	66	Mark Donohue	Sunoco McLaren/Penske / McLaren / Offy	191.400	3:04:05.540	162.962
1973	11	20	Gordon Johncock	STP Double Oil Filter/Patrick / Eagle / Offy	192.550	2:05:26.590	159.036 d
1974	25	3	Johnny Rutherford	McLaren Cars / McLaren / Offy	190.440	3:09:10.060	158.589
1975	3	48	Bobby Unser	Jorgensen/All American Racers / Eagle / Offy	191.070	2:54:55.080	149.213 e
1976	1	2	Johnny Rutherford	Hy-Gain/McLaren / McLaren / Offy	188.950	1:42:52.000	148.725 f
1977	4	14	A.J. Foyt, Jr.	Gilmore Racing/A.J. Foyt / Coyote / Foyt	194.560	3:05:57.160	161.331
1978	5	2	Al Unser	First National City/Chaparral / Lola / Cosworth	196.470	3:05:54.990	161.363
1979	1	9	Rick Mears	The Gould Charge/Penske / Penske / Cosworth	193.730	3:08:47.970	158.899
1980	1	4	Johnny Rutherford	Pennzoil/Chaparral Racing / Chaparral / Cosworth	192.520	3:29:59.560	142.862
1981	1	3	Bobby Unser	The Norton Spirit/Penske / Penske; Cosworth	200.540	3:35:41.780	139.084
1982	5	20	Gordon Johncock	STP Oil Treatment/Patrick Wildcat / Cosworth	201.880	3:05:09.140	162.029
1983	4	5	Tom Sneva	Texaco Star/Bignotti-Cotter / March / Cosworth	203.680	3:05:03.066	162.117
1984	3	6	Rick Mears	Pennzoil Z-7/Penske / March / Cosworth	207.840	3:03:21.660	163.612
1985	8	5	Danny Sullivan	Miller American/Penske / March / Cosworth	210.290	3:16:06.069	152.982
1986	4	3	Bobby Rahal	Budweiser/Truesports / March / Cosworth	213.550	2:55:43.480	170.722
1987	20	25	Al Unser	Cummins-Holset/Penske / March / Cosworth	207.420	3:04:59.147	162.175
1988	1	5	Rick Mears	Pennzoil Z-7/Penske / Penske / Chevy Indy V8	219.190	3:27:10.204	144.809
1989	3	20	Emerson Fittipaldi	Marlboro/Patrick Racing / Penske / Chevy Indy V8	222.320	2:59:01.490	167.581
1990	3	30	Arie Luyendyk	Domino's Pizza/Shierson / Lola / Chevy Indy V8	223.300	2:41:18.404	185.981 *
1991	1	3	Rick Mears	Marlboro Penske Chevy 91 / Penske / Chevy Indy V8	224.113	2:50:00.791	176.457
1992	12	3	Al Unser, Jr.	Valvoline Galmer '92 / Galmer/Chevy Indy V8A	222.989	3:43:05.148	134.477
1993	9	4	Emerson Fittipaldi	Marlboro Penske Chevy '93 / Penske/Chevy Indy V8C	220.150	3:10:49.860	157.207
1994	1	31	Al Unser, Jr.	Marlboro Penske Mercedes / Penske/Mercedes Benz	228.011	3:06:29.006	160.872
1995	5	27	Jacques Villeneuve	Player's LTD/Team Green / Reynard/Ford Cosworth XB	228.397	3:15:17.561	153.616
1996	5	91	Buddy Lazier	Delta Faucet/Montana/Hemelgarn / 95 Reynard/Ford Cosworth XB	231.468	3:22:45.753	147.956
1997	1	5	Arie Luyendyk	Wavephore/Sprint PCS/Miller Lite/Provimi / G Force/Oldsmobile	218.263	3:25:43.388	145.827
1998	17	51	Eddie Cheever, Jr.	Rachel's Potato Chips / Dallara/Oldsmobile	217.334	3:26:40.524	145.155
1999	8	14	Kenny Brack	AJ Foyt Power Team / Dallara/Oldsmobile	222.659	3:15:51.182	153.176
2000	2	1	Juan Montoya	Target / G Force/Oldsmobile	232.372	2:58:59.431	167.607
2001	11	68	Helio Castroneves	Marlboro Team Penske / Dallara/Oldsmobile	224.142	3:31:54.1800	141.574

a 1916 - 300 Miles (Scheduled)   b 1926 - 400 Miles (Rain)   c 1950 - 345 Miles (Rain)
d 1973 - 332.5 Miles (Rain)   e 1975 - 435 Miles (Rain)   f 1976 - 255 Miles (Rain)

*Track Record

INDY
2002
RACING

SAT.	March 2	Homestead-Miami Speedway Miami	ABC	1pm
SUN.	March 17	Phoenix International Raceway Phoenix	ABC	4pm
SUN.	March 24	California Speedway Fontana	ESPN2	3:30pm
SAT.	April 21	Nazareth Speedway Nazareth	ABC	1pm
SUN.	May 26	Indianapolis Motor Speedway Indianapolis	ABC	11am
SAT.	June 8 ·	Texas Motor Speedway Ft. Worth	ESPN	8pm
SUN.	June 16	Pikes Peak International Raceway Pikes Peak	ABC	4pm
SAT.	June 29 ·	Richmond International Raceway Richmond	ESPN	7:30pm
SUN.	July 7	Kansas Speedway Kansas City	ABC	1pm
SAT.	July 20 ·	Nashville Superspeedway Nashville	ESPN	7:30pm
SUN.	July 28	Michigan International Speedway Brooklyn	ABC	2:30pm
SUN.	Aug. 11	Kentucky Speedway Sparta	ABC	1:30pm
SUN.	Aug. 25	Gateway International Raceway St.Louis	ESPN	3pm
SUN.	Sept. 8	Chicagoland Speedway Joliet	ABC	1pm
SUN.	Sept. 15	Texas Motor Speedway Ft Worth	ABC	3pm

· Night Race   **AIR TIMES SUBJECT TO CHANGE**   **ALL TIMES EASTERN**